EAST ASIAN STUDIES IN THE PERSPECTIVE OF REGIONAL INTEGRATION

EAST ASIAN STUDIES IN THE PERSPECTIVE OF REGIONAL INTEGRATION

Editor

Xinbo Wu

Shanghai International Studies University, China

World Century

Published by

World Century Publishing Corporation
27 Warren Street, Suite 401-402, Hackensack, NJ 07601, USA

Library of Congress Cataloging-in-Publication Data
Names: Wu, Xinbo, 1966– editor.
Title: East Asian studies in the perspective of regional integration /
edited by Xinbo Wu (Shanghai International Studies University, China).
Description: New Jersey : World Century Publishing Corporation [2017]
Identifiers: LCCN 2017040694 | ISBN 9781938134968
Subjects: LCSH: Regionalism--East Asia. | East Asia--Economic integration. |
Regionalism (International organization) | International economic integration.
Classification: LCC JQ1499.A38 R433446 2017 | DDC 337.1/5--dc23
LC record available at https://lccn.loc.gov/2017040694

British Library Cataloguing-in-Publication Data
A catalogue record for this book is available from the British Library.

Published by arrangement with Shanghai People's Publishing House.

For any available supplementary material, please visit
http://www.worldscientific.com/worldscibooks/10.1142/U031#t=suppl

Desk Editor: Dong Lixi

Typeset by Stallion Press
Email: enquiries@stallionpress.com

Printed in Singapore

Contents

Preface ix

East Asian Cooperation and its Economic Integration **1**

Chapter 1 Sino-Japanese Cooperation in Economic Integration of East Asia 3
Zhang Jian

Chapter 2 East Asian Regionalism: Issues and Visions 17
Hong Pyo Lee

Chapter 3 Regional Cooperation and Technology Transfer in East Asia: The Case of Myanmar 33
Yuri Sadoi

Chapter 4 The Influence of Japanese Social Ideological Trends Upon East Asia Cooperation 51
Jiang Xudong

Election of Political Leadership in East Asia **65**

Chapter 5 Heredity, Election, and Leadership in Northeast Asia: A Comparative Institutional Analysis of Political Process 67
Hiroki Miura

Chapter 6 Chinese Political Leadership Transition: An Overview and Assessment 93
Wu Xinbo, Wu Di

Chapter 7 What Makes Hereditary Politicians an Issue in Japan? 115
Kwangwook Kim

Chapter 8 Reassessing Incumbency Advantage in Korean Politics: An Evidence from Korean General Elections Since 2000 135
Yeawon Kim

Chapter 9 The Endurance of Political Family in the Philippines: Hereditary Election 153
Yoko Yoshikawa

East Asian Cultural Identity, History, and Norms **189**

Chapter 10 The Construction of Cultural Identity in East Asia and Confucianism 191
Bao Xiaqin

Chapter 11 Do ICTs Change Citizenship Norms? Technological Determinism vs. Social Determinism 201
Seongyi Yun

Chapter 12 Functional Cooperation and Japan's Cultural Diplomacy: A Case Study of the Preservation of Angkor 225
He Ping

East Asia and the Global World **245**

Chapter 13 The Korea Policy of Truman Administration (1945–1948) 247
Fang Xiuyu, Li Li

Chapter 14 China's Proposing Behavior in Global Governance: The Cases of the WTO Doha Round Negotiation and G-20 Process 267
Liu Hongsong

Chapter 15 Analysis of Trade Commodity Structure and Complementarity of the Regional Cooperation between China and Russia 289
Kang Chengwen

Preface

East Asia is now experiencing significant economic growth and social change. Integration of East Asia seems an irresistible trend, as East Asian countries are closely interdependent with each other and share many common interests in economic development. This is the internal factor. Externally, globalization and regional integration are also driving force of East Asia cooperation. However, despite of the complementary advantages and group cohesion among East Asian countries, they still face severe challenges brought by global changes. Enhancing the overall status of East Asia in the international arena is a pressing need.

The first Trilateral Symposium was held in Seoul, South Korea in February 2010, attended by scholars from three universities representing the three East Asian countries. The universities are Fudan University of China, Kyung Hee University of Korea and Meijo University of Japan. Up till now, the Trilateral Symposium has been held successfully for six consecutive years and the scale of the symposium has been expanded with each passing year. In the latest symposium, the participants came from more than 10 universities and institutes, including Kyung Hee University, Incheon National University of Korea, Meijo University, Kyushu University, Gifu Keizai University, Nanzan University, Gakushuin University of Japan, Shanghai International Studies University, Fudan University, Shanghai Academy of Social Sciences, and Harbin University of Commerce of China.

This volume compiles 15 papers which were carefully selected from two Symposiums. One was held at Kyung Hee University in Seoul, South

Korea in 2013 and the other was at Shanghai International Studies University (SISU) in Shanghai, China in 2014. The edited papers now become chapters in this book. The chapters are divided into four sections. The first section discusses the impact of East Asia cooperation and economic integration. The second section emphasizes the election of political leadership in East Asia. Section three covers topics of East Asian cultural identity, history and norms. Section four addresses the issue of relationship between East Asia and the world.

The editors of this volume are most grateful to the contributors, whose fine work and enthusiasm made the completion of this book possible. This volume would never be such fruitful without the intellectual passion presented by each author — Hiroki Miura, Hong Pyo Lee, Seongyi Yun, Jiang Xudong, Kwangwook Kim, Yeawon Kim, Wu Xinbo, Wu Di, Yoko Yoshikawa, Bao Xiaqin, Fang Xiuyu, Li Li, He Ping, Kang Chengwen, Liu Hongsong, Zhang Jian, and Yuri Sadoi. We also thank the anonymous reviewers for their encouragements and suggestions for revision.

In November 2015, SISU Trilateral Cooperation Studies Center was founded by Chinese Ministry of Foreign Affairs within the Trilateral Cooperation Framework. It shows that China is paying increasing attention to the studies of East Asian cooperation. Colleges, universities and research institutes in China, South Korea and Japan will continue to hold regular meetings. The continuous intellectual interaction will drive the trilateral cooperation in areas of higher education, political, economic and cultural exchanges for substantial progress, as well as provide concrete foundation for international friendship making.

East Asian Cooperation and its Economic Integration

Chapter 1

Sino-Japanese Cooperation in Economic Integration of East Asia[1]

*Zhang Jian**

Introduction

The economic integration of East Asia[2] after WW II is the result of the transformation of foreign trade strategy of the region's largest economy — Japan in the 1980s. The direct reason of Japanese foreign trade strategic transformation is the higher yen, trade friction and demand for upgrading of industrial structure. In that context, Japan strived to build "Flying Geese Pattern" (Kojima, 2004), speeding up direct investment in East Asia including ASEAN, South Korea and China which has played a promoting role in the development of export-oriented economy, and it also increased the economic dependence among East Asian countries and regions, promoting the development of economic and trade integration in East Asia. But since the sustained and rapid growth of Chinese economy in East Asia in 21st century with its gross domestic product (GDP) of 2010 exceeding Japan and becoming the region's leading economic power, the original East Asian economic cooperation system dominated by Japan is hard to adapt to present situation and meet the need of regional development. Thus, the new East Asia economic integration framework system cannot wait to be built.

*Zhang Jian, associate professor of School of Japanese Studies, Shanghai International Studies University, China.

As the first and second largest economy in this region, how could China and Japan participate and cooperate to promote the construction of regional economic cooperation mechanism becomes the key point of promoting the regional economic integration naturally. This thesis takes Sino-Japan cooperation in the process of the integration as the research object, to investigate and analyze the following questions. First, the status quo and characteristics of economic integration in East Asia; second, the comparison of cooperation mechanism and frameworks in the areas that the two countries have participated in respectively; third, their focus and position on the issue of the regional economic integration. On the basis of investigation and analysis of the above problems, they try to think about the problems and prospects in constructing the effective East Asia's economic integration cooperation mechanism.

The Development Background of East Asian Regional Economic Integration

Why is economic integration in East Asia promoted? On the one hand it is resulted from the driving force of Japan for being the first economy for its own economic interests consideration, and on the other hand, a wider range of backgrounds and reasons external and internal also paly the role.

First of all, the global trading system is undergoing hard multilateral liberalization talks under the original General Agreement on Tariffs and Trade (GATT) and the new framework of the World Trade Organization (WTO). Uruguay Round negotiations lasted for more than seven years due to opposition in the U.S. and Europe. Before the start of the new round of multilateral negotiations of World Trade Organization (WTO), ministerial meeting talks broke down repeatedly. A new round of the Doha Development Round (DDR) has not come to an agreement because of the great differences in the developed countries and developing countries, and has come across severe challenges in promoting the global multilateral trade liberalization mechanism. Thus, WTO members, including China, Japan, South Korea, and the Asean countries, have to start thinking about other trade liberalization means and mechanism, in order to realize the economic growth.

Second, since the 1990s, global regional and bilateral trade agreements have been hot and brought significant impact on the East Asian economies such as China, Japan and Korea's foreign trade strategy. The establishment of the European Union (EU) in 1993 and the North American Free Trade Area (NAFTA) in 1994 shows that Europe and the United States (U.S.) have switched the focus of promoting the development of foreign trade to bilateral and regional framework. The global trading system has substantial entered the era when multilateralism and regionalism (bilateral) coexist.

Third, judging from the internal development in East Asia, the effect of the labor division pattern emerged gradually in the process of industrial upgrading and international industry transfer in Japan in the 1970s–1980s. Newly Industrial Economics (NIES[3]), ASEAN and China who have achieved high economic growth, have constructed the complementary industrial structure and division of labor system in Japan, South Korea, China and ASEAN based on the division of labor and collaboration using different comparative advantages. This system also drives the economy's explosive growth in East Asia, making East Asia gradually form a new type of regional economic pattern against the two traditional poles — the U.S. and EU. Of course, in the process, geography and location advantages between the East Asian countries and regions, as well as historical and cultural commonality of the region, also greatly promoted the national and regional economic integration.

The Status Quo and Characteristics of East Asian Regional Economic Integration

Because the 10 ASEAN countries decided to set up the ASEAN Free Trade Area (AFTA) as early as in 1992 in the Singapore Declaration, the existing domain in East Asia economic integration framework is mainly divided into China, South Korea and Japan bilateral and trilateral framework, as well as free trade agreement (FTA) framework between the three countries and ASEAN. At the same time, China, South Korea and Japan, and the Association of South-east Asian nations (ASEAN) will also actively promote economic cooperation with the outside countries and regions, to construct bilateral free trade agreement mechanism. By the end of 2014, the bilateral and regional free trade agreement frameworks that

China, Japan, South Korea and the ASEAN have signed or participated in respectively are as follows.

1. South Korea. By the end of 2014, South Korea has signed 12 bilateral free trade agreements with Chile, Singapore, EFTA, ASEAN, India, the European Union, Peru, the United States, Turkey, Colombia, Australia, Canada and other countries and regions. South Korea also ended bilateral free trade agreement negotiations respectively with China, New Zealand, and Vietnam at the end of 2014. In addition, South Korea has also begun or involved in the bilateral free trade agreement negotiations with Indonesia, China, Japan, Mexico and the Gulf Cooperation Council (GCC), free trade agreement of China, South Korea and Japan, Regional Comprehensive Economic Partnership (RCEP) and other countries or regions.[4] South Korea also showed intention to participate in the Trans-Pacific Partnership (TPP) framework.[5]
2. Japan. By the end of 2014, Japan successively signed 14 bilateral Economic Partnership Agreements (EPA) with Singapore, Chile, Mexico, Malaysia, Thailand, Indonesia, Vietnam, Brunei, ASEAN, the Philippines, Switzerland, India, Peru, Australia and other countries and regions. Other countries and regions who are undergoing economic partnership agreement are the gulf cooperation council, Mongolia, Korea, Canada, Colombia, China, Japan and South Korea free trade agreement, the European Union, RCEP and the TPP.
3. China. By the end of 2014, Mainland China has successively signed 12 free trade deals with the ASEAN, Singapore, Pakistan, New Zealand, Chile, Peru, Costa Rica, Iceland, Switzerland, Hong Kong and Macao regions (CEPA), Taiwan region (ECFA). Bilateral free trade agreement negotiations between China and South Korea, Australia, also ended at the end of 2014 basically. In addition, free trade agreement negotiations with GCC, Sri Lanka, Norway, CJKFTA (China-Japan-Korea Free Trade Area), the South African Customs Union (SACU) and RCEP and so on are in progress. China is still in the works to establish bilateral free trade with India and Colombia.
4. The ASEAN. By the end of 2014, the ASEAN has signed bilateral free trade agreement respectively with China, South Korea, India,

Australia, New Zealand and Japan. In addition, with the help of the ASEAN, the free trade agreement negotiation under the framework of RCEP ASEAN "10 + 6" is also ongoing. In addition, there are many countries in the ASEAN signed bilateral free trade agreement with countries outside the region separately, such as Indonesia, Malaysia, the Philippines, Singapore, Thailand and Vietnam. They all signed the bilateral economic cooperation agreement (EPA) with Japan, and Singapore signed bilateral free trade agreements with both China, South Korea and Japan.

From the free trade agreement framework and mechanism that the four main parties in East Asia have been involved in, the current situation of the development of regional economic integration reflects the following five characteristics.

Firstly, although the choice of cooperation framework on host countries or regions are different, foreign trade strategies and policies do not exclude specific areas and countries. They are actively exploring more economic cooperation framework with countries and regions outside, which has obvious "non-exclusive" characteristics. This shows that, different from the mechanism of the EU with strong conceptual meaning and binding powers, the regional economic integration framework that countries in East Asia are promoting is a relatively loose and open mechanism.

Second, the level of economic development gap between regions and countries in East Asian is comparatively large. The formation of original region industry division of labor system based on factor endowments and industrial structure is still largely maintained. At the same time, the motive that countries and regions inside are in pursuit of economic growth is still very strong, thus economic integration cooperation space is huge. In 13 countries of East Asia, only Japan and South Korea joined the organization for economic cooperation development (OECD). In the 10 ASEAN countries except for Singapore, Brunei and Malaysia, the per capita GDP of other countries are at relatively low levels, and there are gaps in the national economy and trade competitiveness level. This also means that it is very important for the region to promote economic integration on the basis of industrial division of labor system, and to expand mutual investment and trade. Meanwhile, there is huge development space.

Third, the existing mechanisms are classified in Balassa "free trade area" level,[6] and the economic integration level is relatively low compared with customs union, common market and economic union. Bilateral and regional free trade agreements appeared crossing and overlapping repeatedly, forming a multi-level and mixed regional economic integration system. What different parties have taken are more practical model of "early harvest". Economic integration is focused on the traditional goods trade liberalization, investment, economic cooperation, and other fields, which also gives attention to the expansion of services, intellectual property and other new areas. At the same time, due to coexistence of bilateral and regional free trade agreements in different levels, their different contents and regulations in the liberalization of time and rules of origin, etc. increased the enterprise cost and burden.[7] Therefore, East Asia economic integration has objectively bred the practical need of integrating countries inside within the framework to cooperate.

Fourth, liberalization ratios of all kinds of existing frameworks remain about 70%–90%, and all countries set more sensitive products or exceptional items in the free negotiations, such as Japan's agricultural "exception 5 items". On the one hand, it reflects the reality of adjustment difficulty in national political and economic interests; on the other hand, it also reflects the necessity of progressive development in the process of economic integration in East Asia, which needs to be based on the actual situation and the ability, and cannot blindly pursue unrealistic high standards and goals.

Fifth, the regional economic integration is vulnerable to countries outside of the territory and non-economic factors. European economic integration greatly enhanced economic integration and foreign policy coordination among countries within the EU, with its trade transformation effect produced by its economic integration. On the one hand, it greatly raised the commodity admittance threshold of countries outside; on the other hand, its influence as a whole on economy is greatly enhanced, which makes the economic influence and speaking right in other countries and areas of the world weakened. Also because of this, the U.S. dominated and quickly set up the North American Free Trade Area (NAFTA) after that the European Union (EU) was founded, and actively promoted the process of American free trade area. At the same time, when China, Japan and South Korea, India and ASEAN, etc. in the most economic active

Asian area tried to set up the mechanism of new economic cooperation in East Asia, the U.S. would not be excluded from the East Asian economic cooperation mechanism from its own economic interests, which is an important economic reason for the U.S. "to return to the Asia-Pacific" strategy. Regional security cooperation mechanism generated under the background that the cold war in East Asia is dominated by the U.S., so the countries in this region are inevitable influenced by the world's only superpower — the U.S., politically and economically. As a result, regional economic integration is extremely vulnerable to the influence of American economy, politics, military, and other non-economic factors. In addition, between Japan and China, South Korea also have territorial and historical issues which are difficult to solve in such a short term. Meanwhile, mutual trust and cooperation mechanism have not been substantially established in the field of politics, which also has brought many uncertain factors for the regional economic integration.

Thus, economic integration in East Asia at present is still centering on economic construction and the early stages of the industrial structure and the economic level of different countries should be considered as well, which means that there is a huge space for development of the regional economic integration and cooperation. Because the regional economic development level is still generally lagged behind North America and the EU, the regional economic integration cannot be separated from the basic reality of economic development of most countries in the region, and "non-exclusivity" characteristics need to be maintained in European and American markets. Considering the influence of politics and other aspects, how to promote the region's economic integration while balanceing the good economic relations with the U.S. at the same time is particularly important.

Comparison between the East Asian Regional Economic Integration Status and Sino-Japan Strategic Framework Negotiation

China and Japan is the world's second largest and the third largest economy respectively. China, being the number one economic power in East Asia, low level of per capita gross national product, is the world's most populous developing country; Japan is the second largest economy in this region, being one of the few advanced economies in this area. The economic and market position of the two countries in the region and the world economy determined that they need to bear main responsibility and play leading roles in the process of regional economic integration. Besides, based on five characteristics of the regional economic integration mentioned above and the actual situation of the region, it is necessary for China and Japan to adhere to the principle of gradualness while promoting regional economic integration. The importance of U.S. market requires the two countries to balance the economic and political relations with the U.S. Therefore, in the construction of East Asia economic integration mechanism, the key is how to reach consensus by reducing the differences between the two countries.

At present, free trade and economic integration frameworks that the two countries have participated in are mainly three kinds of mechanism, system of multilateral liberalization of the WTO, China, Japan and South Korea free trade area, RCEP. Although China has not yet attended TPP negotiations, due to the involvement of Japan, Malaysia, Vietnam, Singapore and other countries in this region, and because the U.S. is the common important trade partner in East Asia, which is an important driver in the TPP negotiations, therefore its progress and framework formation has larger direct or indirect impact on the regional economic integration in East Asia.

This section studies issue in four kinds of framework as the main study object, analyses the negotiations content of the frame and trend of the two countries around each framework of the negotiations, and addresses problem of Sino-Japan cooperation in promoting the region economic integration process.

First of all, from the liberalization issues set by the China-Japan-related free trade agreement framework, the WTO's main negotiation areas focus on agriculture, market access and development, and development issues, which conforms to the fact that developing countries accounted for more in the WTO. It is an amendment for negotiation system in GATT which has long been dominated by Europe, the U.S., and other developed economies, and it is also a result of developing countries' struggle and achievements. Issues set by RCEP framework are only 7 items, which partly reflects that there are gaps in economic development in East Asia, and reflects the consensus that most of the countries and regions in East Asia gradually promoted for regional economic and trade development, based on the actual situation of the regional economy in order to boost economic integration. In general, the RCEP and WTO negotiation areas are relatively small, and their issues are mainly focused on the traditional goods trade, service trade, investment, intellectual property rights and the development of economic and technical cooperation which are related to eliminating economic development gap.

Compared with the RCEP and WTO framework, the number of CJKFTA negotiations issues increased significantly. Including traditional goods, services, trade and investment issues, China, Japan and South Korea free trade area negotiations touch upon many issues related to three countries' economy and trade such as the electronic commerce, industrial cooperation, consumer safety, electronic commerce, energy, mineral resources, fisheries, food, environment, and it also includes high-level market standard issues such as the intellectual property rights, competition policy, government procurement, and transparency etc. We can say that issues set by China, Japan and South Korea free trade area reflect that the three parties have strengthened economic and trade interdependence among the three countries and expanded economic cooperation agreement through this mechanism, as well as being pragmatic of the three countries in cooperation starting from the specific and realistic problems.

There are many fields concerning TPP negotiations, achieving 21 items, and the number and scope of issues related to trade, investment exceeding other agreements, including 15 items — "rules" issues, so "rules" talk is the real focus of TPP negotiations. Japan has decided to join the TPP negotiations because that Japan needs to participate in the framework formulation of broad trade rules as soon as possible. Japan also wants to take the preemptive opportunities in the framework formulation of new trade rules, so as to achieve initiative as the major economies of the BRIC countries such as China, India and Russia in the future negotiations. Of course, on the other hand, to realize the free trade agreement between Japan and the U.S. in the framework of TPP is also one of the important reasons that Japan needs TPP. Because China is not involved in the TPP negotiations, the TPP issues itself does not reflect China's stance, but we will still be able to confirm that there are many similar or common issues between the TPP framework and negotiations among China, Japan and South Korea free trade. Although liberalization standards of the same issues are different, China, Japan and South Korea free trade agenda setting is "high inspiration", which fully reflects China's positive position of promoting the economic and trade cooperation as it is the only developing country among the three countries.

Secondly, China and Japan have made substantial efforts to push forward the above framework talks. Because of the multi-stakeholder coordination difficulties of reaching a package deal under the WTO framework, the two sides therefore have put the focus of promoting trade liberalization on promoting and realizing the framework of bilateral or regional free trade agreement. CJKFTA negotiations officially began in March 2013 and by early 2015, six rounds of negotiations had been held, and the RCEP negotiations officially began in May 2013 and by the end of 2014, six rounds of negotiations had been held, while by early 2015, the TPP negotiations held 14 rounds secretly including ministerial conference since Japan joined in July 2013, reaching certain results in fields of investment, the state-owned enterprises reform, environment, goods trade, rules of origin, food health and quarantine, the labor, etc. Thus, China and Japan showed high enthusiasm in their participation of the main framework and strong desire to break through the framework. But at the same time, since the framework negotiations started, there was no big breakthrough or tangible results achieved, which shows that the two sides respectively adjust problems by domestic interests, so it is difficult to make decisions quickly on the liberalization of sensitive industries and products in their own countries.

As mentioned earlier, China is still a developing country and China's current foreign trade strategy of China is promoting bilateral and regional free trade negotiation effectively and steadily, while the WTO Doha Round multilateral liberalization talk is moving forward at the same time. China currently focused on the China, Japan and South Korea free trade area and RCEP negotiations, which reflects the fact that China actively promotes East Asia regional economic integration. As for Japan, the thinking of paying more attention and giving priority to TPP negotiations can be confirmed while it is involved in China, Japan and South Korea free trade area to negotiate with the RCEP. Since the Japanese government announced to join the TPP talks in 2013, Abe cabinet has vigorously promoted "Abe Economics", carried out the reform in many fields. Many policies such as production of rice (decreased) policy reform, reform of farmland system, the association reform and a number of reforms in the field of agriculture reflected that the Abe cabinet had really prepared for the TPP negotiations. Because the TPP negotiations reflected that Japan wanted to go ahead in setting high standard free trade rules, and tried to apply the pattern to all kinds of frameworks of regional economic cooperation in East Asia, and to revitalize the economy, the TPP has certainly become Japan's focus of free trade agreement strategy in the process of transformation to a new stage in 2013, being the key in advancing the strategy of economic growth and at the same time containing China, Japan and South Korea free trade area and RCEP framework. This strategy in Japan formed powerful challenge for China's free trade agreement strategy which is still mainly based on East Asia.[8]

Conclusion

The foreign trade strategies of China and Japan have entered into a new stage of paying more attention to regional free trade agreement, which is also a new trend of world trade patterns in the 21st century. For the two countries, they not only made active response this trend of world trade, but also attach importance to the two countries' intrinsic demand of economic growth in their trade and economic development. As the region with the largest population, the fastest economic growth and the biggest development potential in the 21st century, East Asia is rapidly growing into an important party in the world economy comparable to Europe and North America, and the construction of East Asia economic integration framework has become a substantial focus of the two countries' trade strategy. As the major economies of East Asia, China and Japan have already started to build a multi-level and comprehensive trade strategies and have participated simultaneously in WTO, RCEP, China, Japan and South Korea free trade area, and gradually expanded the scope of liberalization and marketization on the basis of continuing to pay attention to traditional liberalization issues. Therefore, the core of the Sino-Japanese cooperation in economic integration in East Asia is no longer based on which framework to be the center, but to continue promoting existing multi-level economic integration framework of this region with "non-excludability" gradually at the same time, and strive to build stable mechanism of effective cooperation between the two countries in a multi-level three-dimensional framework. Of course, in the long run, the common goal of the two sides should still be continuously eliminating the gap between the rich and poor, integrate the framework at each level, and push forward the WTO multilateral free trade system.

To build stable mechanism of effective cooperation between the two countries, it is inseparable from the contribution of the two countries and the region's political mutual trust mechanism. But at the same time there are many domains in this region that need participation and cooperation of the countries led by China and Japan, such as agriculture and food security, energy security and environmental issues etc., which objectively requires China and Japan to speed up economic and trade cooperation, stimulate the market potential in this region, promote the stable development of the region's economy, and make greater contribution to the world's economic growth. The framework that Japan has strived to build in the TPP negotiations should consider its own agricultural problems and sensitive items, and how to take other countries in East Asia into account at the same time, particularly the issues of agriculture, food security and poverty problems in developing countries, in order to realize coordinated development of East Asian economic integration. The effective and stable cooperation mechanism in the process of East Asia economic integration built by China and Japan will have a positive and far-reaching influence on East Asian economic integration process.

Notes

1. This chapter is Supported by Innovative Research Team of Shanghai International Studies University.
2. East Asia includes China, Japan, South Korea and ASEAN 10.
3. NIES refer to Singapore, South Korea, Hong Kong and Chinese Taipei.
4. Source: Korean official hompage "Ministry of Foreign Affairs Republic of Korea".
5. Source: Quote from "Korean Daily" chosunonline 2015.1.26.
6. Balassa, B. (1961) *The Theory of Economic Integration*, R.D. Irwin.

7. Koichi Ishikawa "The FTA of East Asia and Its Influence on Japanese Firms," *Intenational Trade and Investment*, Autumn 2013, No. 93.
8. Zhang Jian, "An Analysis on Japan's EPA Strategy and TPP's Negotiation," *International Review*, 2014, No. 5.

References

China Oriental Morning Post, "China has Signed 12 Free Trade Agreements and Hold an Open-mind on TPP," 2013.12.5.

Guan Quan (2012), "Economic Integration of East Asia and TPP — The Game between China and Japan," *Northeast Asia Forum*, No. 2.

Keiichi Umada, Shujiro Urada, Fukunari Kimura (2005), *The New Trade Strategy of Japan — Through WTO and FTA*, Bushindo Press (Japan).

Kiyoshi Kojima (2004), The "Flying Geese" Model of Development Theory (Second Volume): *Asia and the New Order of the World*, Bushindo Press (Japan).

Li Xiangyang (2012), "Trans-Pacific Strategic Economic Partnership Agreement: A Great Challenge in China Rising Process," *International Economic Comment*, No. 2.

Ministry of Agriculture, Forestry and Fisheries of Japan website (http://www.maff.go.jp).

Ministry of Commerce of PRC website (http://www.mofcom.gov.cn).

Ministry of Economy, Trade and Industry of Japan website (http://www.meti.go.jp).

Ministry of Foreign Affairs of Japan website (http://www.mofa.go.jp).

Ministry of Foreign Affairs of South Korea website (http://www.mofa.go.kr/ENG/).

Shen Minghui (2012), "A Cost-benefit Analysis in Trans-Pacific Strategic Economic Partnership Agreement (TPP): A Chinese Perspective," *Journal of Contemporary Asia Pacific Studies*, No. 1.

Shujiro Urada (2002), The FTA Strategy of Japan, Nihon Keizai Shinbun Press (Japan).

The National Diet Library of Japan Issue Brief (2012), "The Tendency and Task of Trans-Pacific Strategic Economic Partnership Agreement (TPP)," *Research and Information*, No. 735.

The World Bank website (http://www.worldbank.org.cn).

Yorizimi Watanabe (2007), *The FTA·EPA Negotiation*, Nihon Keizai Hyoronsha Press (Japan).

Zhang Jian (2014) "A Study on the Possibility of China's TPP Participation," *The AIBS Journal: Society for Asian and International Business Strategy*, No. 7.

Chapter 2

East Asian Regionalism: Issues and Visions

*Hong Pyo Lee**

Introduction

The age of globalization is characterized by the increasing dominance of multilateralism because the world has moved beyond a previously perceived bipolar structure, and statist views have been challenged by the emergence of a variety of actors. Along with this notion of globalization to feature the changes in the international structure, notions such as regionalism and regionalization have increasingly become the subjects of scrutiny in the realms of international relations and global political economy. East Asia, experiencing economic dynamism over the decades in holistic terms, has not been overlooked. In fact, there has been a lively discourse on the issue of regionalism and multilateral institution-building over the decades, especially following the end of the Cold War. In the initial period, the focus had been on economic cooperation, but as a recent move, an increasing attention has been paid to regional security as well.

Nonetheless, the mainstream discourse on the subject has mostly focused on the effectiveness of its regional institutions and whether or not it ought to be compared to other regional cooperation experiments, notably the European Union (EU). In short, East Asian efforts of building

* Hong Pyo Lee, Professor, Faculty of Law, Kyushu University, Japan.

regional institutions have been considered less than successful by most analysts. Although a plethora of efforts to establish regional multilateral institutions has resulted in the creation of such organizations as the Asian-Pacific Economic Cooperation (APEC), the Asian Regional Forum (ARF), the ASEAN plus Three and the East Asian Summit (EAS), these institutions are now frequently referred to as the "talk shops", because they lack specific obligations of enforcement and fail to agree on effective settlement mechanisms of disputes.[1] As a result, the effectiveness of such institutions to play a meaningful role in regional affairs remains a source of debate. Along this line, Europe is frequently used as an example, for some as a model to follow while others to contrast and critique East Asia's regional development. Others still tend to view the comparison as unfair, and that East Asia's regionalization is simply evolving in a manner different from Europe's, or that regionalism in East Asia did not have the same level of hegemonic support from America and Europe.

This chapter attempts to address some critical issues regarding East Asia's efforts to work toward a more intertwined region through the formation of a region-wide cooperative institution. The goal is to highlight why regional institutional building has brought only limited results to date, focusing on some lessons the region can draw on the European experience. It should be noted here that while there are diverse ideas as to what kind of region the term "East Asia" entails, the region under consideration in this chapter includes those nations considered to be a part of Northeast Asian, those of Southeast Asia, as well as Australia and New Zealand. Whether on the basis of geographic constancy, economic interdependence or shared security concerns, all of these nations should be considered together. Besides, while the United States is not geographically a part of this region, it still should be considered a part of the region given its status as a regional hegemon, the linchpin for the security order in East Asia and still the most important economy for the nations in this region. A brief examination of the current existing visions of East Asian regional institutions is in order.

Visions for East Asian Institutions

In the process of searching for a regional mechanism or institution designed to promote multilateral cooperation for the ultimate purpose of maintaining regional stability and prosperity, numerous ideas and suggestions have come to the fore. As for the most basic vision, Acharya argues that the current institutional arrangements like the ASEAN plus Three or EAS, are most likely to continue to be the most prominent regional institutions.[2] In other words, the top leaders of member states gather annually to address regional issues, but leave no binding agreement for the betterment of the given situation in the end. As a result, none of the above meetings is considered to have made a breakthrough in the lingering conflicts deemed to hamper a full-fledged cooperation in the region. One scholar suggests that the status quo of this kind will unlikely change any time soon, at least so long as East Asian institutions continue to defend notions of sovereignty and non-interference. While the current institutional arrangement has arguably been unable to provide much in the way of effective action to regional issues as manifested in the Asian Financial Crisis[3] and the presently ongoing territorial disputes in the region, the South China Sea dispute is the most noteworthy. Nevertheless, many still tend to argue that the current institutional order is not overly maligned and does at least provide an outlet for regional players to discuss issues in a bilateral and multilateral fashion. As a result, it is believed to prevent the existing disputes from developing into a fierce conflict involving military means. Even if they are "talk shops", thus, at least, that is better than nothing.

Given the desire to avoid institutions that might scale back national sovereignty, while at the same time having a desire to strengthen national economic performance through increased economic intercourse, there have been efforts to create regional trade regimes that some think could provide the basis for greater regionalism. An early example of this is APEC, a primarily economic issues-focused institution that was also one of the more successful attempts to broaden the regional definition of East Asia to include nations outside the region in geographical terms. One suggests that the increasing number of Free Trade Agreements (FTAs) between East Asian states will result in a "domino effect" toward more multi-lateralization,[4] and it is possible that the recently proposed trade-focused regimes are an example of this, including the Trans Pacific Partnership (TPP) and the Regional Comprehensive Economic Partnership (RCEP), the first being considered an American-centered trade deal with "WTO-plus" while the other one being considered a more China-centered trade deal with limited "WTO-Plus" aspects.

For those who see the need for a more concerted effort by the larger powers in East Asia to work together over security and economic issues to avoid conflict amidst increasing economic dialogue in the region, the most prominent idea is the notion of a "Concert of East Asia" among the great powers. Among the most notable versions of this is an idea of "condominium" between China and the United States agreeing to share power in the region[5] as insinuated in the concept of "G-2",[6] and a wider version that include Japan, India and Russia. Of relevance here is that Fukuyama suggests the concept of building upon North Korean Six-Party talks to create a regional order more stable than the past, that is, the immediate post-Cold War period characterized by a power vacuum created by the disappearance of the Soviet Union and the subsequent decline of U.S. engagement in regional security.[7]

Another version of this vision seeing the great powers dominating East Asia, is the idea of considering the East Asian region as a hierarchical system ruled by one power, with the other powers appearing below at various levels of the pyramid.[8] It is in this context that Kang sees China's rise to prominence in the region as a return to its traditional place atop the hierarchy in the East Asian region, and thus perfectly acceptable to most other East Asian nations.[9] In a similar vein, Goh suggests that the hierarchy has been one with the United States atop the region since the end of WWII and the establishment of its security alliances, and that its place will continue at the top of the region for the foreseeable future given the lack of trust many East Asian nations have in China.[10] Then one main question that arises is: how will a rising China deal with an American-dominated security order? And how will the U.S. react to China's changing posture vis-à-vis its place in the future?

There are many problems that result from the above visions. Starting with the currently existing institutions mentioned above, they have had difficulty enforcing any sort of meaningful cooperative policy objectives, there has been notable absence of cooperative action in a region-wide crisis situation and/or inter-state lingering disputes over territorial sovereignty. There is also the problem that many of these institutions are quite diverse in terms of the political and legal norms that their members subscribe to. According to Acharya, it is this diversity in its own membership that is part of the reason that even the ASEAN, known as the most successful regional institution, holds on to the ideals of national sovereignty and non-intervention and has been reluctant to adopt more collective ideals like humanitarian intervention or has sought to localize them like with the European concept of common security being reinterpreted as cooperative security.[11]

One important undercurrent in these visions is the expansion of economic dialogue would create a basis, constituting environment conducive for regional integration in the long run. As a practical means, thus, there has recently been mounting calls for the formation of FTA as noted above. The goal is to promote economic cooperation between the parties involved, but a successful FTA is expected to boost up the level of interdependence between them, by extension the less chance for them to get engaged in a military collision over any disputes. Implicit in this observation is the belief that increasing FTA will lead to greater regional integration, paving the way for the creation of a region-wide institution as the countries involved would favor a mechanism designed to assure a win-win or mutually-beneficial relations. However, this seems to have issues of its own.

As Ravenhill suggests, most agreements have been driven by foreign policy goals rather than the desires of domestic businesses, and they have offered mostly shallow integration with little genuine impact on boosting trading between nations.[12] Given that the larger regional trade proposals similarly rest on such factors, it is unlikely that any of the trade-regime proposals will drive any sort of multilateralization fit for the solution of the issues relevant to regional economic cooperation and security. It is in this context that one needs to consider the notion of "capability-legitimacy gap."[13] This notion was first put forward by Acharya who sees that while the region has enjoyed a high level of political will and legitimacy as manifested in the case of ASEAN, its weakness as a region-wide institution stemming from the lack of binding force has had a normative influence on East Asian regionalism since its creation. In addition, the material capabilities needed to solidify such a regional order has failed to come about through the successive failure of regional powers like the United States, China, Japan and India to provide due leadership. Whereas Acharya sees this gap as having prevented East Asia from becoming driven by a "concert of powers" or some other type of hegemonic order,[14] one can see continued weakness in its regional development as making a hegemonic directed order more likely. Here when one wonders if a rising China or India might one day provide the leadership necessary for developing stronger regional institutions, he may rather see the need for leadership to come from those East Asian nations that have the material capabilities to prop up a stable regional order but no longer powerful enough to purse regional hegemony.[15]

When considering the role of the hegemonic regional powers in East Asia, China and the United States, they present many problems to the creation of successful multilateral institutions. As seen in the term of "strategic competitor" that the U.S. often uses in relation to its relations with China, Washington has tended to view Beijing as a potential challenge to its status in the world, let alone East Asia. In return, China has tended to perceive the U.S. as one of the biggest huddles to go over in pursuing its long-term strategic aspirations with East Asia placed in the center. Given this, these hegemonic powers can seek to undermine regional multilateral institutions by pushing for bilateralism instead (consider the U.S. security alliance set-up or the Chinese attempts at settling the South China Sea disputes) or they can seek to play out their rivalry by trying to influence the direction of such institutions or proposing rival regional orders. Certainly when we see the EAS vs. ASEAN plus Three,[16] Shanghai Cooperative Organization (SCO) vs. the Trilateral Security Dialogue (TRD),[17] or the TPP vs. RCEP,[18] we find multiple examples of rival security and economic visions in which one or the other hegemon appears to be shaping the regional order to its own interests. One crucial question that arises in this context is: how can a hegemonic influenced or undermined institution be able to deliver cooperative results? Examples that could constitute an answer to this question abound, but one can point out that Chinese influence undermined the attempt at the 2012 ASEAN meeting to agree to a cooperative framework for the South China Sea dispute.[19]

Another important issue to be addressed here is: why should the rest of East Asia accede to allowing their fates to be shaped by the lager powers? One of the reasons that ASEAN first formed was to give the weaker states of Southeast Asia a stronger position relative to the larger powers like the U.S. and the Soviet Union. In a sense, this question may relate as well to ideals like the "Concert of East Asia" or the traditional hierarchical system. Being sovereign, the majority of states in East Asia would want a say and influence in the direction of the region. Given this, it may be hard to see them accepting any system where they end up in the second class.

In this regard, the status quo might look good to many of these states, since the weaker states are acting as a stronger driving force for regionalism in the current environment.

One last aspect that needs to be mentioned in regards to all the visions discussed is the question of normative ideas, specifically in terms of political and legal values, and how any of these institutions can develop and spread norms in this region. Because if there is one aspect that is noteworthy about the development of the European Union, that is what has been called its normative power, its ability to spread its ideals far beyond its borders; so much so that it is heavily studied in East Asia and Latin America as a model for developing multilateral institutions.

Implications of the European Experience for East Asia

One common fact that is brought up against the idea that Europe should be used as a model for East Asia or other regions is the fact that Europe is more homogeneous as compared to East Asia. This may relate to some of the other problems individuals make when looking at Europe as a model by overlooking the historical development of the European Union (EU) and considering why that model emerged as it did. While the EU today comprises 28 nation-states, its origins can be found in the six nation European Coal and Steel Community (ECSC) formed in 1952,[20] which later led to the European Economic Community (EEC) in 1957. Yet, this was not the only vision for Europe, as the European Free Trade Association was created among other European nations that could not or would not join the EEC. There also existed authoritarian states like Spain, and the Soviet Bloc of nations in Eastern Europe. The fact that the EEC would spread out to encompass many of the nations in this region is not just due to its economic success, but its normative success as well. Its idea for the region was certainly stronger than the other.

A couple of crucial points can be made here on the European experience. First of all, it started small with a core group of six nations. It also avoided the direct participation of hegemonic powers. One of the reasons that the UK did not join until 1973, despite applying first in 1960, was the belief prevalent in France that it might be a way for the U.S. to influence the direction of the EEC.[21] What is important to be noted here is that the first six members shared economic ties, security concerns and normative ideas, especially about political and legal systems in terms of a collective vision in regional matters.[22]

In retrospect, one can only state that the fact that a core membership shared ideas and concerns matters profoundly. What is more is that they set about developing their regional institutional vision before expanding their membership. This allowed them to strengthen the institutional rules in place and made it more likely than what those who had joined did on the basis of such rules, rather than the new members attempting to shape the institution to accept other norms. The result was a supranational institutional order that has been much more effective at establishing and enforcing policy measures, particularly in terms of trade and economic integration. In addition, the norms that have spread from six nations to 28 also influence many of the neighbors of the EU, whether because they have a desire for joining or wish to develop better economic ties with the member states for both intangible and substantial benefits.

As a corollary of this to East Asia, one could contend that instead of coming up with grand and large scale groups that cover all the regional players with a diversity of economic conditions as well as political and legal systems, the goal of developing an effective multilateral institution in this region needs to look at a more modest but realistic group of nations, a small group of nations that should share economic ties (and be economically developed enough to handle economic integration), share security concerns, and hold similar normative values in terms of legal and political set-ups. Such an institution must also avoid, at least at its inception, the direct involvement of one of the hegemonic regional powers for the reasons outlined above. To put it differently, allowing hegemonic influence would likely undermine any attempt at developing collective rules or allowing the institution to strengthen the position of weaker states vis-a-vis the hegemonic states as evident in the recent episode of ASEAN involving China and other smaller claimants over the South China Sea Dispute.

Now the question is where we can find region the potential for an effective multilateral institutional order in the East Asian. In light of its achievements to date, can ASEAN still have a role to play in developing regionalism in East Asia? To put it differently, is there any room for ASEAN to serve as a springboard to accelerate the process toward the formation of a region-wide institution. By all accounts, it is the most successful of all the multilateral institutions in this region, and at least in its beginnings it managed to be a small organization with similar interests among its members like the case of the EU. However, over time it has broadened its membership that has made it a more heterogeneous organization, while its adherence to the principle of sovereignty has meant a lack of meaningful integration among its members. Another aspect to consider is if ASEAN was always hampered by being only made up of weak regional states, particularly in terms of economic power. Given that deeper economic integration may be something that is more beneficial to developed economics rather than developing ones, and given that we are more likely to see well developed political and legal norms in developed economies, maybe we need to turn to a strong, developed nation to see where a core group could emerge to spur meaningful multilateralism.

In line with the aforementioned concept of capability-legitimacy gap, accordingly, one can argue that any hope for an East Asian regional order must see (1) stronger institutional order emerge, particularly with a greater commitment to collective action by ASEAN, while (2) seeing leadership emerge from nations other than regional hegemons such as the United States and China, strong powers that are willing to provide the material capabilities necessary to strengthen a successful regional institution without trying to dominate it. In this aspect, Japan appears to be one of the most likely powers to fill this gap, but only if it can lead through weakness of its own.

Certainly, Japan is a strong nation that in many ways seems to be a hinge at the core of the region. According to Baldwin who introduced "the domino theory" mentioned above,[23] the idea of expanding trade in East Asia is centered around the notion that a trade deal with Japan and another larger East Asian economy (most likely South Korea) would be the critical starting point for deeper regional economic integration because of the size and developed nature of Japan's economy.[24] According to Ravenhill, however, the idea has some merit if one considers this integration happening among a smaller group, one with members developed enough to handle integration.[25] Goh also suggests that when we consider the security concerns existing in the region, especially between China and the U.S., one only finds that Japan has a central and thus critical role to play in regional security.[26] There are certainly a number of nations in the region that share many of Japan's security concerns, notably North Korea's nuclear threat and the rise of China. In terms of political and legal norms, as one of the most developed nations in the region, it is strong on both counts and shares such norms with other well-developed nations in the region. Yet, one can question Japan's increased role pertaining to the formation of a regional institution for various reasons.

The problem with Japan is simple but compelling, that is, the lack of leadership stemming from both its own policy proclivity and the regional circumstance unfavorable to its re-assumption of major responsibility in the dimension of regional security in particular. As a result, it continues to prefer deferring to the U.S. in shaping its foreign policy and regional vision, and has been incapable of any sort of political will to develop a different regional vision with itself assuming a bigger responsibility.[27] Moreover, judging from the ever-escalating feud between Japan and its two most important neighbors, viz., China and Korea, over the said territorial disputes originating in Japan's past role in the region, one cannot but deduce a conclusion that Japan's radius of action would only likely shrink even when it wishes to amplify its role pertaining to regional institution-building. As a recent move, Japan has endeavored to introduce a change in its regional and global role as well, but suffice it to say that Japan's such efforts have brought about repercussions, making its neighbors alarmingly wary of its enhanced role in the region.

Conclusion

While East Asia presently stands as one of the most dynamic region in economic growth, it remains a region full of unresolved security issues which in turn would prevent the region from maintaining its current dynamism in the long run. Accordingly, East Asia cannot afford to be left out of the global trend toward regionalism. If East Asia were to see its regional institutions to grow in strength and power, however, it might need to see the aforementioned "capability-legitimacy gap" closed more than anything else. It is certainly true that the easiest way to do so is likely through one of the "Concert of East Asia" type concepts, which can achieve this without much regard for the wishes of smaller regional nations. If the goal is to see an institutional structure develop that is non-hegemonic, however, then this gap must be bridged in a more intricate way.

This is most likely to happen not with the creation of a new institution, but with the strengthening of the existing institution that enjoys the greatest ability to generate legitimacy in the region, that is, ASEAN. It is all clear that ASEAN has the ambition to become a stronger entity, and many of those within ASEAN recognize the need to put greater effort in strengthening and expanding their institutions. There seems to be an acknowledgment ASEAN needs to put a greater emphasis on developing a more legalistic character to the institutions, must show a greater willingness to break away from consensus and a greater desire to implement monitoring and compliance mechanisms while shifting away from the principles of sovereignty and non-interference. All these actions will be a challenge to meet, especially in terms of finding a balance to ensure that the weakest members of ASEAN can buy into these efforts and not fear being victimized by the stronger members of ASEAN.[28]

One main problem with the approach that ASEAN has taken in the past toward regional integration and cooperation, one that is protective of national interests above all else, is that it is a product of a different time, when ASEAN nations first were gaining their independence and looking to shield themselves from the adverse influence of colonial powers. The principles of sovereignty and non-interference that have formed the basis of ASEAN were understandable in those circumstances and gave the member nations strength in defending their interests. However, times have changed and without stronger institutional structure, one made stronger with the adoption of more legalistic norms, then the influence of ASEAN and its member nations in the region is likely to shrink, and with it any hope of a non-hegemonic international order.

On the other hand, a stronger nation like Japan faces many difficulties as noted above if it intends to position itself as a regional hegemon, while South Korea and Australia are middle powers for whom such a goal seems out of reach. Be that as it may, on the basis of sheer power interests, all three would seem to be better off in contributing to a regional framework that encourages collective action through non-hegemonic institutions. They can play a large technical role in assisting in ASEAN's institutional development while also establishing tighter bonds with each other. Essentially, the need is to develop two spheres, with these more powerful nations developing a greater basis for public goods sharing with ASEAN in return for its stronger and more liberal institutional development. These more powerful nations can also help maintain and develop regional talk shops like the EAS, the purpose of which would be to allow for more expanded regional discussions within such forums, while ASEAN-led efforts would be put aside as it focused more on developing itself.

If these poles of influence can strengthen themselves and eventually come together, it is possible for the capability-legitimacy gap to be overcome in a non-hegemonic way. Otherwise, it is hard to see East Asia developing in a manner in which the interests of smaller nations will influence regional institutional development, and the future of East Asia will most likely be dictated by the interests of hegemonic nations more likely to favor a regional order hierarchical in structure. In the final analysis, the externally-oriented economic structure of most countries in the region who have contributed to regional economic dynamism to date and the eve-complicatedness of regional security landscape together suggests that the future of East Asia will likely hinge upon the success of regional cooperation. One main feature of East Asian international politics and political economy, that is, the nexus of economics, security, and international relations in East Asia demands greater attention as numerous examples constitute evidence conclusively confirm the security implications of flourishing economic relations in East Asia, and vice-versa as well.[29] In this situation, the evolving rivalry between the United States and China behooves us to analyze its impact on regional security and economic climate as well as the on-going search for a formula which would help us to form a multilateral regional institution. Then the remaining question is whether East Asian countries will be willing and able to come together not only for their own security and economic prosperity but also for regional common goals with any hegemonic or dominance powers engaged in the process minimal, if not nil.

Notes

1. Kai He, *Institutional Balance in the Asia Pacific: Economic Interdependence and China's Rise* (London and New York: Routledge, 2009), pp. 127–139.
2. Amitav Acharya, *Foundations of Collective Action in Asia: Theory and Practice of Regional Cooperation* (Asian Development Bank Institute Working Paper Series, No. 344, February 2012), pp. 3–5.
3. Kevin G. Gai, *The Political Economy of East Asia: Regional and National Dimensions* (New York: Palgrave Macmillan, 2008), pp. 204–205.

4. Richard E. Baldwin, "Asian Regionalism: Promises and Pitfalls," in Choong Yong Ahn, Inkyo Cheong and Richard E. Baldwin, eds., *East Asian Economic Regionalism* (Netherlands, Spring 2005), p. 157.
5. Brendan Taylor, "Asia's Century and the Problem of Japan's Centrality," *International Affairs*, Vol. 87, No. 4 (July 2011), p. 880.
6. Similar to "Chimerica," which would put the U.S. and China at the forefront of international affairs, the idea of a G2 grouping has recently attracted wide attention both in the media and the academic circles. Examples are too many to cite.
7. Francis Fukuyama, "The Security Architecture in Asia and American Foreign Policy," in Kent E. Caldor and Francis Fukuyama, *East Asian Multilateralism: Prospects for Regional Stability* (Baltimore: Johns Hopkins University Press, 2008), pp. 249–250.
8. David Kang, "Why China's Rise Will be Peaceful: Hierarchy and Stability in the East Asian Region," *Perspectives in Politics*, Vol. 3, No. 3 (September 2005), p. 551.
9. Ibid.
10. Evelyn Goh, "Great Powers and Hierarchical Order in Southeast Asia: Analyzing Regional Security Strategies," *International Security*, Vol. 32, No. 3 (Winter 2007/08), pp. 150–152.
11. Amitav Acharya, "Can Asia Lead? Power Ambitions and Global Governance in the Twenty-first Century," *International Affairs*, Vol. 87, No. 4 (July 2011), p. 852.
12. John Ravenhill, "Extending the TPP: The Political Economy of Multilateralization in Asia," Paper for Asia Pacific Trade Economists' Conference <ArtNet> (United Nations Economic and Social Commission for Asia and the Pacific, Bangkok, November 2–3, 2009).
13. Amitav Acharya, *Foundations of Collective Action in Asia: Theory and Practice of Regional Cooperation* (Asian Development Bank Institute Working Paper Series, No. 344, February 2012).
14. Ibid.
15. Ibid., p. 16.
16. These two examples of expanding regionalism in East Asia can be seen as reflecting the competition between China and Japan. The Chinese response to the EAS has been to suggest that Japan is attempting to bring nations outside the region into regional affairs in an attempt to counterbalance China. Michael Wesley, "Asia-Pacific Institutions," in William T. Tow, ed., *Security Politics in the Asia-Pacific: A Regional-Global Nexus?* (Cambridge: Cambridge University Press, 2009), p. 63.

17. The Trilateral Security Dialogue can be interpreted as an attempt by the United States to contain China within East Asia, and thus the Shanghai Cooperative Organization can be seen as China's attempt to push back against this and assert its own power in the region. Wesley, *op.cit.* p. 64.
18. When we look at the TPP or the RCEP, we can also see worrying elements of great power rivalry. The first is a U.S.-led effort at a regional trade pact that notably does not include China at this time, while the other is ostensibly an ASEAN-led effort but includes China as a key partner with the U.S. excluded. Beginda Pakpahan, "Will RCEP Compete with the TPP?" (November 28, 2012) http://www.eastasiaforum.org/2012/11/28/will-rcep-compete-with-the-top (Date of Access: March 3, 2014).
19. "ASEAN Appears More United on South China Sea Issues," The Japan Times (November 15, 2012).
20. This paragraph is largely drawn on EUROPA, "Treaty establishing the European Coal and Steel Community, ESCS Treaty," European Union, http://europa.ed/legislationsummaries/institutionalaffairs/treaties/treatiesecsc en.htm (Date of Access: March 3, 2014).
21. Ibid.
22. Ian Manners, "Normative Power Europe: A Contradiction in Terms," *Journal of Common Market Studies*, Vol. 30, No. 2 (2002), pp. 235–258.
23. Baldwin, *op.cit.* p. 157
24. Ibid.
25. Ravenhill, *op.cit.* pp. 3–4.
26. Goh, *op.cit.* p. 900.
27. Brendan Taylor, "Asia's Century and the Problem of Japan's Century," *International Affairs*, Vol. 87, No. 4 (2011), p. 885.
28. He, *op.cit.* pp. 115–129.
29. Avery Goldstein and Edward D. Mansfield, "The Political Economy of Regional Security in East Asia," in Every Goldstein and Edward D. Mansfield, eds., *The Nexus of Economics, Security, and International Relations in East Asia* (Stanford: Stanford University Press, 2012), pp. 1–31.

References

Acharya, Amitav (2011), "Can Asia Lead? Power Ambitions and Global Governance in the Twenty-first Century," *International Affairs*, Vol. 87, No. 4, July.

Acharya, Amitav (2012), *Foundations of Collective Action in Asia: Theory and Practice of Regional Cooperation*, Asian Development Bank Institute Working Paper Series, No. 344, February.

Baldwin, Richard E. (2005), "Asian Regionalism: Promises and Pitfalls," in Choong Yong Ahn, Inkyo Cheong and Richard E. Baldwin, eds., *East Asian Economic Regionalism*, Netherlands, Spring.

EUROPA, "Treaty establishing the European Coal and Steel Community, ESCS Treaty," European Union, http://europa.ed/legislation summaries/institutional affairs/treaties/treaties ecsc en.htm.

Fukuyama, Francis (2008), "The Security Architecture in Asia and American Foreign Policy," in Kent E. Caldor and Francis Fukuyama, *East Asian Multilateralism: Prospects for Regional Stability*, Baltimore: Johns Hopkins University Press.

Gai, Kevin G. (2008), *The Political Economy of East Asia: Regional and National Dimensions*, New York: Palgrave Macmillan.

Goh, Evelyn (2007/2008), "Great Powers and Hierarchical Order in Southeast Asia: Analyzing Regional Security Strategies," *International Security*, Vol. 32, No. 3 (Winter).

Goldstein, Avery Goldstein and Mansfield, Edward D. (2012), "The Political Economy of Regional Security in East Asia," in Every Goldstein and Edward D. Mansfield, eds., *The Nexus of Economics, Security, and International Relations in East Asia*, Stanford: Stanford University Press.

He, Kai (2009), *Institutional Balance in the Asia Pacific: Economic Interdependence and China's Rise*, London and New York: Routledge.

Kang, David (2005), "Why China's Rise Will be Peaceful: Hierarchy and Stability in the East Asian Region," *Perspectives in Politics*, Vol. 3, No. 3 (September).

Manners, Ian (2002), "Normative Power Europe: A Contradiction in Terms," *Journal of Common Market Studies*, Vol. 30, No. 2.

Pakpahan, Beginda (2012), "Will RCEP Compete with the TPP?" *East Asia Forum* (November 28).

Park, Ariella (2012), "Explainer: What is the Trans-Pacific-Partnership?" *America's Society* (April 26).

Ravenhill, John (2009), "Extending the TPP: The Political Economy of Multilateralization in Asia," Paper for Asia Pacific Trade Economists' Conference <ArtNet> (United Nations Economic and Social Commission for Asia and the Pacific, Bangkok, November 2–3).

Taylor, Brendan (2011), "Asia's Century and the Problem of Japan's Centrality," *International Affairs*, Vol. 87, No. 4, July 2011.

Wesley, Michael (2009), "Asia-Pacific Institutions," in William T. Tow, ed., *Security Politics in the Asia-Pacific: A Regional-Global Nexus?* Cambridge: Cambridge University Press.

Chapter 3

Regional Cooperation and Technology Transfer in East Asia: The Case of Myanmar

*Yuri Sadoi**

Introduction

Sustainable development in East Asia requires stable economic development, which is possible with continuous technological upgrading led by human resource development and innovation. Human resource development is indispensable for sustainable development and is powered by innovation in many ways. Innovation is not a new phenomenon. People have always thought about new and better ways of doing things and tried them out in practice. Without innovation, or new and better ways of performing tasks, the world looks different. Not only are there highly technological innovations; but also there are fundamental innovations and many ways to improve performance.

The technology development of automobile firms shows an evolutionary process, from manufacturing prompted by simple customer requests, then moving to a strict policy of quality and later becoming a key player in the automotive market with an innovation and technology development cycle consisting of design, prototype, validation and fulfillment. This

*Yuri Sadoi, Professor, Faculty of Economics, Meijo University, Japan.

long-term process has allowed firms to consolidate their innovation and technology development efforts.

Technological capability building is an important issue for developing countries in terms of economic development. Technology and knowledge have moved across enterprises and countries. Since the 1980s, Japan's foreign direct investment has accelerated because of the appreciation of the yen, and Japan has been a major contributor of technology transfer to Asian countries. Especially in the ASEAN countries, the Japanese technology transfer to the automobile industry has been intensive and has played an important role in the development of the manufacturing industry and its human resources.

The ASEAN Economic Community (AEC), currently undergoing its finalization process, which is due to be completed by 2015, is expected to achieve regional economic integration. The AEC envisages the following key parts: a single market and production base, a highly competitive economic region, a region of equitable economic development, and a region that is fully integrated into the global economy. The AEC areas of cooperation include human resources development and capacity building, among the most important issues considered in this chapter.

However, for the late developing countries in the ASEAN, the AEC is their opportunity as well as their threat. Those countries face an urgent need to catch up in their industries or to find their competitive fields by liberalization.

This chapter examines the regional cooperation in the sustainable development of East Asian countries, especially focusing on the key roles of China, South Korea and Japan in the ASEAN countries. In 2015, the ASEAN countries are aiming to complete the AEC. Under these circumstances, the roles of China, South Korea and Japan in relation to the ASEAN countries area major issue for the sustainable economic development in East Asia. The aim of this chapter is to analyze the technology transfer from Japan, compared with that from China and South Korea.

The automobile industry plays an important role in terms of technology transfer. In those three countries, China, South Korea and Japan, the automobile industries have been actively engaging in foreign direct investment and technology transfer to ASEAN countries.

Followed by theoretical studies on technology transfer, the issues of the AEC are discussed. As an example of the three countries' approaches, Myanmar, the least developed country and the last frontier in the ASEAN, is discussed as an empirical study. The empirical survey in this chapter examines the differences in the social and cultural perspectives of regional cooperation. The Myanmar case may show characteristics of the strategies of China, South Korea and Japan in regional cooperation and technology transfer.

Theoretical Framework

Technology transfer in Asia has been actively discussed, especially since the 1985 Plaza Accord. The application of the yen and the industrialization policies of the Asian countries accelerated the Japanese transplantation to Asian countries. The industrialization of Asian countries was largely accomplished by the Japanese transplants and the Japanese technology transfer through them (Taniura 1990). The growth of the Japanese automobile industry in the 1980s was conspicuous for more than the speed of the increase in production volumes. The rapid expansion of overseas production, the integration of overseas operation into a global production network and the accompanying expansion of integrated global supply networks also attracted attention (Busser and Sadoi 2004).

With regard to its product architecture and organizational capabilities, the automotive industry has the characteristics of integral architecture, and its technical innovation is relatively moderate but requires wide experience and coordination with other members and processes (Fujimoto 2003). Therefore, the expansion of the Japanese global production networks in Asian countries, especially NIEs and ASEAN countries, including Thailand, Malaysia, Indonesia, the Philippines and Vietnam, has been studied and the cases of technology transfer evaluated (Koike and Inoki 1990; Taniura 1990; Itagaki 1997; Busser and Sadoi 2004). The technology transfer of Japanese enterprises, in the automobile, electric, electronics and other various industries, has been studied as cases (Okamoto 1998). The host governments have applied industrial strategies to create a cluster policy in their automotive sectors, which draw on multinational enterprises (MNEs) to enhance the automotive industries (Taniura 1990; Sadoi 2003).

The technology transfer of the Japanese production system has been studied in various ways. Itagaki (1997) presented surveys of technology transfer of the Japanese production system in NIEs and suggested the importance of human resource management in those cases. In particular, the Japanese skill formation system is a key to the successful technology transfer (Koike and Inoki 1990). Japan developed a skill formation system from the early years of development. In other Asian countries, as Japanese technology was transferred, the importance of human resource development in industries began to be evaluated and introduced, starting with Asian NIEs.

Japan has been successful in achieving high skill-based industries. Japan is known for its extensive, firm-based system of training, strongly associated with complementary personnel policies, such as seniority wages and internal career ladders (Thelen 2004; Sadoi 2009). However, Japan, as well as other Asian NIEs, has experienced falling competitiveness in export markets due to a rise in labor costs since the 1980s and the rapid development of China. The rising labor costs have driven the relocation of a significant share of production from Japan to China and Southeast Asia. Japan, which has developed high skill- and technology-based industries, has expanded its production in the ASEAN and transferred its skills and technology in the process, with important ramifications for the international division of labor of firms in both countries.

In many developing countries, the foreign direct investment (FDI) of multinational enterprises has become a major source of technology. In Thailand, where in recent years Chinese, South Korean and Japanese direct investment have been concentrated, the economic growth rate in the 1980s and 1990s paralleled those of its more technologically sophisticated neighbors, such as Malaysia, Singapore, and South Korea, yet its technological development lags behind quite significantly (Wang and Chien 2007).

Sadoi (2010) focuses on the development of technological capability and aims to investigate how organizational capability and human resources have been developed. Technological capability is judged focusing on engineering-related jobs in the R&D and engineering divisions in the Thai automobile industry. According to the *Frascati Manual* (OECD 2002),

R&D comprises creative work undertaken on a systematic basis in order to increase the stock of knowledge and the use of this stock of knowledge to devise new applications. R&D covers basic research, applied research and experimental development.

What will happen after the AEC is completed? China, South Korea and Japan will see the ASEAN as a single market. Thailand will continuously play an important role as a hub of automobile production in the AEC. Each ASEAN country will have to find and upgrade its strength to survive in the AEC. The countries in the AEC that lack a specific strength will urgently need to acquire one.

Comparative Analysis of Regional Cooperation through the Case of Myanmar

The previous section explained the Japanese case of FDI and technology transfer to the ASEAN. South Korea and China are increasing their FDI to ASEAN countries as well as Japan. The South Korean investment in the ASEAN started since the 1990s, especially in the electric industries. In the case of China, direct investment in the ASEAN began since the 2000s. By focusing on the case of Myanmar, this section tries to analyze the differences in the three countries' FDI and technology transfer approaches.

Myanmar is the developing country with the lowest GDP per capita in the ASEAN. Since March 2011, the new Government of Myanmar has anticipated sustained economic development through advancing democratization domestically and moving toward a market economy. Myanmar has been attracting foreign investment opportunities and attention from all over the world since then.

Figure 1 reveals the low level of economic development in Myanmar. It shows the GDP per capita in major countries. As shown here, Myanmar is in the lowest group among the ASEAN.

The trading information can show the current industrial situation of Myanmar. Table 1 provides the breakdown of exports by trading partner in 2012. As shown here, the major import partners are Thailand, China and India. They are all connecting lands with Myanmar. Japan is in the fourth place and South Korea is in the sixth place, representing 5% and 3% of the total exports from Myanmar.

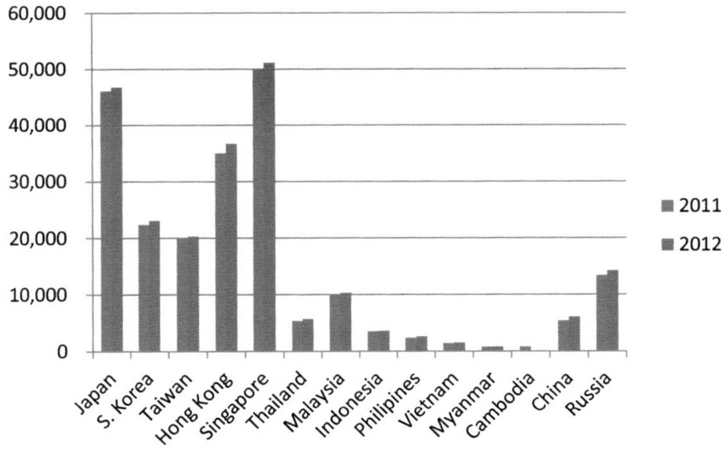

Figure 1. GDP Per Capita in 2011 and 2012 by Country (US$).

Source: Data obtained from JETRO (2014).

Table 1. Breakdown of Myanmar's Exports (by trading partner).

FY 2012 Exports: 8098 million (US$)	
Name of Country	%
Thailand	45
China	25
India	11
Japan	5
Singapore	3
South Korea	3
Malaysia	1
Germany	1
Indonesia	0
United Kingdom	0
Hong Kong	0
Others	6

Source: Myanmar Central Statistical Organization.

Table 2. Breakdown of Myanmar's Imports (by trading partner).

FY 2012 Imports: 9.07 Billion (US$)	
Name of Country	%
China	30
Singapore	28
Japan	12
Thailand	8
Malaysia	4
South Korea	4
India	3
Indonesia	2
Germany	2
United States	1
United Kingdom	0
Others	6

Source: Myanmar Central Statistical Organization.

Considering imports, the situation is different from that of exports. Table 2 shows the breakdown of imports by trading partner in 2012. China is the biggest import partner, with 30% of the total imports, followed by Singapore with 28%, Japan with 12% and Thailand with 8%. South Korea is in sixth place, accounting for 4%.

What kinds of products are exported from Myanmar? Table 3 shows the breakdown of exports from Myanmar by product in 2012. As shown here, natural gas accounts for 41% of the total exports from Myanmar, followed by agricultural products, such as pulse crops, rice, seafood and sesame. In the manufacturing industry, sewn products and labor-intensive products make up 8% of the total exports.

Regarding imports, general and transportation equipment accounts for 29%, followed by petroleum products with 18%, metal products with 11%, electronics and electric appliances with 5%, plastics with 4% and so on, as shown in Table 4. Here, we can see that automobile imports have represented a large part of the imports since Myanmar liberalized automobile

Table 3. Breakdown of Myanmar's Exports (by product).

FY 2012 Exports: 8098 million (US$)	
Items	%
Natural gas	41
Pulse crops	11
Sewn products	8
Rice	6
Seafood	5
Teak	4
Sesame	3
Hardwood	3
Jade	3
Rubber	2
Others	14

Source: Myanmar Central Statistical Organization.

Table 4. Breakdown of Exports (by product).

FY 2012 Exports: 9.07 Billion (US$)	
General and transportation equipment	29%
Petroleum products	18%
Base metal and base metal products	11%
Electronics and electric appliances	5%
Plastics	4%
Synthetic fabrics	4%
Vegetable oil	3%
Medical supplies	3%
Fertilizer	2%
Cement	2%
Others	19%

Source: Myanmar Central Statistical Organization.

imports in March 2011 under the new government. Although Myanmar still faces import barriers, compared with the prior government, the import tariffs and limitations of importers have been lowered considerably.

We have looked at imports and exports so far. The trading pattern of Myanmar typically shows the initial phase of developing countries' trading pattern, which is largely observed in the ASEAN, that is, pre-industrialized countries' trading pattern, such as exporting natural resources and importing industrial products. Indonesia and Malaysia, following independence, show similar patterns to Myanmar. The Malaysian case might be the role model for development policies and patterns for Myanmar.

Myanmar is starting to attract foreign direct investment. Table 5 shows the foreign investment approved in Myanmar from April 2012 to

Table 5. Approved Foreign Investment in Myanmar (April 2013 – March 2013) Foreign Direct Investment in Myanmar (MIC Approved Basis).

(Units: US$ million, %)

	FY 2011		FY 2012			
	No	Amount	No	Amount	%	Increase
China	2	4,346	14	407	28.7	Δ90.6
Vietnam	1	18	3	329	23.2	1715.1
Singapore	—	—	14	248	17.5	
United Kingdom	1	100	5	233	16.4	133.1
Hong Kong	—	—	9	81	5.7	
Japan	2	4	11	54	3.8	1,152.0
South Korea	2	26	28	38	2.7	48.4
India	1	73	2	12	0.8	Δ84.2
The Netherlands	—	—	2	10	0.7	
Malaysia	3	52	2	4	0.3	Δ91.7
Thailand	—	—	2	1	0.1	
Canada	—	—	1	1	0.1	
Brunei	—	—	1	1	0.1	
Panama	1	26	—	—	—	
	13	4,644	94	1,419	100	Δ69.4

Source: Myanmar Central Statistical Organization.

March 2013. The three countries focused on in this paper, China, South Korea and Japan, show active investment in Myanmar. China accounts for the largest investment, with 29%. The number of investments has increased 7 times from that of FY 2011, although the amount of investments is smaller than that of 2011. FDI from South Korea and Japan show a significant increase both in the number and in the amount of investments.

The breakdown of FDI by items is shown in Table 6. It indicates manufacturing in the first place, followed by electric utility, oil and gas, and hotels and tourism. The investments in Myanmar in the form of partnerships with local companies are not included in this table. Therefore, including those investments with local companies, it is obvious that Myanmar is starting to attract large investments. The large parts of the investments come from China, South Korea and Japan, as they are the

Table 6. Foreign Direct Investment in Myanmar (MIC approved basis).

(Units: US$ million, %)

	FY 2011		FY 2012			
	No	Amount	No	Amount	%	Increase
Manufacturing	5	32	78	401	28.2	1142.4
Electric utility	1	4,344	1	364	25.7	Δ91.6
Oil and gas	5	248	6	309	21.8	24.8
Hotels and tourism	—	—	1	300	21.1	
Mining	2	20	1	15	1.1	Δ22.9
Others	—	—	4	15	1	
Agriculture	—	—	2	10	0.7	
Fishery	—	—	1	6	0.4	
Transportation	—	1	—	—	—	—
Construction	—	—	—	—	—	—
Real estate development	—	—	—	—	—	—
Industrial complex	—	—	—	—	—	—
	13	4,644	94	1,419	100	Δ69.4

Source: Myanmar Central Statistical Organization.

major players, especially in manufacturing industries in electric appliances and automobiles.

The situation of Japanese investment in Myanmar was surveyed by the author in March 2012 and February 2014. The methodology of the survey was mainly an interview survey conducted by visiting the offices and manufacturing sites of investors. In this chapter, a summary of the findings is introduced.

In the case of Japanese investment, the number of companies registered at the Japanese Chamber of Commerce and Industry, Yangon, can be used as one indicator. The number was 60 in the fiscal year of 1996. It increased to 86 by 1998, but dropped to 70 in 1999 because of the political problems in Myanmar. The numbers continued to drop for more than ten years until 2011. A drastic change came in 2012. The number of the companies increased by more than double: 53 companies in 2011 increased to 133 by the end of March 2013. About half of the companies are in the distribution and services sectors.

As shown in the previous data, Myanmar is attracting many investors from Japan. The major investing sectors are the distribution and services sectors. Their investments might be for pre-investment and feasibility study purposes before starting manufacturing in Myanmar. The electric and automobile industries are only included in imports and distribution centers.

Japanese manufacturers are interested in investing in Myanmar to search for better locations with lower labor costs. As shown in Table 7, the labor cost in Myanmar is the lowest in the Asian countries listed below. Small and medium-sized enterprises (SMEs) act quickly to relocate their production sites. Many of them operate in the labor-intensive garment industry. For the electric and automobile industry, in which most of the players are large corporations, the entry speed is rather slow. However, firms are setting up their distribution centers and service centers as an initial phase.

In the case of automobile manufacturers in Myanmar, Japan has a long history after World War II. From 1962 to 1988, Mazuda and Hino contributed their automobile technology to Myanmar Automobile and Diesel Engine Industries (MADI) as the import substitution industrialization policy of Myanmar under the social planned economy as part of the

Table 7. Monthly Basic Salary of Workers in Manufacturing (questionnaire survey of foreign-based Japanese companies: October–November 2012).

(Unit: US$)

Hong Kong (21)	1,619
South Korea (46)	1,517
Singapore (29)	1,230
Taiwan (44)	1,051
Thailand (395)	345
Malaysia (140)	344
China (457)	328
India (86)	290
The Philippines (55)	253
Indonesia (103)	229
Pakistan (9)	173
Vietnam (153)	145
Laos (10)	132
Sri Lanka (16)	118
Cambodia (11)	74
Bangladesh (16)	74
Myanmar (5)	53

Source: JETRO (2012).

compensation for WWII. However, from 1988, following Myanmar's open market policy, MADI stopped production. From 1998, MADI recommenced production based on the strict control of imports. At that time, MADI, SPA and Suzuki established Myanmar Suzuki and produced the Wagon R locally. However, as it was difficult to import knock-down parts from Japan, Myanmar Suzuki stopped production in 2010 and closed the company.

The situation has changed in Myanmar since the open policy in September 2011. Suzuki has again started production and plans to open a new production site in the Thilawa industrial area. As of February 2014, at the time of the author's survey, the production volume of Suzuki is still small, about 300 vehicles per month. However, Suzuki has re-employed most of its former employees at the time of Myanmar Suzuki and trained them following the Japanese human resource development system. Its non-automated production system has helped the workers to develop their skills in on-the-job training. The Japanese managers evaluated the re-employed workers' loyalty and working attitude toward skill formation highly.

In summary, Japanese technology transfer is just starting in Myanmar. Except for the case of Suzuki, most Japanese manufacturers are still waiting to start making big investments by setting up small operations to conduct feasibility studies and check the opportunities.

Chinese investment in Myanmar has a long history. Currently, there are mainly two types of investment moving from China to Myanmar. One is big energy projects and the other is labor-intensive projects.

One of the major Chinese energy investments in Myanmar is the pipelines of oil and gas from Myanmar's western coast to China's southwestern Yunnan province. In order to avoid the risk of oil and gas transport by ship through the Strait of Malacca, in 2009, two state-owned energy giants, China National Petroleum and Myanmar Oil & Gas Enterprise, agreed a $2.5 billion project to lay down more than 500 miles of oil and gas pipelines from Myanmar's western coast to China's southwestern Yunnan province. When the oil pipeline is activated later this year, tankers carrying crude oil from the Middle East and Africa will be able to dock at Myanmar's port of Kyaukpyu and send as many as 440,000 barrels of oil a day overland to China. The industry news service Platts (MHFI) reports that the oil pipeline is 75% complete and should be operational by June 2014.

The situation has changed from the time when the project was agreed in 2009. At that time, Myanmar was still ruled by a military junta and acted as a de facto vassal state to China. Since then, Myanmar's remarkable democratic transition has been changing the situation.

The other type of Chinese investment is in labor-intensive manufacturing. As shown in Table 7, the labor cost in China is rapidly increasing and was about six times higher than that in Myanmar in 2012. In addition, the trade imbalance of China, as well as the export surplus from China, might cause a trade imbalance with other major countries. In order to avoid this situation, Chinese garment industries started production in

Myanmar and now export their products as made-in-Myanmar products rather than made-in-China products. Those investments are very active, especially in the Mandalay area.

South Korea shows different strategies from those of China and Japan, that is, the cultural approach to influence marketing and consumer interests. First, South Korean dramas were introduced to Myanmar and became very popular among Myanmar's population. The popularity of South Korean dramas is used effectively as a marketing strategy. For example, in the case of modern dramas, attractive actors and actresses use modern electric appliances in their urban lifestyle. They use the latest Samsung or LG TVs, refrigerators and other electric devices. They drive Hyundai or Kia automobiles. In addition, South Korean cosmetics attract Myanmar women instead of traditional Myanmar cosmetics, called Tanaka. Those cultural approaches appeal very strongly to consumers in Myanmar.

Along with the cultural approach, the South Korean automobile maker Kia signed a contract with Super Seven Star Motors in Myanmar, for the production and sales of imported Kia cars. It set up modern showrooms in Yangon and provides the high status of South Korean cars with good service and maintenance. The company even provides an automobile loan system to customers where the banking system is not yet developed.

The government support in South Korea is strong. South Korea and Myanmar agreed to provide a $500 million loan to Myanmar for the years 2013 to 2017 from the Economic Development Cooperation Funds. They discussed eight areas of cooperation covering 39 projects, inclusive of those related to the infrastructure development, promoting services and sports sectors.

The government support enhances the private sector's investment activities. The Long Luck Group of Companies of Myanmar and HANBAEK ITC Co., Ltd of South Korea signed a memorandum of understanding on economic cooperation from manufacturing to energy projects. In the IT sector, South Korea launched an information access center (IAC) in Nay Pyi Taw in order to support Myanmar's ICT development and infrastructure development for the introduction of an e-government system.

The South Korean International Cooperation Agency (KOICA) is helping Myanmar to develop many projects, such as a road network, a land reform scheme to introduce mechanized farming, a master plan for arterial road network development, strengthening the statistical system and strengthening the capacity for convention management. In the latest development, the South Korean Government is planning to build a friendship bridge crossing the Yangon River to link urban Yangon with Dala, from where nearly 50,000 workers cross the Yangon River everyday by ferry to work in urban Yangon as there are no bridges between the two river banks. Along with the building of the bridge, an industrial park is also planned in Dala, where there is plenty of land and a workforce to enable South Korean companies to invest in the industrial park (Xinhua 2013).

Conclusions

This chapter examined the cases of regional cooperation in East Asia from the viewpoint of technology transfer. Technology transfer is an important issue and, especially in relation to human resource development, will contribute to sustainable development in the greater region.

For the ASEAN countries, the AEC in 2015 will be the urgent target for building capability. Under these circumstances, this chapter focused on China, South Korea and Japan and their strategies in technology transfer and investment in Myanmar, the potential market and so-called last frontier of the ASEAN.

There are various means of regional cooperation: state-oriented or private companies' initiatives, international support for human beings and welfare, and contributions for infrastructure or cost reduction purposes of products. We focused on how they are contributing to the industrialization of Myanmar using Chinese, South Korean and Japanese expertise in the field. Those three countries have experienced their own industrialization processes, Japan in the 1960s, South Korea in the 1980s and China in recent years. All three countries are currently shifting their roles from precipitants of technology to donors.

In the case of Myanmar, all three countries are important partners and donors of technology and industrialization for Myanmar. According to the findings, Japanese investments are becoming active, but they have so far been in the labor-intensive garment industries of SMEs or distribution and service centers. However, Japan is preparing and processing feasibility studies concerning the best timing and strategies. JICA and JETRO are contributing human resource development for managers.

China has strong ties with Myanmar historically. Large energy-related projects are in progress as the same time as the private sector is actively investing in labor-intensive manufacturing, especially in sawing.

South Korea has a unique cultural approach that attracts customers by using Korean drama. The Korean Government is assertive in investing in Myanmar in many ways, along with South Korean Samsung in the electronics industry and Hyundai Kia in the automobile industry.

This chapter shows the initial phase of investment in Myanmar by three major Asian players, China, South Korea and Japan. Continuous research on this topic is planned and will lead to more detailed data to be presented in the near future.

References

Busser, R. and Y. Sadoi (2004), *Production Networks in Asia and Europe*, London: Routledge.

Fujimoto, T. (2003), "Sosikinoryoku to seihinakitekucha" ["Organizational capabilities and product architecture"], *Sosiki Kagaku*, Vol. 36, No. 4, pp. 11–22.

Itagaki, H. (1997), *Nihonteki Keiei Seisan Shisutemu to Higashiajia [Japanese Management and Production System in East Asia]*, Tokyo: Mineruba Syobo.

JETRO (2012), *Survey on Activities of Japanese Companies Operating in Asia and Oceania*, October–November.

JETRO (2014), "The Japan External Trade Organization (JETRO)" http://www.jetro.go.jp/ (Accessed in March 2014).

Koike, K. and T. Inoki, eds. (1990), *Skill Formation in Japan and Southeast Asia*, Tokyo: University of Tokyo Press.

OECD (2002), *Frascati Manual 2002: Proposed Standard Practice for Surveys on Research and Experimental Development, The Measurement of Scientific and Technological Activities*, OECD Publishing.

Okamoto, Y. (1998), *Nihon Kigyo No Gijyutsuiten [Technology Transfer by Japanese Enterprises]*, Tokyo: Nihon Keizai Hyoronsha.

Sadoi, Y. (2009), "Japanese Skill and Knowledge Transfer: The Case of Exporting High-Precision Production Technology to China and Vietnam," *Meijo Ronso*, Vol. 19, No. 4, pp. 39–50.

Sadoi, Y. (2003), *Skill Formation in Malaysian Auto Parts Industry*, Selangor Malaysia: University Kabangsaan Malaysia (UKM) Press, pp. 1–177.

Sadoi, Y. (2010), "Technology Capability of Automobile Parts Suppliers in Thailand," *Journal of Asia Pacific Economy*, Vol. 15, No. 3, pp. 320–334.

Taniura, T. (1990), *Asia no kougyouka to gijyutsuiten [Industrialization and Technology Transfer in Asia]*, Tokyo: Asia Keizai Kenkyusho.

Thelen, K. (2004), *How Institutions Evolve — The Political Economy of Skills in Germany, Britain, the United States, and Japan*, Cambridge: Cambridge University Press.

Wang, T.Y. and S.C. Chien (2007), "The Influence of Technology Development on Economic Performance: The Example of ASEAN Countries," *Technovation*, Vol. 27, No. 8, pp. 471–488.

Xinhua (2013), "Myanmar South Korea Economic Cooperation Warms Up Myanmar Business Network," July 8. http://www.myanmar-business.org/2013/07/myanmar-south-korea-economic.html (Accessed on March 10, 2014).

Chapter 4

The Influence of Japanese Social Ideological Trends Upon East Asia Cooperation

*Jiang Xudong**

As one of the most vibrant areas in the world, East Asian countries have shown extremely strong interdependence among each other, especially in economic affairs. However, East Asian region is facing with a situation that politics is departing from economy. In terms of economy, the economic and trade development among China, Japan and South Korea is growing with each passing day. In politics, however, East Asian countries have not shown enough trust towards each other, especially between China-Japan, and Japan-South Korea. On the other hand, Japanese politicians' irresponsible remarks on issues about war and history worthened the distrust of both sides. This distrust, in turn, resulted in the stagnation of economic cooperation of East Asian countries.

If one gets to the bottom and asks why these Japanese politicians made those irresponsible remarks, one point cannot be ignored is the change of social ideological trend in current Japan. French historian Marc Broch thought, "the potential factors that control the human destiny consist of the fluctuation of social ideological trend, technological update and change of social and economic structures, whose influence upon history is no less than a coup or a war."[1] Chinese scholar Jiang Lifeng held that

* Jiang Xudong, Ph.D of International Politics, Shanghai International Studies University, China.

"Social ideological trend is a trend in a specific period of relatively the majority of Japanese people of one class or cross classes, a trend reflected the social and economic situations of that time especially the theme of the times, a trend that embodied their benefits and requirements, and therefore brought about far reaching and extensive significance and echo around the society."[2]

Elected by the public power, Japanese politicians' discourses and deeds should cater to the psychological demands of the electorate. The analysis of Japanese social ideological trend is conducive to better understanding of current Japanese politics and judgment of the future of cooperation of East Asian countries.

Japanese Three Social Ideology since Modern Times and Their Influence

1. The Nationalism at the End of the Tokugawa Shogunate

With the decline of power of the Shogunate, Perry led a U.S. naval and diplomatic expedition to Japan in 1853. Japan was caught in unprecedented crisis. Japanese wise people who cared for the fate of the nation thought the decadent Tokugawa Shogunate could not assume the responsibility of leading Japan in defending exterior invasion any more. Only the national wide unity could realize the rebellion of the barbarians. To realize national wide unity, respecting the emperor was demanded. That is to say, the authority of Japanese emperor should be established and the country should be reined by the emperor to form and unite "300 Dukes" of the nation to realize the goal of defending Japan. Through returning the region versions, abolishing fan and setting up county, Japan realized national unity.

Japanese modern plan, led by Meiji Restoration, was rooted in non-axial, immanentist Ontologies. Meiji Restoration led the main formation process of the Meiji state and even the development of post-Modern Japanese society ... among which the most important feature was the strong tendency of national community, uniting nation with society.[3] This tendency contributed to the formation of single-nationality state — Japan, the driving force behind which was no other than Japanese Nationalism formed in the end of 19th century.

2. The Militarism that Provoked WWII

After the Meiji Restoration, Japan was confronted with trebling goals: state industrialization, national cohesion, and the realization of democratization that was in line with world trends. However, "industrialization, nationalism and democratization, were once the founding philosophy of Meiji Restoration after reforms. The problem lied in the fact that the leaders of Meiji Restoration did not integrate the three founding philosophies, neither did they reach a consensus".[4] Finally, Japan started its industrialized course with nationalism as the forerunner, while democratization was put in the last step.

At the outset of Meiji Restoration, Japan who was seeking reform ran into a fundamental problem: lack of money for reform. Through imposing heavy tax upon the peasants, Japan should secure finance and accumulate the original capital in no time so as to realize industrialization. Weighing up the situation, Japan had exploited the domestic public to the fullest, now the only way out was to seek out of Japan. It was impossible for foreign people to hand their money to Japan, and the only way out for Japan was military expansion.

The two victories in the war of 1895 and 1905, not only granted the Japanese nation confidence, but also yielded real benefits toward Japanese industrial development. A case in point was that the initial accumulation of industrial capital of Mitsubishi resulted from the orders of the Japanese government during the first Sino-Japanese War, together with the postwar claim obtained by the Japanese government. The favored Japanese domestic capitalists quickly converged with rising Japanese militarists, suppressing the voices of Japanese democratic faction. Especially after the Tokyo Earthquake in the 1929, in order to get rid of domestic economic crisis and to shift contradiction, Japan invaded China, which directly led to the Mukden Incident. Ever since, Japan was heading toward a road of no return, until its defeat in the war.

3. The Pacifism that Accompanied with Postwar Introspection

The heavy loss suffered by defeated Japan was followed by the rise of Pacifism. Seemingly, the rise of Pacifism was a "Pacifist Constitution" brought by Mac Arthur; essentially, it signaled the Japanese fear of suffering the loss of war as well. As Masao Maruyama remarked, "the survival rights of Japanese people included two: one was the right to enjoy freedom from honor and deprivation; the other one was the right of the Japanese people to live peacefully".[5] Therefore, the routes advocated by Yoshida Shigeru such as "Yoshida Doctrine", "Economy first, then Military" were very prevailing. At the beginning of the postwar period, the opposition to Japanese armament was very strong. In times of Kishi Nobusuke, Kishi once attempted to strengthen armament, only to incur the demonstration of anti-arms by 600,000 Japanese public, who sieged the Japanese parliament and directly led to the collapse of Kishi Nobusuke Cabinet.

Pacifism had been Japanese mainstream ideology since postwar. The most important was that the Japanese public who benefited from "Pacifism" has strengthened cognition and reverence towards this ideology, and directly resisted to the "Extreme Right", "Amend the Constitution", "Arms Expansion" put forward by Japanese postwar politicians. However, with the decline of Japanese bubble economy, Japanese ordinary people were going from bad to worse. The fact that less dividend of "Pacifism" was shared triggered new transformation towards Japanese social ideological trend.

New Nationalism in Contemporary Japan Emerges

Either Junichiro Koizumi's visit to Yasukuni Shrine or Shinzo Abe's hail of long live the Emperor, in essence, both signify the emerging new nationalism of Japan. The series of "Right" movements since Abe's taking office were not isolated. If we connect this with the following instances, we would find that the whole political ecology has undergone a huge transformation. They are the public "Anti-human" speech on sex slave delivered by Toru Hashimoto from Osaka Restoration Association, secret and Nazi-like attempt to amend constitution requested by Taro Aso, a series of remarks brazenly denying Nanking Massacre by Kawamura magistrate of Aichi-ken last year.

In the 1990s, with the decline power of "Left Wing" and an end of "1955 System", we thought that general conservative trend has taken shape, but would not change the main guideline under Pacifism, which remains the mainstream of Japan's society. This judgment was probably right ten years ago, however, today's "Pacifism" is confronted with a formidable challenge by New Nationalism.

New Nationalism, focusing on "Japan's postwar political final accounts" and "be a great power" put forward by Masahiro Nakazone, implies the vision to restore Japan's influence as a political power. In the eyes of politicians represented by Ichiro Ozawa contending New Nationalism, the most emergent thing is to realize the "Be a normal state" of Japan. Conservative politicians held the viewpoint that Japan should not maintain the identity of a defeated country, playing a passive and insignificant role in the international arena. On the contrary, Japan should strive to become an influential country in various areas including economy, politics, military, etc.[6]

If New Nationalism of the 1980s and 1990s was barely known and hardly accepted, except by some politicians in the "Top design" of "Superstructure", then in the first ten years of 21st century, New Nationalism has turned into an ideological trend that could sheer the development direction of Japan's future. This is best represented in the following three aspects.

1. Gradual Consensus on Amending the Constitution

According to the investigation by Mainichi Shimbun in 2005, 62% subjects objected the amendment of rule in the ninth clause of the constitution and there were only 30% supporters. In addition, in the view of 80% Japanese public, the Ninth Clause made its contribution to Japan's maintaining peaceful road after WWII.

In 2007, Asahi Shimbun conducted telephone surveys of 1807 people from April 14 to April 15. The result announced on May 2 revealed that over 78% interviewees believed that the Ninth Clause made its contribution to national peace over the 60 years; 49% interviews hoped not to amend peace clauses, while only 33% held the opposite attitude. When asked whether parts of the constitution needed amendment, 58% thought it necessary with 27% showing objection.

In the 2013 opinion poll delivered to 3,000 electors by Asahi Shimbun and University of Tokyo, almost 1900 replies were received. The poll revealed that about 50% electors were in favor of amending the constitution to strengthen national defense power, 10% higher than the percentage (41%) of 2009, and 45% electors were for Japanese united self-defense with other countries to counter external attack, 8% higher than that of 2009.

From the above statistics, we could observe that after WWII Japanese public scarcely raised doubts about current constitution. Over half of the ordinary people would not carry on with lessons learnt by their ancestors through blood and sweat. It is predictable that with the fading memory of Japanese young generation toward WWII and the worsening economy, more and more ordinary Japanese hope to change their lives through politics, for example, through amending the constitution. Ordinary people thought in this way, let alone Japanese politicians. In political circle of Japan, 89% parliament members are for constitution amendment, while 79% are in favor of Japanese government's setting up Defense League.

2. The Influence of Regional Parliament Members towards Central Parliament

After its taking office, the Democratic party carried out a series of "regional reform" to regulate "relations between the central government and regional government", to enlarge "region privilege" and to realize regional self-autonomy, aiming to realize the situation that Ichiro Ozawa envisioned as "300 New Dukes". These reforms expected to bring about central development through regional development and final realization of maximizing national benefited through regional benefits. With the anchorage of Osaka reform and Toru Hashimoto's coming to power, Japanese ordinary people caught sight of a ray of hope. Meanwhile, the popularity of either Tokyo's Ishiwara or Aichi's magistrate had surpassed that of politicians of "Kasumigaseki". However, these "capable" regional parliament members attempted to march into the central, instead of marching in the direction of becoming a regional "Daimyo" designated by Ozawa, which best elucidated by the confluence of Toru Hashimoto and Ishihara. It was obvious that Japanese politicians did not sway in nationalism, and their temporary slogan was for the sake of gaining more votes with the ultimate goal of guiding regional construction with the help of the nation.

3. Marching towards Military Power

In 2007, Self defense mandate updated to the division on self defence; Japanese 2010 national defense program guidelines put forward "proactive defense" for the first time, changing its 70 year old "static defense" guideline. A series of measurements such as three principles of relaxing restrictions on weapon export, increasing the number and competence of U.S. troops in Japan, improving the armament of Japanese naval, constructing missile defense system in the name of defending DPRK's missile, amending self defense law, and etc. had in fact broke Japanese self defense forces away from the scope of "Self Defense", signifying its essential march toward troops. The prewar inspiring and encouraging situations propelled by troops reappeared.

The Appearance of New Nationalism and Change of Japanese Geopolitical Perspective

1. From Internationalism to Nationalism

In the time of Pacifism, Japan pursued the developing road of "Economy first, then politics" with the focus on economic development and goal of realizing the internationalization of Japan. Japan is the "World's Japan". However, in the perspective of New Nationalism, Japan is returning to "Japanese Japan". Focusing more and more on Japan itself, Japan is emphasizing more and more on the benefits of the public, looking inside instead of outside, making longitudinal comparison instead of horizontal, more apt to be incited by nationalism, and in turn conducive to Japanese politicians' manipulation of public opinions.

2. From Globalization to Regionalization

In the time of Pacifism, Japan has held a global outlook. Meanwhile, in terms of geopolitical perspective, Japan pursued the global outlook by treating itself as "Ocean Country" and restricting itself with the identity of trade country. However, with the emerging of new nationalism, Japanese perspective is becoming more and more narrow. Japan found itself not the winner of globalization. The real winner is China whom Japans once made every effort to preach to join the WTO. In the past ten years, China has surpassed Japan, while Japan has been relatively stagnant during this period. Globalization is not the tool for Japanese victory, but perhaps regionalization is.

This point could be attested to by East Asian Community put forward by Japan. The proposal of TPP is out of the same consideration. Judging by appearance, TPP has shown a wider scope of application. In reality, Japan was going back to the era of Yukiti Fukuzawa, departing Asia for Europe and adhere stubbornly to old ideas of 100 years ago by deliberately "denying" the world economic center is moving eastward. This can only be explained by the fact that despite the beneficial impact of Asia in the era of globalization upon Japan's economy, it's detrimental to Japan's plan to become a political power. Therefore, TPP was neglected by Japan on purpose. On the contrary, Japan was provocative and aggressive in regional issues and dividing regional process of globalization and integration.

3. From "Returning to Asia" to "Holding the U.S."

After WWII, from the prime minister Shigeru Yoshida to Takeo Fuda, and to Yokio Hatoyama, all without exception valued Asian influence on Japan's economy. From Fukuda Doctrine (Peace, Heart to Heart, Equivalence) to "East Asian Community", Japan was actually clearly realizing the significance of a rising Asia to Japanese future development. However, this "impulse" to return to Asia was restrained. Literally, it was due to Diaoyu Island dispute that disillusioned the envision of "East Asian Community". As a matter of fact, it was the Japanese parochial thought that once East Asian Community was established, the benefactor was China not Japan, which will influence Japanese political power instead of Japanese economy. For example, if Japan negotiated with China to establish the East Asia Community, it would probably depend upon China in politics and economy comprehensively. As a consequence, Japan would be reduced to a second rate country in Asia, unable to become the global power as envisioned in the new nationalism. If Japan were to become a strong power as planned to be, it needed to take advantage of the Sino-U.S. contradictions to seek for favorable opportunities to return to East China and to realize world power.

4. From Liberalism to Realism

Rising by virtue of free trade, Japan once thought as long as the world was trading with itself, the world's attention was out of question. By means of

"Pacifist Constitution", Japan was the "Pacifist Angel" of the world, having the qualification "not to promote war" to the world. However, all these took place in the glorious past of Japan. For the time being, Japanese economy is in recession with a slumping world rank. Apart from China and South Korean, once Japan's colony has shown a trend of surpassing, the dividend of free trade and liberalism no long existed. In the perspective of new nationalism, Japan tended to consider questions in a realistic thinking mode, attempting to balance and seize power, using security dilemma to take the place of security community. This led to the futility of "Proactive Pacifism", once advocated by Japan all the time.

The Setback of East Asian Community

When Japanese New Nationalism brought about even more conservative geopolitical perspective, Japan was not without the thought of change. Once in 2005, Japan actively put forward the conception of East Asian Community. Especially after the DPJ came to power in 2009, the progress of East Asian Community was accelerated.

After the regime transition in 2009, the Democratic Party of Japan came to power and started to exert huge influence on the political circle. "A new broom sweeps clean" goes the Chinese old saying, so did the Democratic Party of Japan. Long Okada, the staff member of the DPJ, once declared in an interview that the DPJ was no more different from the LDP in terms of diplomatic policies. As the boss rod of Japanese foreign affairs, Japan-U.S. Alliance was of equal importance to the relation with China. The relations between the DPJ and the LDP were not similar to the ideological antagonism under the "1955 system" of the cold war.[7] However, Okada also expressed that the DPJ would also make some different decisions since the regime transition, after having emphasized the successive characteristics of the DPJ. "However, at the time of attaching importance to succession, the policies in need of change were not a few, which meant that the DPJ had great desire to carry out new foreign policies."[8]

In East Asian countries, Mr. Hatoyama's cabinet executed Love Foreign Policy, actively "Involving into Asia". During the UN Conference on Climate Change in September 2009, Hatoyama held a meeting with

Chinese President Hu Jintao, which lasted as long as one hour, illustrating the conception of "The East Asian Community". On September 17, 2009, Chinese Ministry of Foreign Affairs responded with endorsement. During the trilateral summit on September 28, 2009, Hatoyama reconfirmed the conception of "East Asian Community". On December 10, 2009, then staff member of the DPJ Ichiro Ozawa led a delegation of over 600 people to visit China, which not only raised a new climax of civil communication between China and Japan in the DPJ administration, but also broke the historic record of the dispatch number of Parliament members during international exchanges.[9]

Obviously, Prime Minister Hatoyama was more willing to take the rise of China as an opportunity to obtain the independence of foreign affairs. Therefore, Hatoyama took a more practical and up-to-date method to deal with Sino-Japanese relation. For Hatoyama, China provided more of an opportunity than of a threat. Hence, Prime Minister Hatoyama showed a pro-China decision tendency with an emphasis on Asia in diplomatic policies.[10] It was fair to say that in the period of Hatoyama Cabinet, Sino-Japanese relation was gradually heading toward the journey of deepening the systematic partnership between China and Japan, following the "Ice-breaking", "Ice-thawing", and "Warm Spring" periods represented by the governance of Abe, Fukuda, and Aso.

However, the Sino-Japanese relation showed as strong tenacity as its extreme fragility. More importantly, the Sino-Japanese relation could not bring expected or immediate effect on Japan. As a newborn party in power, the DPJ pursued to be a long-lived party in power like the LDP, making every effort to avoid becoming another ephemeral power. Showing diplomatic estrangement to the U.S. was to meet the growing nationalistic spirits of domestic China, while to show intimacy to China resulted from the huge unexpected business opportunity brought by China's rapid rise, and the global power shift brought by China's rise, which made Japan realize the immense change of world "trend of the times" and the need to keep a close relationship with China, instead of an estranged one, so as not to miss the benefits that would bring about by the rise of China.

At the same time, to be on good terms with China would force the U.S. to make concessions in some critical issues, especially in issues like Futenma. If the American military power in Futenma were all evacuated, the safety guarantee was left to Japan itself to a large extent. The increase of Japanese political and diplomatic independence, was necessary if Japan was to retain a peaceful regional environment. Otherwise, Japan needed to spend more money on defense and was forced to speed up its rearmament process. And the speed up of Japanese armament would be a total disaster, if not understood by China. Especially under the circumstance of American evacuation, if Japan regarded China as an enemy, which would necessarily slow down the progress of Japanese economic construction. This would not help Japan get rid of the "Lost Twenty Years", instead it would make Japan fall deeper into the loss.

However, the real situation was more complicated than the DPJ had thought. U.S. control upon Japan was not only in military. U.S. Marines in Futenma was only superficial, with an essential aim to include Japan in its political and economic system at the outset of postwar, just like putting Japan in a cell encircled by transparent glass, which seemingly showed no barrier, but hard to escape in essence.

What the DPJ did was not unprecedented. In the middle of 1950s, the Hatoyama Ichiro Administration once underwent similar experience. After Hatoyama Ichiro came to power, in order to placate domestic discontent caused by Yoshida's "absolute support of the U.S.", Hatoyama made an active contact with the Soviet Unions to coordinate with the amendment of Treaty of Mutual Cooperation and Security between the U.S. and Japan, which was thought unequal by domestic Japanese politicians. Marnoru Shigemitsu, then foreign minister, put forward a 12-year long evacuation plan to the U.S., which raised the fury of U.S. Secretary of State Dulles and naturally met refusal from the U.S. authorities. Finally, Mr. Hatoyama's cabinet withdrawed the proposal of Shigemitsu Kwai.

Yukio Hatoyama, the grandson of Ichiro Hatoyama, followed suit. However, the result was equally tragic. Due to the negligence in choosing diplomatic direction and failure in Futenma issue, the DPJ of Mr. Hatoyama's cabinet had to depart tearfully. The DPJ authorities soon realized that it was extremely perilous (even threatening to the power of the DPJ) to take advantage of China to seek "Independence", while bypassing the U.S. Nobutaka Machimura, senator of the LDP, thought, "even though Japan realized regime shift in its true sense, Mr. Hatoyama's cabinet nearly denied the power of the LDP in politics and diplomacy ... The most important issue was that it worsened the Japan-U.S. alliance ... It was a show for the public".[11]

Seemingly, the disillusionment of the conception of East Asian Community was caused by the DPJ's diplomatic failure towards the U.S. However, in essence, the potential reason was due to the conservative mindset of Japanese public. To Japanese, the longer success lasted, the deeper they would be caught in "The Burden of Success", the easier they would become over dependent on the Japanese modes such as systems, habits, policies that supported previous successes, and even psychological indifference. What is frightening is that even though Japanese existing development modes were no longer easy to adapt to the huge change at home and abroad, Japanese people still found it hard to walk out of the fixed previous success inertia, and were easy to form the "Resisting Forces" that refused to abdicate benefits, which would deviate various Japanese systems from the needs of the Era.[12]

Conclusion

Seemingly, the conflict between Pacifism and New Nationalism is the theory of games between two different social ideologies; in fact, it expressed Japanese identification crisis: whether Japan should continue to be a "Rich and Small" medium country according to Pacifism or to be a "Strong and Big" political power under the influence of New Nationalism.

From the national level, behind the conservative emergence of New Nationalism, there is the deep anxiety of Japan's future and self-recognition. During the 50 years of postwar economic boom, Japanese were immersed in the urban prosperity and money bubbles, thinking that hard work could get affluent life in return and temporarily forget to think about its own identity and orientation.

However, Japan suddenly lost its direction since the crash of economic bubbles of the 1990s. Neither did Japan walk out of the economic stagnation, nor did it create a new path from the political and foreign plight. What Japan did was constant repetition of past behavior, emphasizing U.S.-Japan Alliance and Japanese specialty, disclaiming its liability in historic issues and even speaking for itself for the past. Just like Martin Jacques's comment on Japan, "when the aim of Meiji Restoration was achieved, what's the next step? Japan has no answer, caught in a survival crisis. People used to explain Japanese economic bubbles from the point of pure economy, however, there is a more essential cultural and psychological explanantion: for this nation, together with its organizations, including companies, completely lost its sense of direction."[13]

Currently, Japan looked more to the past, or history, immersed in the past wonderful life, losing the ability and courage to rush forward. The more people reminisce the past, the more conservative they would be. Japan in the new century thinks in its own conceit that it boasts the world-class economic power with affluent life and improved social security level, unable to have a clear understanding of the development of neighboring countries and the progress of power shifts in international system. Looking in retrospect, Japan also had a long history of being secluded from the outside world and the historic tradition of refusing to make progresses. The traditional consciousness of a sacred country strengthened Japanese recognition of Japanese citizens towards its own specialty. Used to the affluent life, Japan is afraid to lose the life and status it boasts now, but fails to find a good way out. Having wasted precious 20 years' time, Japan turned around helplessly, attempting to find an answer with the help of history and ancestor.

Objectively, Japan has always been looking for the methods to get rid of economic stagnation and to realize renaissance. Japanese think tank are also fully aware of the fact that "the third rise" is not only the rise of Japanese unilateral act to walk out of Japan, neither was it the rise of copying foreign countries; instead, it was the internationalization combined with "walk out" and "invite in". That would be an era when there is no need to distinguish Japanese from foreigners, or foreign enterprises from Japanese enterprises.[14] With the deepening of globalization and against the backdrop of the rise of China, if Japan could not accurately position itself in the world stage, making its own contribution to East Asian cooperation, then Japan would necessarily find it difficult to walk out of the plight.

Notes

1. Marc Bloc, *Apologie pour l'histoire ou Metier D'Historien*, Shanghai Academy of Social Science Press, 1992, p. 6.
2. Jiang Lifeng, *The Contemporary Japanese Society Ideological Trend*, World Affairs Press, pp. 12–14.

3. S.N. Eisenstadt, *The Great Revolutions and the Civilization of Modernity*, Shanghai People's Publishing House, 2012, p. 147.
4. Jyonji Banno, *The Idea of Modern Japan's National: 1871–1936*, Social Sciences Academic Press, 2014, p. 2.
5. Makiyo Hori, *Japan Democracy Analects*, Iwanami Shoten, 2013, p. 134.
6. Wu Jinan, *Japanese New Generational Politicians*, Current Press, 2002, p. 343.
7. "The Era of Discussion Focusing on Reality has Come", *Diplomatic Interview*, Vol. 9, p. 10.
8. Ibid.
9. Li Guangmin and Ou Bin, "The Political and Diplomatic Policies of Chinese Communist Party in the Communication with the DPJ," *Studies on the History of Chinese Communist Party*, Vol. 2, 2010, p. 101.
10. "Could Hatoyama Move the Base of Japan-US Alliance?" *Xinhua News Agency*, November 2, 2009.
11. Nobutaka Machimura, "The Diplomacy of the DPJ that Lost the 'Asset' of Trust," *Diplomacy*, Vol. 9, p. 27.
12. Akira Kosima, *Japan's Choice*, Oriental Press, 2010, p. 2.
13. Martin Jacques, *When China Rules the World: The Rise of the Middle Kingdom and the End of the Western World*, China CTTIC Press, 2010, p. 71.
14. Nomura Research Institute, *2015 Nenno Nihon*, China CITIC Press, 2012, p. 112.

Election of Political Leadership in East Asia

Chapter 5

Heredity, Election, and Leadership in Northeast Asia: A Comparative Institutional Analysis of Political Process[1]

*Hiroki Miura**

Introduction

This chapter compares the institutions for selecting political leaders in China, Japan, and South Korea (CJK), aiming to elaborate common and critical aspects of the political process in Northeast Asia. Though there are a number of institutions concerning the selection of political leaders, this chapter focuses on the significant ones. That is, the electoral systems as formal legal procedures, hereditary or factional politics as informal socio-cultural customs, and the channels of political communication as cognitive foundation for running different institutions. Each of them has its own operative orientation and reasons to be considered as a significant factor in selecting political leaders at different levels. This chapter compares these institutions of CJK by combining several approaches of "new institutionalism", premising that the real difficulty of comparison lies not in the apparent difference of their institutional arrangements, but in the diversity of viewpoints or standards for evaluating political leaders and

* Hiroki Miura, research professor of Kyung Hee University, South Korea.

institutions, which is clouding our insight on what after all should be compared in the topic of leadership. Put it simply, the excellence of institution does not necessarily result in the excellent performance of political leaders who are selected by these institutions. A large part of this conceptual problem would be associated with the complex, uncertain, and multidimensional reality of political leadership itself. Thus, deliberative as well as holistic approach is needed to meaningfully discuss "good institution" or "good leader" under the complicated social reality in the three countries. The comparison and arguments on such critical aspects would help understand the characteristics of leadership institutions in each country and the possibility of their common regional model.

The three countries in East Asia are often viewed as de fact integrated socio-economic region or a familiar set of actors in East Asian international relations (Fouquin *et al.* 2006). Tripartite cooperation has evolved rapidly in a number of societal fields, creating various interactive patterns and biding them together as a certain form of socio-economic community. However, the increase of interdependence and the geopolitical settings do not necessarily mean that they firmly share somewhat common political system or a set of political values that make their political livelihood unique and remarkable in the world politics. In fact, East Asia once experienced such moment. Developmental state, flying gees model, and corporatist political system of East Asian counties received worldwide attention particularly in terms of their effective administrative performance for rapid economic growth. Since then, however, the academic inquiry for their domestic political economic systems seems to have received less attention compared to their ever evolving inter-states dynamism.[2]

As Almond *et al.* (2008, 28) assert that comparing countries or polities "deepens our understanding of our own institutions and ... helps expand our awareness of possibilities of politics", it is an important task for the three countries to re-discover and broaden their political possibility to overcome the internal and external socio-economic challenges and to reaffirm their unique, regional, or universal significance in the world politics. The institutional design of leadership selection is one of the most relevant and important issues in this regard.

This chapter first summarizes the new institutionalism and a theoretical framework to compare the leadership institutions of CJK. Second, it gives a general view of empirical data about their basic political structure, selection process, and socio-political performance of leaders, which are the important components of the theoretical framework. Finally, it discusses the common and critical aspects of their institutional operation, based on the theories, empirical conditions, and the insights from relevant preceding studies. The scope of the discussion here will be fairly limited, compared to the broadness of the issue. However, it is a primarily concern in this chapter to search for a creative and alternative perspective of the comparative politics of CJK today.

Approaches for Comparing the Institutional Operation in CJK

1. New Institutionalism and Its Sub-level Approaches

Comparative research begins from setting abstract concepts and equivalent cases which should be neither completely unique nor universal. A meaningful comparison is possible by establishing a standard concept and adjusting its degree of abstraction appropriately between these two levels.[3] For example, saying that "Shinzo Abe, present prime minister of Japan, is grandson of a former prime minister" is a simple and unique fact. However, the fact can be an important case by comparing it under the perspective of "hereditary politics".

From past to present, comparative politics has searched for the middle level concepts between uniqueness and universality of political phenomena. Those include "political system", "political development", "democratization", "dependency", "public choice", "governance", etc.[4] In its recent theoretical trend, various influential concepts and theories seem to converge into "new institutionalism" (March and Olsen 1984, 2006; 3–5; Schmitter 2009, 39; Bara 2009, 1–4; Lim 2010, 93–97).[5] According to *The Oxford Handbook of Political Institutions*, institutions are "collections of structures, rules, and standard operating procedures that have a partly autonomous role in political life" (March and Olsen 2006, 4). At their practical level, institutions are categorized into formal and informal or soft and hard ones ranging from cultural norms to legal or constitutional articles. Consequently, institutions are viewed as the foundation of all types of political behavior which were once dealt differently by the various concepts and theories aforementioned (Bara 2009, 1; Pennington 2009, 14–15). Then, institutionalism is "a set of theoretical ideas and hypotheses concerning the relations between institutional characteristics and political agency, performance, and change" (March and Olsen 2006, 4). While old institutionalism sought to describe political phenomena by mainly focusing on formal institutions, new institutionalism seeks to explain them by incorporating various informal institutions and under wider context of social dynamism emerged around institutions (Peters 1996, 206; Wiarda 2006).[6]

When applied as a research framework at operational level, new institutionalism is often decomposed into several sub-level approaches. Major three of them are briefly summarized here. The first approach focuses on the interactions among different explanatory variables. Traditionally, there are three schools of thought in this approach: rational choice institutionalism, structural institutionalism, and cultural institutionalism (Peters 2008, 49; Pennington 2009, 16–30; Lim 2010, 77–93. Drogus and Orvis 2012, 18–27). Three schools highlight different variables to explain institutional dynamism. They are respectively (1) rational judgment and strategies of individual actors or groups, (2) cultures, customs, social trends, and norms that influence their preference formation, and (3) various underlying and external structures surround them. Significance of this approach is not a threefold classification itself as sub-sub-level of division, but their interactive aspect which would more meaningfully reflect the complex reality. The effective comparison of institutions can be possible by investigating how those different variable are substantially linked and mutually reinforced together (Peters 2008, 57–58; Pennington 2009, 30–37; Lichbach and Zuckerman 2009, 16; Lim 2010, 96–97).

The second approach searches for the alternative and synthetic aspects of institutional dynamism beyond mere interactions of the variables aforementioned. New institutionalism has another sub-division, namely, simplicity vs. complexity of causal explanation. Basically speaking, while the rational choice institutionalism prefers the parsimony of causal argument, structural and cultural schools pay more attention to the complex and complicated social dynamism lying at the deep dimensions of reality. However, the combination of simple explanations can produce complex arguments and an analysis of the complexity can result in a simple conclusion or concept, vice versa. Simplicity and complexity, as paradigms of science, constitutes another theoretical frontier in comparative politics (Schmitter 2009; Lichbach and Zuckerman 2009). In practice, the contemporary discourse, which focuses on investigating the globalized and diversified political systems, tends to seek for more sophisticated complex approach rather than simple reductionist one (Schmitter 2009, 59; Lichbach and Zuckerman 2009, 1; Huckfeldt 2009). "Reasonableness" rather than "rationality" is necessary to effectively understand, explain, and compare the multi-dimensional social reality (Schmitter 2009, 41). Thus, the major goal of the second approach is to elaborate the critical aspects of the target institutional operation, which can more reasonably explain its complex causal dynamism.

The third approach attaches importance to the holistic "model" and its applicability beyond comparing partial aspects of cases or facts. "Great Systems Debate" has been one of important topics in comparative politics.[7] Once popular concepts such as democratization, corporatism, and developmental states were all holistic political models based on the empirical studies of Eastern Europe, Asia, South America etc. East Asia has a popular tradition to associate its political system and democracy with Confucianism and other traditional Asian cultures (Tu 2000, Huang 2001; 2010; Berman 2010). It will be our interests to inquire whether the characteristics of institutional dynamism explained by previous approaches can be viewed as East Asian model in the world politics.

2. Framework and Critical Questions for Comparing CJK

Heredity and electoral system can be understood as informal and formal institution for selecting political leaders. Hereditary politics is an informal selecting process based on the principles of personal succession by family members, offspring, kinship, or dynasty. Electoral system, which is mostly based on the ballot and majority rule, involves a set of institutions operating at national and local levels and in private organizations such as political party. Political leaders here include formal politicians, government officials, and politically influential individuals.

There are other institutions concerning leadership selection; the nomination and approval system, the factions and group politics based on interpersonal networks configured along with the hometowns or schools, the lobbying systems and various channels of communication between state and civil society, etc. Moreover, a general theory of leadership explains that particular social circumstances produce a particular leader. Thus, it will be safe to say that the reality of leadership selection process consists of a mixture of various institutions and no single institution can completely dominate in the whole process.

To mitigate the problem of internal diversity of leadership institutions, it will be helpful to investigate the external constraints and the operational results. The following three points for comparison will be relevant in this context (Figure 1). Firstly, the institutional operation is generally under the influence of higher political system which architects basic power and authorities at the constitutional level. That is, "basic political structure" constrains the overall institutional operation. In particular, the basic political structures of CJK vest particular group of people with formal decision-making authorities at different levels, which substantially regulate the institutional dynamism. In the case of national top leader, the members of the National Peoples' Congress and House of Representatives execute the final vote in China and Japan, and general public directly vote to

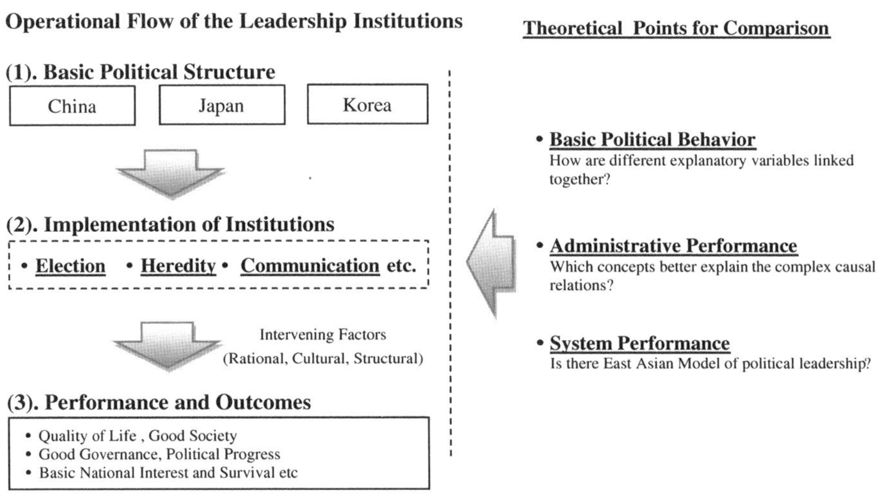

Figure 1. Framework for Comparing Leadership Institutions of CJK.

presidential candidates in Korea. Of course, the processes are intervened by various factors which are theoretically classified into rational, structural, and cultural as aforementioned. The members of politburo of Communist Party are generally viewed as the most substantial stakeholders for leadership selection in China. General public and party politics may be decisive factors in Japan. Socio-economic structure or political culture may be more important in Korea. Thus, the political behavior of the substantial stakeholders under the basic political system is the first point for comparing leadership selection.

Second, the evaluation of a particular institution is closely related to the personal or administrative performance of political leaders selected through the institution. Their relations are notably important in the modern democratic political systems. Arguments for "good leader" or "bad leader" presuppose sufficient empirical grounds about their leadership performance, which eventually reflect the arguments for better institutional arrangement and operation. In the modern democratic system, such consequential indicators include not only national economic development, but also more comprehensive and hybrid ones such as "national happiness", "quality of life", "good governance", "good society" etc. (Zhang 2010; Inoguchi and Shin 2010; Draper and Ramsay 2012). Various factors can intervene the relations between the personal or institutional attributes of leaders and their performance, too. The second point for comparing CJK will be the operation of this complex causal mechanism.

Thirdly, from a broader perspective, the relations between the different basic political structures and the different administrative performance will also provide meaningful implications for the leadership institutions. The holistic analysis is particularly important in order to discuss the national, regional, or universal "model" of political leaders and the institutional arrangement. In other words, "system performance" is a critical point for comparing CJK. For example, "Asian Value Debate" in the middle 1990s took up major aspects of system performance of East Asian countries including the positive and negative roles of political leaders, their institutional arrangements, characteristics of followership, etc. from which the Debate elaborated an Asian model of democracy.[8]

Three sub-level approaches of the new institutionalism can be applied respectively to aforementioned three points for comparison, formulating nine theoretical focus points in total. Among them, the most relevant and important sets for comparing the cases of CJK are picked up and summarized as follows. By answering these questions, this chapter tries to articulate the critical aspects of the operation of leadership institutions in CJK.

Basic Political Behavior: How are different explanatory variables linked together?

The selection process of political leaders is largely constrained by the basic political structure in each country. However, its substantial aspects are influenced by the rational, structural and cultural variables which regulate the decision-making process of core stakeholders in each country. How are these different variable linked together in the reality of CJK?

Administrative Performance: Which concepts better explain the complex causal relations?

The different political leaders in CJK have shown different socio-political performance measured by various indicators. This process also involves various intervening variables. Which concepts better and more reasonably explain the complex causal relations between the selected leaders and their work?

System Performance: Is there any East Asian model of leadership?

Taking all things considered, our biggest intellectual interest will be whether there is East Asian model or CJK model of political leadership in either positive or negative sense.

Overview of the Institutional Arrangements and their Operation

1. Basic Political Structure

Basic political structures of the three countries can be roughly illustrated as in Figure 2, Figure 3, and Figure 4, which regulate the formal legal

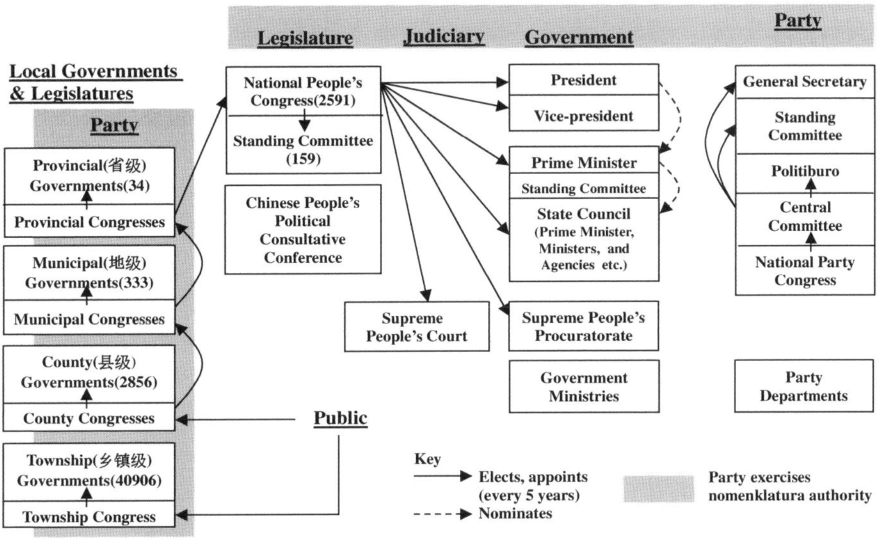

Figure 2. Basic Political Structure of China.

Source: Revised from Manion (2008, 417); National Bureau of Statistics of China (2011).

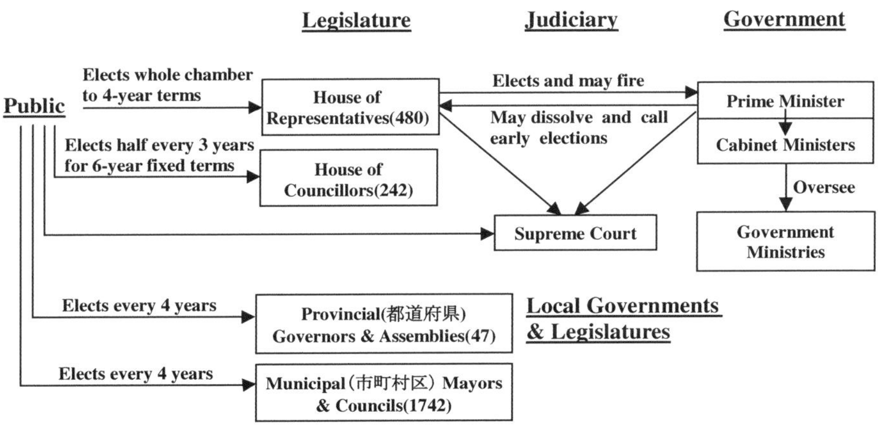

Figure 3. Basic Political Structure of Japan.

Source: Revised from Rosenbluth and Thies (2008, 316); Ministry of Internal Affairs and Communications of Japan (2013).

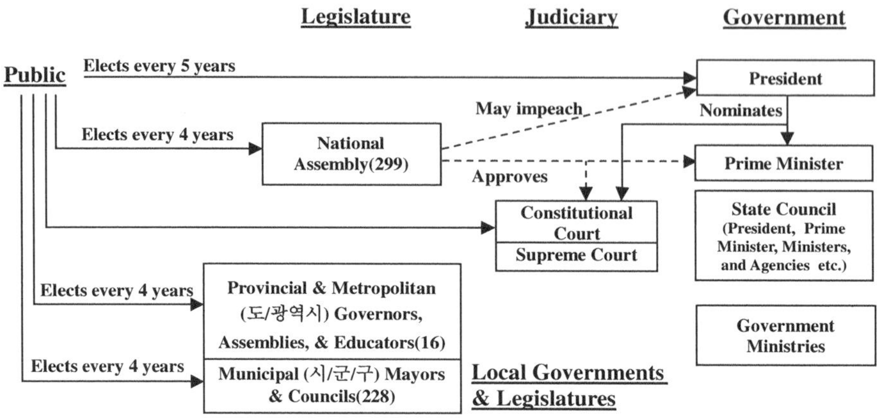

Figure 4. Basic Political Structure of South Korea.

Source: Revised from Huang (2008, 110); Minister of Public Administration and Security of Korea (2012).

procedures of leadership selection at the highest level. The modern constitution was enacted in 1954 in China, 1946 in Japan, and 1948 in Korea respectively. The most recent major revisions concerning the selection of political leaders took place in 1982 in China and in 1987 in Korea. Japan has no single revision ever.

Beside those shown in the figures, the constitution of each country prescribes a number of basic principles guidelines, and norms which also regulate leadership and relevant institutions including roles of state, party systems, civic participation, local autonomy, etc. For example, the Preamble of Chinese constitution states "leadership of the Communist Party of China", "Marxism-Leninism", "people's democratic dictatorship", "socialist democracy", etc. as her essential guidelines of national political management.

2. Selection Process: Rational, Cultural, and Structural Factors

A number of national and local political leaders have been elected at the three countries under each basic political structure. The nominal position of head of the state has changed several times since the chairman Mao inaugurated in 1954 under her first constitution. Shinzo Abe was inaugurated as the 51st prime minister of Japan in December 2012 after the 46th general election of the House of Representatives. Korea elected the 19th

National Assembly members and the 18th president in 2012. Formal electoral institutions are complicatedly interrelated with nomination institutions, party-level elections for candidates, local and community structures etc. The number of seat, service terms, and the frequency of member change are largely different among the three countries. The number of NPC membership exceeds 2,000 in China. Japan has experienced numerous changes of political leaders in her modern history, not withstanding the notable dominant-party system led by the Liberal Democratic Party of Japan.These facts suggest that two countries have particularly produced diverse types of leader. Hereditary politics has got into the regional news in 2012. Japan elected hereditary politician as her new prime minister. Korea's new president, Park Guen-hye, is daughter of past dictator, Park Chuang-Hee. In addition, hereditary politics can be also seen in North Korea, Malaysia, Indonesia, the Philippines, etc.

However, different domestic circumstances and processes in those Asian countries must be considered to sufficiently understand and evaluate the hereditary aspect of their politics. Furthermore, it should be noted that the family succession is much more popular in business rather than politics. In order to understand the political one, the different social background must be taken into account.

Theoretically, the substantial selection processes are explained with three types of intervening factors. Rationalists and cultural institutionalists attach importance to the attributes and preferences of the stakeholders in the voting or nominating process. Orthodox rationalists often explain the process by grouping and comparing individual stakeholders in terms of their educational level, income, age, hometown, political belief and so on. Table 2 is an example of comparative survey that shows how the individual attributes provide rational logic to explaining a potential tendency of leadership selection among the three countries. The three countries combined, the survey result indicates that "educational level" is statistically significant in the preference formation of Chinese, Japanese, and Korean people regarding the ideal type of political leader. However, general as well as partial tendencies should also be noted, too. While democratic leader is overwhelmingly supported in the three countries, its tendency is comparatively weaker in Korea and stronger in China and Japan. In addition, Korea seems to have the widest generational gap among three.

Culturalists pay more attention to the wide-range context under which the preference of individual stakeholders is transformed. Cultural factors include the conditions of group politics, politics in local communities, traditions and customs of party politics, communication channels, prevailing political values and social trends, etc. Social capital is one of the persuasive explanatory factors in the recent researches. On the other hand, structuralists elaborate the influence of multi-layered structures which supplementally reinforce the constitutional system. According to their viewpoint, difference and similarity of CJK can be efficiently explained in terms of the arrangement of party system, economic and industrial structure, foreign relations, institutions regulating state-society relations, conditions of public sphere, etc. To sum up, under the relatively stable basic political structure, the substantial selection processes in the three countries are varied by these rational, cultural, and structural factors.

3. Performance and Outcomes

Major socio-political outcomes of political leaders are summarized below Figure 5 and Figure 6. Good and bad leaders and effective and ineffective institutions can be evaluated by referring to these facts.

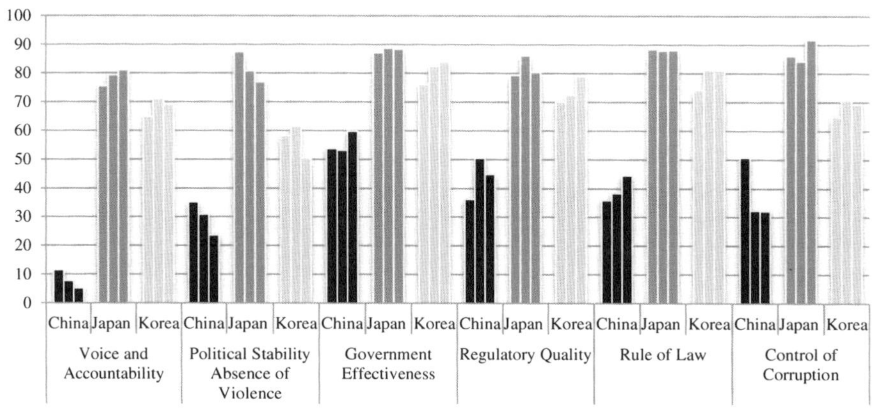

Figure 5. Good Governance: the World Governance Index* (2000, 2005, 2010).

*The World Governance Index, the research project led by the World Bank, compiles and summarizes information from 30 existing data sources on 6 broad dimensions of governance for over 200 countries over the period 1996–2011.

Source: World Bank (2013).

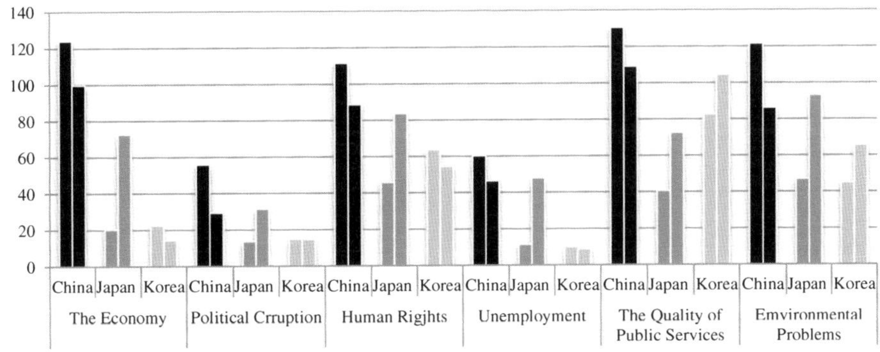

Figure 6. Subjective Evaluation of the Governments' Performance (2003, 2006).

*The number is the total balance of calculating the percentage of each items: very well (+), fairly well (+), not so well (–), and not well at all (–).

Source: Inoguchi *et al.* Asia Barometer Survey Data 2003 and 2006.

Q: How well do you think your government is dealing with the following issues?

However, as shown in two figures, the objective and subjective indicators seem to suggest inconsistent patters of outcomes. That is, it may be difficult to rationally judge which government has better performance than others. Other relevant indicators such as quality of life or feeling of happiness indicates similar tendency as well.[9] Better performance of government in terms of the objective political development do not necessarily mean higher satisfaction and higher level of subjective evaluation of its people.

Searching for the Critical Aspects of Leadership Institutions in CJK

1. Basic Political Behaviors: Cognitive Aspect of Stakeholders' Preference Formation

The overview of the difference of the basic political structures of CJK suggests that a proper theoretical approach to explain their institutional dynamism can be different to each of them. Structural approach would be appropriate for the Chinese case because of her multi-layered election and nomination systems and the complicated institutional relations between state and Communist party. Rational choice and cultural approaches can be supplementarily used to explain the detailed and partial processes such as the decision-making in the politburo members. In Korea's case, rational choice institutionalism would better explain the trend of her direct and simple election system. The major part of her leadership selection process can be meaningfully explained by analyzing the voting behavior and preference of the electorate. Structural and cultural perspectives would effectively reinforce additional important aspects of institutional operation. Traditional "regionalism", involvement of civil society, and external conditions of economy and security are the popular items to explain Korean electoral politics. Japan may be located in between two cases. The indirect election system, multi-party system, tradition of factional politics, loosely decentralized system, strategies of particular private schools which trains future political leaders, and low level of public voting rate and civic participation, etc. have been combined complicatedly in Japan, shaping her partly flexible and partly rigid politics. These national traits are also emphasized in the comparative studies at the regional and the world level (Rosenbluth and Thies 2008; Manion, Melanie 2008; Huang 2010).

Then, the reality of institutional operation in CJK can be meaningfully "compared" by investigating the difference of gravity between structural factors and stakeholders' rational choice, acknowledging the various cultural factors lying in the middle of this alignment. In other words, the moderate and expanded cultural institutionalism may be useful as a standard concept to compare the three countries.

Pennington (2009, 33) argues that, in order to analyze the interplay and the synthesis of three approaches of new institutionalism, one should focus on the "capacity for actors to transform the rules from within". It would be beneficial to search for such transformative capacity as a form of cultural factor in the case of CJK comparison. A key aspect is the cognitive and informational foundation of stakeholders as an important political culture. Both general public and the small numbers of political elite build up their preference based on the information which is created and transformed through various activated communication channels around them. *The World Value Survey* supports this point. People in CJK commonly prefer the secular and rational value to traditional one, which characterizes them as "Confucian countries" (Inglehart and Welzel 2005, 63) in the world. That is, people in CJK takes much care of the modernity, development, the latest social trends, and the ever changing economic and social conditions around their livelihood than the people in other region of the world. The interplay between structural and rational factors in CJK may be meaningful analyzed by investigating the flow of influential information which creates social norms or trends that ultimately constrain the overall behavior of core stakeholders in the three countries.

"Public opinion" is notably one of the most important and relevant factors concerning the informational foundation of politics. It influences both the voting behavior of individuals and the decision-making of political elites or representatives at different levels. As suggested in Figure 7, it is common in the three countries that the mass-communication devices such as TV programs and newspapers are much more influential than the channels of inter-personal communication. Significance of public opinion, in whatever degree, is surely a common sense for every individual in the three countries. However, by reevaluating the role and influence of these major communication channels as overarching cultural factors between the structural and rational ones, more meaningful and dynamic analysis may be possible.

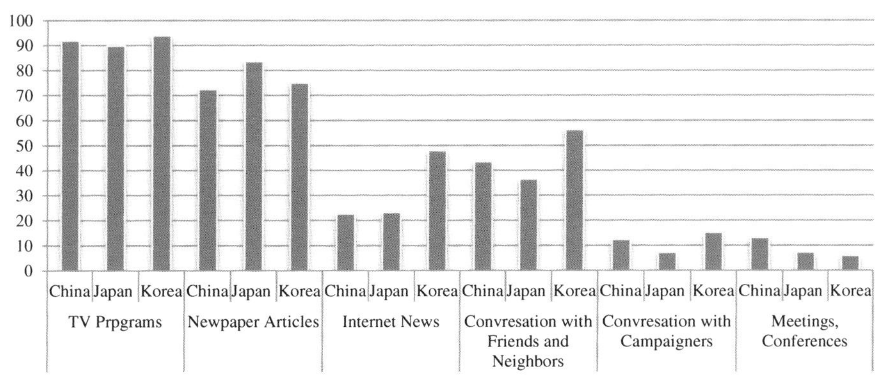

Figure 7. Comparison of Major Information Sources in CJK (2006).

Source: Inoguchi *et al.* Asia Barometer Survey Data 2006.

Q: When you shape your opinions about social and political issues, which of the following media influence your opinions most? (multiple answers)

2. Administrative Performance: Contextual and Adoptive Aspect of Institutional Operation

Flow of information and public opinion are the influential factors in selecting political leaders. However, public opinion do not always select "good leader". The actual performance of formal political leaders is often disappointing in the eyes of general public. Mahbubani (2013) points out that the comeback of hereditary politic in East Asia does not promise to solve the difficult domestic problems in each country. The public opinion itself changes over the times along with the changes of various conditions. Therefore, in order to evaluate the leadership institutions meaningfully, it is necessary to consider much deeper aspect of politics.

One of the most remarkable facts concerning the administrative performance shown in Figure 5 and Figure 6 is its inconsistency. While Japan and Korea have recorded better performance in the objective index of governance, Chinese people show much higher level of satisfaction to their government's performance. In addition, difference among sub-items of indexes and historical trend should not be ignored either. Table 1 also shows that Chinese people's preference for democratic system is higher than that of Korean people despite her relatively successful democratic governance of South Korea. These facts clearly indicate that the relationship between objective and subjective evaluation of political performance is fundamentally complex. Under this condition, it may be impossible to "rationally" discuss good and bad leaders and selecting institutions.

However, the apparent inconsistency may be "reasonably" understandable if we take into consideration different circumstances of each country and depend less on strictly rational standard for comparison. For instance, it may be obvious for Chinese people that China is so big country that the government and politics face various limitations and problems, thus, people less expect the high performance for their leader from the beginning. It is often discussed that Japan lacks "energy" for her further growth, which may be the source of dissatisfaction of people and psychological standard to evaluate their government. Korea has been known as a successful example of simultaneously achieving the economic development and democratization. However, the rapid growth has brought about deep confusion and by-products to its society, which may be the more important standards for Korean people to evaluate their political leaders.

Table 1. Rational Choice Approach to Prefer Type of Political Leader.
Q For each political system, would you say it is a very good, fairly good, fairly bad or very bad way of governing this country?
a. Having a strong leader who does not have to bother with parliament and elections.
b. Having experts, not government, make decisions according to what they think is best for the country.
c. Having a democratic political system.

		Strong Leader			Experts			Democratic System		
		China	Japan	Korea	China	Japan	Korea	China	Japan	Korea
Average	**Balance**	**–27.8**	**–51.4**	**–4.8**	**0.6**	**7.4**	**4.7**	**87.4**	**77.0**	**54.3**
Age	15–29	–22.7	–59.3	–5.4	–2.6	32.8	–3.8	82.4	70.4	47.9
	30–49	–31.6	–49.0	–10.2	4.2	23.3	9.5	86.0	75.8	47.5
	50 and more	–25.6	–50.6	4.2	–2.6	–12.0	3.4	91.9	79.8	69.5
Employment status	Full time	–31.5	–45.2	9.5	4.6	16.8	12.9	88.8	81.0	52.4
	Part time	–30.8	–69.5	–18.6	–36.2	22.0	–17.0	86.7	72.3	57.8
	Retired	–28.8	–44.7	–11.9	–10.8	–20.4	–26.0	90.2	85.2	53.8
	Unemployed	5.5	–75.1	11.4	–9.4	33.4	–9.8	80.4	71.5	45.7
Educational Level Attained	Elementary School	–23.7	–44.1	5.3	1.5	–12.9	–1.3	87.6	73.5	64.6
	Secondary School	–33.3	–51.0	–9.8	–0.7	7.7	5.9	87.5	73.1	48.4
	Higher Education	–19.2	–55.2	–4.1	8.7	12.8	6.6	87.0	87.7	56.6

*The number is the total balance of calculating the percentage of each items: very good (+), fairly good (+), fairly bad (–), and very bad (–).

**The Survey conducted face-to-face interview to about one thousand individuals in each Asian countries.

Source: Inoguchi *et al.* Asia Barometer Survey Data 2006.

"Ineffectiveness of rational analysis" and "usefulness of reasonable analysis" suggest that a key to the meaningful discussion of good and bad leader and selecting institutions is in a reactive, adoptive or contextual aspect of institutional operation. In other words, the adoptive capacity of intuitions for leadership selection may be an effective criterion under the condition of uncertainty and consecutive changes of critical variables. Such capacity involves the aspects regarding, for example, how well and quickly the institutions react to the internal and external changes and challenges and select better political leaders. In this context, inconsistency between objective and subjective evaluations can be reasonably viewed as a winding process of balancing and adjusting the institutional operation to meet the society's various needs.

In the recent discourse of social progress and leadership, several illuminative concepts have been suggested concerning the adoptive capacity of leadership institutions. Nye (2008) proposes "contextual intelligence" as an important trait of leader in modern politics.10 "Social resilience" indicates that the sound cycle of stability and internal institutional innovation is necessary to maintain sustainable growth of political system (Westley *et al.* 2007). Complex political systems and their models have been discussed from various perspectives, which commonly understand our political system as somewhat like a living organism, highlighting particular aspects such as local interactions, adoptive behavior, simple alternative rules, etc. (Axelrod and Cohen 1999; Earnest and Rosenau 2006; Geyer and Rihani 2010; Innes and Booher 2010). These illuminative concepts seem to formulate another and endogenous "messy center" of institutionalist thinking in comparative politics.

To sum up, in order to meaningfully evaluate the operation of leadership institutions of CJK, it is necessary to focus on their reactive, adoptive, and contextual aspects, because there is no fixed relationship between the characteristics of individual political leaders selected through specific institutional path and their socio-political performance which is evaluated by people in various ways. Meaningful argument for good or bad political leaders and their institutions in CJK can be possible by comparing the adoptive capacity of those institutions.

3. System Performance: Pragmatic and Innovative Aspect of Asian Political Culture

The final question is whether we can identify East Asia model of leadership in either positive or negative sense. Despite the obvious difference in the basic political structures, are there any common characteristics in the political leaders and in their selection process which are remarkable in the comparison with other regions of the world? In particular, the point of argument is whether aforementioned informational politics and adoptive capacity of institutions in CJK can be acknowledged as regional political model.

Traditionally, "Asian value debate" tried to answer this question in the 1990s. Studies such as Tu (2000), Huang (2001, 2010), and Berman (2010, 22–23) continue to champion certain Confucianist aspects of Asian countries to proclaim Asian model of politics and public administration.[11] In their argument, Confucian Asia is different from Western countries regarding the organizational culture which attaches importance to the interpersonal relationship and family.[12] This characteristics might be a key to sustain the moderate balance between the rigid stability and adoptive innovation in institutional operation.

On the other hand, from survey and statistical analysis about the quality of life, Shin and Inoguchi (2010, 243) conclude that "[c]onfucian Asia is more alike, rather than different from, all other regions of the world" on the ground that, nevertheless the region has a tradition to respect to interpersonal relationship, this particular preference does not matter in the end as a single decisive variable to their quality of life.

In order to analyze the East Asia model of leadership, some new aspects of Asian and Confucian political culture should be elaborated. The Asian Value Debate and the preceding studies mainly concern the several remarkable characteristics of Confucianism such as a perception of power, authority, and inter-personal moral order. However, the possibility of a refreshed version of Asian political model is still remained by associating various Asian political cultures with the political communication, endogenous institutional innovation, the way of balancing the programmed system performance and the variable mind of people, etc. In this context, Sen (2003, 29–32) asserts that Asian countries traditionally have their own roots and sources of democracy such as deliberative political communication and respect for public discussion. The accumulation of study and data collection is expected to discuss these potential and inspiring aspects of political leadership in CJK.

Conclusion

As the interdependence among China, Japan and South Korea is getting deeper, the demand for more sufficient knowledge concerning the political system of each country increases. It is also true that the three countries are seeking for understanding the deep dimension of their own political characteristics and their significance in the world politics. However, though there is a number of comparative studies at the thematic and single or two country level, the recent trend of comparative politics of CJK at its comprehensive and fundamental level does not sufficiently catch up with these goals.

This chapter tries to compare the institutions for selecting political leaders in the three countries from a perspective of new institutionalism and suggested several critical aspects which should be elaborated for envisioning more meaningful operation and evaluation of political leadership in the three countries. In particular, the chapter suggested that investigating synthetic aspects such as cognitive and informational foundation of core stakeholders and adoptive capacity of institutional operation is important for meaningfully compare, understand, and evaluate the leadership institutions of CJK. The argument is largely grounded on the prevailing complex conditions that CJK share more or less different basic political structures and that the performance of political leaders can be evaluated in various ways. Through the accumulation of study and collection of data concerning these critical aspects, the political livelihood of CJK is expected to provide another remarkable and interesting knowledge and models to the Comparative Politics, as they did in the past.

Notes

1. This work was supported by the National Research Foundation of Korea Grant funded by the Korean Government (NRF-2011-413-B00006).
2. There are a number of thematic comparative studies, two-country comparison, and single country studies regarding comparative politics in East Asia. Global and Asia-pacific level of comparative studies also involves the comparison of CJK. However, sufficient study has been lacking regarding the three countries comparison from broad and in-depth political perspective.
3. See Sartori's famous argument on "ladder of abstraction" (Sartori 1970; Newton and van Deth 2010, 410–413).

4. For theoretical development of Comparative Politics, see Wiarda (2007, 8–12); Munck (2007, 38–39); Lim (2010, 77).
5. Lichbach and Zuckerman (2009, 1–5) describe this convergent point as "messy center" of comparative politics, where paradigmatic or methodological frictions as well as creative arguments have been interacting.
6. March and Olsen (2006, 5) elaborates the core assumption of institutionalism as follows: "institutions create elements of order and predictability. They fashion, enable and constrain political actors as they act within a logic of appropriate action. Institutions are carriers of identities and roles and they are markers of a polity's character, history and visions. They provide bonds that tie citizens together in spite of the many things that divide them."
7. On "Great System Debate," see Wiarda (2007, 5, 265). He argues that three great systems or paradigms of organizing politics have been tested in our modern history: revolutionary socialism, reactionary conservatism or authoritarianism in various manifestations, and liberal democracy. Today, he adds, the system debate was largely ended up with confirming the prevailing excellence of democracy, however, the distinct forms, theoretical bases, and institutional arrangements of democracy in distinct countries and regions are still important issues in comparative politics.
8. According to Huang (2001, 8), the Asian Value Debate and Asia model of democracy mainly deal with following four aspects of politics: (1) unique institutional arrangement such as corporatist state-society relations, (2) growth strategy such as export-oriented one, (3) independent variable outside Asia such as cold war security environment, and (4) cultural uniqueness and cohesiveness in Asian countries.
9. As examples of those non-materialistic and post-modern indicators, see *Economists* (2005); ASEP/JDS (2010); OECD (2012).
10. According to Nye (2009, 85–108), contextual intelligence implies "both a capability to discern trends in the face of complexity and adoptability while trying to shape events," requiring intuitive skills to deal with cultural context, distribution of power resource, followers' needs and demands, time urgency, and information flow.
11. Tu (2000, 205–206) advocates Confucian model of politics as follows:

    - Government leadership in a market economy is not only necessary but desirable.

- Although law is the essential minimum requirement for social stability, "organic solidarity" can only result from humane rites of interaction.
- The family as the basic unit of society is the locus from which core values are transmitted.
- That civil society flourishes is not because it is an autonomous arena above the family and beyond the state. Its inner strength lies in its dynamic interplay between the family and the state.
- Education ought to be the civil religion of society.
- Since self-cultivation is the common root of the regulation of the family, of the governance of the state and peace under Heaven, the quality of life of particular society depends on the level of self-cultivation of its members.

12. Berman (2010, 22–23) points out distinctive elements such as emphasis on familism, a favorable orientation toward hierarchy and duty, strong group culture, the culture of courtesy and pragmatism, very broad-based, bottom-up consultation, and so on. The style of public administration in East Asia is "duty-based consultative pragmatism" compared to "powerful, accountable minimalism" of the United States.

References

Almond, Gabriel A., G. Bingham Powell, Jr., Russel J. Dalton, and Kaare Strom (2008), "Comparing Political Systems," in Gabriel A. Almond, G. Bingham Powell, Jr., Russel J. Dalton, and Kaare Strom, eds., *Comparative Politics Today: A World View,* 9th Edition, NY.: Pearson Longman, pp. 28–42.

ASEP/JDS (2010, "Map of Happiness," http://www.jdsurvey.net/jds/jdsurveyMaps.jsp?Idioma=I&SeccionTexto=0404&NOID=103 (Accessed on Jan. 20, 2013).

Axelrod, Robert and Michael D. Cohen (1999), *Harnessing Complexity: Organizational Implications of a Scientific Frontier*, New York: Free Press.

Bara, Judith (2009), "Introduction," in Judith Bara and Mark Pennington, eds., *Comparative Politics*, London: SAGE Publications Inc., pp. 1–9.

Bara, Judith (2009), "Methodologies for Comparative Politics," in Judith Bara and Mark Pennington, eds., *Comparative Politics*, London: SAGE Publications Inc. pp. 41–65.

Berman, Evan (2010), *Public Administration in East Asia: Japan, South Korea, Chinese Mainland and Taiwan*, NY.: Taylor & Francis Group.

Caramani, Daniele (2008), "Introduction to Comparative Politics," in Daniele Caramani, ed., *Comparative Politics*, Oxford: Oxford University Press, pp. 1–23.

China Statistics Press (2011), 《全国行政区划 (2010年底)》, http://www.stats.gov.cn/tjsj/ndsj/2011/indexch.htm (Accessed on Jan. 10, 2013).

Draper, Alan and Ansil Ramsay (2012), *The Good Society: An Introduction to Comparative Politics,* 2nd Edition, NY.: Longman.

Drogus, Carol Ann and Stephen Orvis (2012), *Introducing Comparative Politics: Concepts and Cases in Context*, 2nd Edition, LA.: Sage.

Earnest, David C. and James N. Rosenau (2006), "Signifying Nothing: What Complex Systems Theory Can and Cannot Tell Us about Global Politics," in Neil. E. Harriosn, ed., *Complexity in World Politics: Concepts and Methods of a New Paradigm*, NY.: State University of New York Press, pp. 143–163.

Economists (2005), "The Economist Intelligence Unit's Quality-of-life Index," http://www.economist.com/media/pdf/QUALITY_OF_LIFE.pdf (Accessed on Jan. 20, 2013).

Fouquin, Michel, Daisuke Hiratsuka and Fukunari Kimura (2006), "Introduction: East Asia's De Facto Economic Integration," in Daisuke Hirastuka, ed., *East Asia's De Facto Economic Integration*, Hampshire: Palgrave Macmillan. pp. 1–15.

Geyer, Robert and Samir Rihani (2010), *Complexity and Public Policy: A New Approach to 21st Century Politics*, Policy and Society, London: Routledge.

Hayes, Louis D. (2012), *Political Systems of East Asia: China, Korea, and Japan*, NY.: M. E. Sharp.

Huang, Xiaoming (2001), "Between the State and the Market: The Problem of Transition in East Asia," in Xiaoming Huang, ed., *The Political and Economic Transiton in East Asia: Strong Market*, Weakening State, Richmond: Curzon, pp. 3–23.

Huang, Xiaoming (2009), *Politics in Pacific Asia: An Introduction*, London: Palgrave Macmillan.

Inglehart, Ronald and Christian Welzel (2005), *Modernization, Cultural Change, and Democracy: The Human Development Sequence*, NY.: Cambridge University Press.

Innes, Judith E. and David E. Booher (2010), *Planning With Complexity: An Introduction to Collaborative Rationality for Public Policy*, NY.: Routledge.

Inoguchi, Tadashi and Doh Chull Shin (2010), "The Quality of Life in Confucian Asia: From Physical Welfare to Sibjective Well-being," in Doh Chull Shin and Tadashi Inoguchi, eds., *The Quality of Life in Confucian Asia: From Physical Welfare to Subjective Well-being*, NY.: Springer, pp. 1–9.

Inoguchi, Takashi, *et al. Asia Barometer Survey Data 2003 and 2006* [computer file]. Asia Barometer Project http://www.asiabarometer.org (Accessed on January 10, 2013). Asia Barometer is a registered trademark of Professor Takashi Inoguchi, Chuo University, Japan, Director of the Asia Barometer Project.

Lichbach, Mark Irving and Alan S. Zuckerman (2009), "Paradigms and Pragmatism: Comparative Politics during the Past Decade," in Mark Irving Lichbach and Alan S. Zuckerman, eds., *Comparative Politics: Rationality, Culture, and Structure*, NY.: Cambridge University Press. pp. 1–17.

Lim, Timothy C (2010), *Doing Comparative Politics: An Introduction to Approaches and Issues*, 2nd Edition, London: Lynne Rienner Publishers.

Mahbubani, Kishore (2013), "Dynastic Succession in Asian Politics is no Guarantee of Success," http://www.scmp.com/comment/insight-opinion/article/1122209/dynastic-succession-asian-politics-no-guarantee-success (Accessed on Jan. 10, 2013).

Manion, Melanie (2008), "Politics in China," in Gabriel A. Almond, G. Bingham Powell, Jr., Russel J. Dalton, and Kaare Strom, eds., *Comparative Politics Today: A World View*, 9th Edition, NY.: Pearson Longman, pp. 406–453.

March, James G. and Johan P. Olsen (2006), "Elaborating the New Institutionalism," in R. A. W. Rhodes, Sarah A. Binder, and Bert A. Rockman, eds., *The Oxford Handbook of Political Institutions*, Oxford: Oxford University Press, pp. 3–20.

March, James G. and Johan P. Olsen (1984), "The New Institutionalism: Organizational Factors in Political Life," *American Political Science Review* 78 (5), pp. 734–749.

McAdam, Doug, Sidney Tarrow, and Charles Tilly (2009), "Comparative Perspectives on Contentious Politics," in Mark Irving Lichbach and Alan S. Zuckerman, eds., *Comparative Politics: Rationality, Culture, and Structure*, NY.: Cambridge University Press, pp. 260–290.

Minister of Public Administration and Security of Korea (2012), "2012. 행정통계연보" http://www.mopas.go.kr/gpms/ns/mogaha/user/userlayout/bulletin/userBtView.action?userBtBean.bbsSeq=1022484&userBtBean.ctxCd=1290&userBtBean.ctxType=21010002&-userBtBean.categoryCd= (Accessed on Jan. 10, 2013).

Ministry of Internal Affairs and Communications of Japan (2013), "広域行政·市町村合併" http://www.soumu.go.jp/kouiki/kouiki.html (Accessed on Jan. 10, 2013).

Munck, Gerardo D (2007), "The Past and Present of Comparative Politics," in Gerard L. Munck and Richard Snyder, eds., *Passion, Craft, and Method in*

Comparative Politics, Baltimore ML.: The Johns Hopkins University Press, pp. 32–59.

Newton, Kenneth and Jan W. van Deth (2010), *Foundations of Comparative Politics*, 2nd Edition, NY.: Cambridge University Press.

Nye Jr., Joseph S. (2008), *The Powers to Lead*, NY.: Oxford University Press.

OECD (2012), *Health at a Glance: Asia/Pacific 2012*, Paris: OECD.

Pennington, Mark (2009), "Theory, Institutions and Comparative Politics," in Judith Bara and Mark Pennington, eds., *Comparative Politics*, London: SAGE Publications Inc. pp. 13–40.

Peters, B. Guy (2008), "Approaches in Comparative Politics," in Daniele Caramani, ed., *Comparative Politics*, Oxford: Oxford University Press. pp. 44–62.

Rosenbluth, Frances and Michael F. Thies (2008), "Politics in Japan," in Gabriel A. Almond, G. Bingham Powell, Jr., Russel J. Dalton, and Kaare Strom, eds., *Comparative Politics Today: A World View*, 9th Edition, NY.: Pearson Longman, pp. 308–357.

Sartori, Giovanni (1970), "Concept Misformation in Comparative Politics," *American Political Science Review* 64(4), pp. 1033–1053.

Schmitter, Philippe (2009), "The Nature and Future of Comparative Politics," *European Political Science Review* 1(1), pp. 33–61.

Sen, Amartya (2003), "Democracy and Its Global Roots," *New Republic* 229(4) (October), pp. 28–35.

Shin, Doh Chull and Tadashi Inoguchi (2010), "Avowed Happiness in Confucian Asia: Ascertaining its Distribution, Patterns, and Sources," in Doh Chull Shin and Tadashi Inoguchi, eds., *The Quality of Life in Confucian Asia: From Physical Welfare to Subjective Well-being*, NY.: Springer, pp. 223–245.

Snyder, Richard (2007), "The Human Dimension of Comparative Research," Gerard L. Munck and Richard Snyder, eds., *Passion, Craft, and Method in Comparative Politics*, Baltimore ML.: The Johns Hopkins University Press, pp. 1–31.

Tu, Weiming (2001), "Implication of the Rise of 'Confucian' in East Asia," *Daedalus* 129(1) (Winter), pp. 195–218.

Westley, Frances, Brenda Zimmerman, and Michael Quinn Patton (2007), *Getting to Maybe: How the World is Changed*, Toronto: Vintage Canada.

Wiarda, Howard J. (2007), *Comparative Politics: Approaches and Issues*, Lanham: Rowman & Littlefield Publishers, Inc.

World Bank (2013), "World Governance Index," http://info.worldbank.org/governance/wgi/index.asp (Accessed on Jan. 10, 2013).

Zhang, Baohui (2010), "Beyond Electoral Democracy: Promoting Good Governance in East Asia," in Brian Bridges and Lok Sang Ho, eds., *Public Governance in Asia and the Limits of Electoral Democracy*, Cheltenham: Edward Elgar, pp. 31–53.

Zuckerman, Aaln S. (2009), "Advancing Explanation in Comparative Politics: Social Mechanism, Endogeneous Process, and Empirical Rigor," in Mark Irving Lichbach and Alan S. Zuckerman, eds., *Comparative Politics: Rationality, Culture, and Structure*, NY.: Cambridge University Press, pp. 72–95.

Chapter 6

Chinese Political Leadership Transition: An Overview and Assessment

*Wu Xinbo, Wu Di**

Introduction

The recent Chinese leadership transition in 2012 received much attention from the international community. Xi Jinping was elected as the highest political leader, CPC General Secretary, President of China, Chairman of Central Military Commission, and Central Politburo Standing Committee member. As Xi had already been a member of the central leadership for five years, it was not surprising to see him elected as the president. This recent transition has put the Chinese leadership system under the spotlight, raising curiosity about the Chinese political leadership system and leadership transition processes. As China's international influence grows, the influence of Chinese leaders on international issues also increases. As policy-makers, Chinese leaders have crucial influence not only on domestic affairs but also on international issues. This chapter is going to introduce the Chinese political leadership transition from a historical perspective and provide analysis on characters of the current leadership transition process.

*Wu Xinbo, Executive Vice Dean and Professor, Shanghai International Studies University, China. Wu Di, Doctorate Student, American University, USA.

This chapter is organized as follows. In the first section, we introduce the Chinese political system. Since Chinese political structure is unique from other major regime types in the world, we feel the need to explicitly explain the system by examining power sources. The second section outlines the political transition in Mao and Deng's time, focusing on leaders and leadership formation. The third section introduces the current leadership system and explains the process of leadership transition from Jiang Zemin to Hu Jintao and then to Xi Jinping. In the fourth section, we provide our analysis on current leadership transition as well as the collective leadership system. Chinese current leadership transition is a product of history, informal mechanisms, and institutionalized democracy. Our conclusion will also shed lights on the future of Chinese leadership transition.

Current Chinese Political Leadership Systems and Their Evolvements

Since its founding in 1949, the PRC has experienced three major leadership transitions before Hu Jintao and Xi Jinping. Mao Zedong was the supreme leader until his demise. Deng Xiaoping was the behind-the-scenes leader during Chinese reform and opening up. Jiang Zemin was the first leader who took the highest position in CPC, the state, and the military. The leadership transitions of two recent leaders, Hu Jintao and Xi Jinping followed Jiang Zemin's process. Over the past six decades, China has witnessed dramatic changes in its leadership system and transition. In order to understand the changes, we have to first understand the political leadership systems in China. As these systems are not rigid and have been changing since the founding of the People's Republic of China, the boundaries of the duties and powers of political leaders have changed along the way. In other words, the history of Chinese political leadership systems is not only a matter of political structure, but more importantly it also relates closely to the leaders themselves. The method of historical analysis and process tracing is very important in understanding Chinese leadership transition, because the current leadership system has evolved over time, changing from individual dominance to collective leadership. Therefore, historical analysis is not only feasible but also necessary. At the same time, the Chinese form of government is so unique and distinct from political structures in Western countries that it is almost impossible to understand leadership transitions without having knowledge of the whole system. Therefore, it is necessary to begin by looking at the Chinese political system.

1. Chinese Regime and Main Leaders

(1) *The Chinese Regime*

China is led by the Communist Party. In categories defined by comparative politics theorists, China is identified as a communist regime (Kopstein and Lichbach 2005, 261), which is true and exact. The Chinese communist regime is unique and one of a kind. After War of Resistance Against Japan and more than a decade of civil war between CPC and Kuomintang (KMT), CPC established the People's Republic of China and became the ruling party in 1949. According to the current Chinese Constitution, "The People's Republic of China is a socialist state under the people's democratic dictatorship led by the working class and based on the alliance of workers and peasants. The socialist system is the basic system of the People's Republic of China." "The system of multi-party cooperation and political consultation led by the Communist Party of China will exist and develop in China for a long time to come (Chinese Constitution 1982)." From the Constitution, we can see there are three important elements that constitute the Chinese communist regime: people (National People's Congress or NPC), the CPC, and multi-party cooperation (Chinese People's Political Consultative Conference or CPPCC).

The relationship among the Party, NPC, and CPPCC is straightforward on paper, yet complex in practice, which is the reason that understanding the leadership system is so important. The relationships among important political parts in Chinese politics can be revealed by looking into different Chinese political leadership systems. According to the Chinese Constitution and the Constitution of the CPC, the CPC serves as a leader, guiding people and the state toward an ultimate goal of a "prosperous, democratic, civilized and harmonious modern socialist country" (Constitution of CPC 2012). One of Deng Xiaoping's Four Cardinal Principles was "the principle of upholding the leadership of the Communist Party of China". Jiang Zemin also emphasized the leading role of CPC in an important meeting in 2001, which was reaffirmed during the 16th CPC Central Committee in 2002 (16th Party Congress Report 2006).

The CPC leads the NPC through political guidance by setting political principles, political orientations, and major decisions, and recommending important talents to organs of political power. This is because, according to official documents and reports from the Party and the NPC, the CPC represents the interests of the majority of the Chinese people (Wu Bangguo 2011). In terms of exercising the legislative power, the NPC makes sure that "the views of the Party become the will of the state as well as the standards and norms of conduct the whole society abides by" (Wu Bangguo 2011).

The main functions of the CPPCC are political consultation, democratic supervision, and participation in politics, which are well explained in the Preamble of the Constitution,

> The Chinese People's Political Consultative Conference is a broadly representative organization of the united front, which has played a significant historical role and will continue to do so in the political and social life of the country, in promoting friendship with the people of other countries and in the struggle for socialist modernization and for the reunification and unity of the country.

The relationship between the CPC and CPPCC has been summarized into the following principles, "long-term coexistence, mutual supervision, utter mutual devotion, and sharing weal and woe". Yu Zhengsheng, Chairman of the 12th National Committee of the CPPCC, said at the closing meeting of the 12th National Committee that, "we need to steadfastly uphold the leadership of the Communist Party of China, adhere to and improve the system of multiparty cooperation and political consultation under the leadership of the CPC" (Xinhua 2013).

The military is another key political body under the leadership of the CPC. The CPC's leadership over the military was also written into the Constitution of the CPC,

> The Communist Party of China persists in its leadership over the People's Liberation Army and other armed forces of the people, builds up the strength of the People's Liberation Army, ensures that it

> accomplishes its historic missions at this new stage in the new century, and gives full play to its role in consolidating national defense, defending the motherland and participating in the socialist modernization drive.

Mao has his famous quote, "Political power grows out of the barrel of a gun." Deng Xiaoping reaffirmed this strategy by making the point that the Party's absolute leadership over the military is significant to China's stability and enduring social order.

The preceding analysis suggests that the CPC has an overarching leading role in Chinese politics, which is the reason that CPC leader has the highest political power in China. In the current Chinese political system, the highest Party leader, military leader, and state leader is one person, while in the past, before Jiang Zeming took all three titles, these three positions were occupied by different leaders, which caused political struggles among them. In order to prevent this from happening, in the end, the three powers were concentrated into one person, the head of the CPC.

(2) *Main Leaderships*

The Communist Party and Military

The CPC central leadership mainly consists of three important bodies: the Central Committee, the Politburo (Standing Committee of the Politburo), and the General Secretary. The Central Committee is the highest authority within the CPC and the members are elected by the Party Congress. The Politburo members are elected by the Central Committee. The Standing Committee of the Politburo represents the Politburo when the full Politburo is prorogued. The Politburo represents the Central Committee when the full Committee is prorogued. Similarly, the Committee represents the whole CPC National Congress when it is prorogued. The Standing Committee of the Politburo consists of seven or nine members and it is currently the de facto the highest decision-making body in China. The title of CPC leader changed from "Chairman of the Central Committee of the CPC" to "General Secretary of the CPC" in 1982, when the 12th National Congress of the CPC decided to abolish the title of Chairman of the Central Committee and establish the General Secretary as the most important and powerful position in the Party (Bartke and Schier 1985, 11).

Since its founding in 1949, China has gone through seven Party leaders. They are Mao Zedong (1949–1976), Hua Guofeng (1976–1981), Hu Yaobang (1982–1987), Zhao Ziyang (1987–1989), Jiang Zemin (1989–2002), Hu Jintao (2002–2012), and Xi Jinping (2012-present). However, not all leaders had the same power over the Party and state. Some of them only served as the Party Secretary; others were heads of the Party, military, and state in one. Deng Xiaoping is a special case. Although he was never head of the CPC, his prestige in the Party made him the most powerful person in China after Mao. The Standing Committee, on the other hand, is the manifestation of the collective leadership and is also the place where decision are made on power transition, where committee members vote for the next Party leader. This mechanism will be discussed in the following section.

Like other countries in the world, in China the person holding the military power is always the most powerful figure. Just like the relationship between the CPC and other Chinese political bodies, the Chairman of the Central Military Commission (CMC) is also the highest Party leader in the current system.

As written above, Deng Xiaoping was never to be General Secretary of the CPC, but he was the military leader from 1983 to 1990, which is another way of proving that he was actually the most powerful person in China. His special prestige and influence made him the "big boss" behind the scene. At the same time, the positions of military leader and Party leader did not belong to one person. Hu Yaobang and Zhao Ziyang were only Party leaders, but they did not have military power in hand. After Jiang Zemin took office in 1989, the former arrangement was back on the table again. Jiang was not only the Party leader, but also the military leader and the president. This arrangement passed down to Hu Jintao and recently to Xi Jinping, which signifies an institutionalized leadership transition.

The State, Government, NPC, and CPPCC

According to the Constitution, the President of China is elected by the NPC, and he has power to appoint the Chinese Premier, head of the government. The president acts as diplomatic representatives on behalf of the People's Republic of China. The President and the CPC General Secretary are usually the same person. For example, Mao was the president of PRC from 1954 to 1959, even though he had been the acting President since

1949. Liu Shaoqi was the President from 1959 to 1968. However, the third and fourth Presidents did not hold the post of CPC General Secretary (Li Xiannian and Yang Shangkun). This situation was again changed and has been officially institutionalized since Jiang Zemin took office. Since then, three tittles, president, general secretary, and chairman of the Central Military Commission, have concentrated in one person.

The Chinese Premier, appointed by the President and proved by the NPC, is the head of the central government, also called the State Council. The Premier and CPC system usually have a clear line, meaning that the head of CPC and the head of government can never be the same person, except Hua Guofeng, who held two posts at the same time. But before him, Zhou Enlai was the Premier when Mao was in office. The premiers after Hua also did not have titles in the Party when they were Premiers. However, some of them either had posts in the NPC or CPC before or after their term as Premiers. Again, since 1983, the institutionalized system required that the current Premier work as the first Vice-Premier before being appointed as Premier. In other words, usually the current first Vice-Premier will be the next Premier.

According to the Constitution, "The National People's Congress of the People's Republic of China is the highest organ of state power. Its permanent body is the Standing Committee of the National People's Congress" (Chinese Constitution 1982). The leader of NPC usually refers to the Chairman of the Standing Committee of the NPC. "The Chairman of the Standing Committee of the National People's Congress presides over the work of the Standing Committee and convenes its meetings (Chinese Constitution 1982)." An important fact about the Chairman is that he/she is also a member of the Standing Committee of the Politburo. This arrangement has been in place since 1993. The Chairman is appointed by the NPC Presidium, which consists of 178 members (Xinhua News Agency 2013) who are senior officials in CPC and elected by NPC (Cheng and Zheng 2011, 68).

As mentioned above, the CPPCC is a political advisory body under the leadership of the CPC. The CPPCC leader is the Chairman/ Chairwoman of the National Committee of the CPPCC. Mao Zedong, Zhou Enlai, and Deng Xiaoping were the first three Chairmen, which indicates the close relationship between the CPC and CPPCC at the beginning. Li Xiannian was the Chairman of CPPCC after he left his position as the Chinese President. Since 1993 when Li Ruihuan took the position of the Chairman, the institutionalized system has been in place until now. The CPPCC Chairman can never be the same person as the General Secretary. The Chairman of CPPCC is also a member of the Standing Committee of the Politburo, ranked at number four.

2. Chinese Collective Leadership System

(1) *The Central Politburo Standing Committee*

As important as the General Secretary is individual, the collective political power of the Central Politburo Standing Committee (CPSC) wields the highest collective authority in China. CPSC is the core decision-making body in the CPC as well as for the whole state. They exercise power and oversee the Party and the state collectively. CPSC contains seven to nine members, and they "respectively represent different leading organs of the Party and the state. They have clear division of labor while they also coordinate with each other (Hu 2013)". This is very different from the presidential system in the United States, where the executive power is held by the President. Whereas in the Chinese collective leadership system, the "decisions are made based on collective rather than individual wisdom" (Hu 2013). With the consideration of interests from all parts of the Party, members of CPSC are elected by the Central Committee of the CPC, meaning that they are drawn from the Central Committee.

According to Lee (2000), the Chinese leadership system has both formal and informal characteristics. From the formal functional perspective, the leadership is "illustrated by the 'democratic centralism,' in which a decision made by discussion, consultation, and consensus-making in a committee setting, operating via majority rule but respecting minority views" (Dittmer, Fukui and Lee 2000, 171). Lee also pointed out that informal style includes "leadership core". In his book on post-Mao reform, Tang Tsou described the Chinese party-state system as "concentric circles" with multiple layers (Tsou 1986, 249). Obviously, CPSC, including the CPC General Secretary, is the internal kernel of the party center.

(2) *The Central Advisory Commission*

The Central Advisory Commission (CAC) does not exist in the current political system. It exercised power from 1982 to 1992 when the central leadership system was going through the process of replacements by young and new leaders. It was established after the twelfth Party Congress in 1982 for the purpose of providing consultation to the new leaders, and at the same time giving posts to the old and retiring leaders that had more than forty years of service to the Party. In the post-Mao reform era, Deng was in favor of demolishing the life tenure system. But before the establishment of a retirement system for senior leaders, China adopted the CAC to place them. The chairman was elected from the CPSC. The first Chairman of the CAC was Deng Xiaoping and the second was Chen Yun.

According to the CPC Constitution passed by the twelfth CPC National Congress, CAC's function is to assist and consult for the Central Committee (Deng 1982). It was also a place provided for the older leaders where they could still play a significant role for the Party and the state. CAC members could join the Central Committee meetings, while the Vice-Chairman could join the CPSC meetings. In this sense, CAC members had equal status as Central Committee members. CAC Vice-Chairman and standing committee members were equal to members of the Central Politburo. The CAC chairman was a member of CPSC. Since CAC members were senior leaders of CPC, they usually held more power than members of the Central Committee (Deng 1982).

From the above, it is obvious that in terms of political leaders, the state and Party lies within the same structure, meaning that leaders of the NPC, the CPPCC, and government should have political positions in the CPC. In other words, these leaders must be CPSC members; and China's highest leader must be the CPC General Secretary, except in Deng's era when he did not hold the position of General Secretary. Therefore, the leadership transition this paper is going to analyze focuses on China's highest leadership and the transition of the CPSC.

Leadership Formation during First and Second Generations of Leadership

1. Leadership in Mao Zedong's Era

(1) *Main Leaders in Mao Zedong's Era*

Immediately after its founding, China established a system of leadership transition based on the model of the Soviet Union and other Communist countries. However, as a young state, this system was not perfect and was not well implemented because of many constraints at the time. At the same time, because of Mao's charisma and general public support, he had a great say on leader nomination. On the one hand, Lin Biao was the reserved leader that was supposed to take Mao's position. Because Lin had different visions of Chinese future from Mao and lost public support, Lin did not become the Chinese leader after Mao. Hua Guofeng, on the other hand, was the successor nominated by Mao in the last month before Mao's demise, and his appointment was agreed and made by the Central Politburo. "With you in charge, I'm at ease" is the note Mao given for Hua. His most well-known credit was that he ousted "the Gang of Four" from political power. Hua had a short term leadership of only five years. Deng became the defacto Chinese leader from then on.

(2) *Formation of Leaderships*

Mao's leadership status within the CPC and the whole nation was the result of both the victory of the CPC fighting against the KMT during the Civil War and political struggle within the Party. The establishment of Mao's power began at the Zunyi conference in 1935. Prior to that, the CPC was dominated by communists trained in the Soviet Union, especially Wang Ming.

Liu Shaoqi and Lin Biao experienced similar fates when they became second-in-command in the CPC under Mao. They were both nominated by Mao and voted by the Party Congress, NPC, and CPPCC. The formal routinization and institutionalization of succession was established at the Eighth Party Congress, where it showed Liu's talent on leading the country. However, Liu's disagreements with Mao as well as public support for Mao cost him stepping down. Lin was chosen to be the next leader, but Lin betrayed Mao and the Party. Hua was a special case because he was made the Party leader just before Mao's demise, so he experienced two political transitions in China: one is the power vacuum after Mao's death with the residual power of "the Gang of Four"; the other is the rise of Deng's power. An interesting and unique phenomenon worth pointing out is that Liu's, Lin's, and Hua's successions were explicitly supported under different occasions by Mao. For example, Lin's nomination was written into the Party's Constitution, and Hua had Mao's personal comment. But Mao's decisions also gained public and Party support. The nominations all went through official process by NPC, Central Politburo, and Party Congress. After Mao's demise, the Chinese leader transition system became more institutionalized.

2. Leadership Formation in Deng Xiaoping's Era

(1) *Transition from Personality Cult to Collective Leadership*

Deng's era was a transition from strong individual leadership to collective leadership, the evidence of which was that Deng never took the position as the first-hand leader, giving power to young upcoming politicians. "During the reform era, Deng made explicit reference to the leadership core for the first time, reiterating that in the party's fine tradition, a balance should be maintained between the role of the leadership core and the proper functions of collective leadership" (Dittmer, Fukui and Lee 2000, 171). Deng made a very important speech during a Central Politburo meeting, in which he criticized the political leadership system, saying that, "as far as the leadership and cadre systems of our Party and state are concerned, the major problems are bureaucracy, over-concentration of power, patriarchal methods, life tenure in leading posts and privileges of various kinds" (Deng Xiaoping 1980). He then proposed the retiring system for senior Party leaders, which was also the drive for establishing the CAC. Deng also considered the Eighth Party Congress a model for constraints on the single leader's authority as "the separation of party and state functions, the strengthening of supervisory organs (for example, the Central Discipline Inspection Commission-CDIC), and the 'standardization' of party committee procedures at all organizational levels" (Sullivan 1986–1987, 606). The leadership system in Deng's time was a mix of personal charisma and the beginning of an impersonal organization. It was the reality of the Party structure with a fully functioning CAC, where elite senior Party leaders still had their power influencing domestic politics.

(2) *The Formation of Leaderships*

Deng stepped up as the actual highest leader after Hua left the position, but Deng never took the post as the Party General Secretary. Although Deng was in favor of non-life-tenure leadership system, he was still much in control of the highest leaderships along with the CAC. Deng was never the Party leader and the President, but he was the Chairman of the CAC and held military power, which made him the defacto highest leader from the Third Plenary Session of the 11th CPC Central Committee in 1978 until Jiang took office in 1989. Two Party leaders (Hu Yaobang and Zhao Ziyang) following Hua were both designated and demoted by Deng and CAC members for different reasons and their terms lasted no more than 5 years.

If we say that Mao established the Chinese political system, then it was Deng who played a crucial role in institutionalizing political leadership transitions. Hu and Zhao's downfalls were due to the inconsistency between their policies and the CAC. Their step-down both went through institutionalized processes rather than by political struggle or political coup. At the same time, this period witnessed both the establishment and abolishment of the CAC. Although Deng was Chairman of the CAC, he did not have the overarching power like Mao did. For example, other senior party elites such as Chen Yun and Peng Zhen were both very influential. In terms of appointing successors, Deng had to consider the interests of other CAC members. Finally, the combination of Jiang Zemin, Li Peng, and Qiao Shi was considered the result of compromise inside the Party, signifying the establishment of intra-Party democracy. However, we should point out that although intra-Party democracy was gradually established, such democracy was confined to a limited scope, including only members of the CPSC and CAC. They were in charge of decision-making, while the Party Congress and the NPC were only formalities. There were never competitive elections.

Current Institutionalized Leadership Formation

1. Jiang Zemin's Leadership Core and Institutionalization of Political Leadership

There were some chances that Jiang would not be the highest leader in China, because he was not a member of the CPSC at the time, and he was only the Party Secretary of Shanghai. However, the 1989 incident changed the whole situation. Deng and CAC members were looking for a replacement. Popular candidates were Li Peng, Qiao Shi, and Yao Yilin, who were all CPSC members and Vice Premiers. It was more reasonable to promote one of them to be the General Secretary. The fact that Jiang Zemin finally became the highest leader was a surprise to many people. However, it was seen as the best decision at the time. Plus, Deng preferred Jiang, which gained Jiang much public support. It is also worth pointing out that although Deng played a major role in determining Jiang as the highest leader, there were legitimate voting processes in both NPC and Central Party Congress.

Deng claimed his fully retirement in 1989. After that, he made several moves to ensure Jiang's leadership. As we explained above, Jiang did not have experience at the central Party, meaning that he did not have much support in the Party and military. With Deng's support, Jiang quickly established his authority. As Lee summarized,

> First, with his [Deng's] full support, the CAC was abolished in the 14th Party Congress in 1992 ... Second, Deng was involved in retiring General Yang Shangkun, the first vice chairman of the CMC, and his half-brother, General Yang Baibing, vice chairman of the CMC and concurrently secretary of the CMC. The "clan of General Yang" was persuaded to step down in 1992, mainly because Deng did not want any powerful military men in the way as power was being passed to Jiang. In addition, Deng skillfully played down and set aside his policy differences with Yangs, for example, the nationalization of the PLA as well as the matter of appointments ... Third, Deng played a key role in the policy change toward the property-rights-centered reform of state-owned enterprises by calling for the establishment of a socialist market economy in his "inspection tour to the South". In the meantime, he provided substantial support to Zhu Rongji to assume the post of the fist vice premier of the State Council at the 14th Party Congress in 1992 to ensure the success of market-oriented reform (Dittmer, Fukui and Lee 2000, 180–181).

From the standpoint of power, the difference between Deng and Jiang, as the core of the third generation leadership, is huge.[1] In other words, Jiang was less powerful than Mao and Deng. According to Yushan Wu, "Deng was less powerful than Mao because he mustered fewer power resources, but in many respects these two men were still comparable. The difference between Deng and his successor is much striking" (Kopstein and Lichbach 2000, 248). He calls Jiang the "representative of a new generation of bureaucrats", who wielded much less power than their predecessors. As a result, "imprint of Jiang or any other third generation leader on Chinese politics and society will be markedly lighter than that of Mao or Deng" (Kopstein and Lichbach 2000, 248). David Bachman (1992) gave an explanation for such a power decrease. He explains that during Mao and Deng's era, talents in the technocratic field were so few that they could not fulfill the task of serving the government. By the late 1980s, technocratic talents had benefited from the education system implemented by Mao and began to fill the positions (Bachman 1992, 1050–1051). This marked the transformation of the Chinese leadership system from a single dominant leader to collective power. Collective power meant that big decision will come not only from the general secretary but also from the CPSC, and the new leader will have to bargain and compromise with other elite officials. We will explain the power distribution in the following discussion.

2. Formations of Current Leadership and CPSC

Since Jiang took office in the central government, China has not experienced any significant political unrest. Leadership transition has entered a stage of institutionalization. Official processes of leadership elections go through the Party National Congress. CPSC members have been elected and placed into posts from the General Secretary, Premier, Chairman of NPC, and Chairman of CPPCC, etc. Of course, these placements have to go through the election processes in NPC and CPPCC. The appointment of Jiang, Hu, Xi and CPSC members during their terms all went through this election process. Usually the top leader stays in position for two terms, or ten years. However, Jiang held on to military power for two more years after he retired from general secretaryship. This "tradition" was considered passed down by Deng. Deng was still the Chairman of CMC after his retirement. Hu's retirement in 2012 broke this cycle. He passed military power to Xi at the same time with general secretaryship. Hu's move also signifies the further institutionalization of Chinese leadership transition.

Informal mechanisms also have a big role in current leadership transition. For example, Jiang's path from Shanghai to Beijing set the precedent for his successors. Officials from Shanghai have been put under the spotlight. Many of Jiang's successors in Hu Jintao and Xi Jinping's administrations had experience in Shanghai before entering the central office. For example, Zhu Rongji (Premier during Jiang's second term), Wu Bangguo (former Chairman of the Standing Committee of NPC), and Xi Jinping all had worked in Shanghai. Moreover, we can find clues about the next leadership from current members of the CPSC. In other words, the next highest leader is inevitably a current CPSC member. This is the case for both Hu and Xi. Hu became a CPSC member at the 14th Party Congress and stayed for four terms. Placing Hu in the CPSC was considered a move of training him as a next generation leader. After ten years of "training", Hu was elected as the party General Secretary in 2002. Xi's path to central government was even more predictable than Hu's. After Chen Liangyu was dismissed from Shanghai for corruption charges in 2006, Xi was transferred to Shanghai. In the 17th Party Congress, Xi was elected as a CPSC member. He was also the new leader who enjoyed highest ranking in CPSC. At the age of 54 he entered the CPSC, which met the Party age standard for CPC central leaders. Many people's guesses were confirmed by the fact that Xi was elected as the general secretary in 2012.

Besides the General Secretary, CPSC member transitions are also important because of the nature of China's collective leadership system. The General Secretary does not have the ultimate decision-making power. He has to bargain, compromise, and cooperate with other CPSC members. Sometimes the decision-making power even lies in the whole Central Politburo. The CPSC usually consists of seven to nine members. The General Secretary ranks first, followed by the NPC Chairman, Premier, and CPPCC Chairman. There are no fixed arrangements from fifth member on, but they usually include one leader in charge of central discipline inspection and one Vice Premier.[2] Here, formal and informal mechanisms function at the same time. On the one hand, their appointments have to go through the legal election of Party Congress, NPC, and CPPCC. Moreover, CPSC members are all formal members of the Central Politburo. The terms of CPSC members depends on their age. CPSC members usually have no more than two terms. Hu Jintao was a special case because he was relatively young when he entered the CPSC. Resulting from the rule of age, he stayed in CPSC for four terms. On the other hand, the CPSC members' local linkages are well known as the informal practice of power inheritance. From the members of the current CPSC, we can also sense the power influence of formal leaders. In addition, the party secretaries of four municipalities directly under the central government — Beijing, Shanghai, Tianjin, and Chongqing — are necessarily members of the Central Politburo and they are also considered as popular candidates for central leadership. In other words, Central Politburo finalists all have gone through years of local services until finally promoted by the Central Politburo.

Assessment and Future Direction

1. Informal Mechanism of Leadership Transition

The current Chinese political leadership transition has unique characteristics, the most important of which is the duality of formal democratic institutionalization and informal personal influence. At least apparently, Chinese political leadership transition appears as a democratic system. No matter if it is through the Party Congress, NPC, or CPPCC, leadership transitions all happen through elections, displaying the democratic centralism inherited from Leninists. However, individual influence has been a very important factor in leadership formation, especially during Mao and Deng's eras. Although there is no dominant individual leader who can exert such influence now, the ability to nominate is still confined within the top leadership. The voting representatives (voters) at these conferences/congresses only provide a yes or no option for the new leader. They do not provide any options of different leaders for voters. Therefore, there is no competitive election at the highest level. Competitive election has been brought up often by media, and it has been practiced since the 16th Party Congress in 2002 with the percentage of nominees for primary elections more than the elected members is getting higher (Xinhua News Agency 2012).

At the same time, from the standpoint of Chinese political rhetoric, there has been a transition from the terms "Closely rally around the Party Central Committee with Comrade Jiang Zemin at its core" to "Closely rally around the Party Central Committee with Comrade Hu Jintao (Xi

Jinping) as general secretary." In fact, Mao was called the "Great Leader, Great Teacher, Great Supreme Commander, and Great Helmsman" (Yan Changgui 2006) when he was in power, but now the CPC calls the leaders of Mao's era "the first leadership around Mao Zedong at its core". Deng was called the "chief architect of reform and opening up" (Song Yijun 2013). CPC also used the word "core" to refer to leaders in Deng's time. The word change from "core" to "general secretary" reiterates the fact that personal influence is reducing its power and institution of collective leadership is taking shape in the Chinese political system. "Core" emphasizes individual power, while "general secretary" stressed the role of party organization and collective leadership. As our analysis above on power decrease indicates, from Mao and Deng to Jiang, Hu, and Xi, Jiang, Hu, and Xi have relatively less power than Mao and Deng. From the standpoint of power transition, Mao, Deng, and Jiang held decisive power on nominations of their successors, but Hu's personal influence on Xi was much less than leaders before him. The decision-making power was spread to the Central Politburo and CPSC. In other words, simply by examining the general secretary himself is not enough to understand Chinese policymaking. Members of CPSC and Central Politburo should all be taken into consideration.

2. Institutionalized Collective Leadership System

China's collective leadership system has a long tradition tracing back to Mao's era. According to Kopstein and Lichbach,

> The post-1949 politics of China can best be understood in terms of the ideas and policies of its top leaders. However, this does not mean that individuals determined China's political development by dint of their personalities and particular political inclinations. As strong as Mao's and Deng's influence on the political process may have been, they nevertheless reflected underlying forces that propelled a communist regime through the kinds of different developmental stages that one can also find in the Soviet Union and other communist countries. In this sense, both Mao and Deng (and Jiang Zemin and Hu Jintao, who succeeded Deng) were more representative of the underlying trend than they were creators of such a trend (Kopstein and Lichbach 2005, 261).

Other leaders, such as Liu Shaoqi, also confirmed that political leadership is "not an individual but a collective one" to the point that leaders were virtually interchangeable (Liu Shaoqi 1969, 171). If Mao and Deng were not able to determine completely the highest leadership from their personal preference, then the personal influence on successors of Jiang and Hu was much less dominant. In addition, with the weakening of individual authority, the actual power of China's highest leaders is reducing. In other words, even though the general secretary is able to determine the next leadership, he is not capable of solely making the final decision on CPSC candidates. Therefore, nomination of the next leadership is no longer the call of the previous leader. Negotiation and compromise within the Party have become a more important way to leadership formation.

Some Chinese scholars believe that this collective leadership system and leadership transition under this system meet Chinese current political and social condition and is superior to Western presidential system. Hu Angang provides five advantages,

> First is the mechanism of collective appraisal of candidates, and collective withdrawal and succession of membership, which both terminates the tradition of individual succession of power seen in China's history and prevents selection of politicians totally through election as practiced abroad.
>
> Second, the mechanism of collective coordination and distribution of responsibilities, is an effective firewall against indecision, buck-passing and opposition in the decision-making process.
>
> The mechanism of collective study, the third one, leads to common view through sharing of decision-making wisdom and expertise.
>
> Fourth, the mechanism of collective inspection and investigation, gives the members a solid ground to speak, to propose and to decide.
>
> And the last one, the mechanism of collective decision-making, prevents an individual from making decisions on major issues and allows timely correction of mistakes (Hu Angang 2012).

China's current political system has in fact guaranteed China's rapid development in the past two decades, especially since Deng's policy of reform and opening up. The CPC did experience unrest in leadership transition at the beginning of the "reform and opening up" and immediately after the 1989 incident, but overall the transitions from one generation to another have been quite smooth. This has allowed implementation of consistent policies. Presidential systems, on the other hand, have limitations on policy consistency. For example, in the United States, recent anti-Obama care moves in the Republican camp indicates that it is possible if a Republican sits in the president's seat, he/she will overturn Obama's health care plan. In this regard, China's collective leadership system has its own merits.

Compared to Communist countries like the Soviet Union and North Korea, China broke the rule of life tenure for highest leaders. Deng was the first person to realize the problem of life tenure in 1979, so he proposed retirement plans in the CPC for elite Party officials. Within 74 years of existence, the Soviet Union had only one leader, Nikita Khrushchev, who did not stay in the highest position until his death. Gorbachev wanted political reform to change the situation, but he failed in the end.

China's collective leadership system also provides opportunity for the next leaders to become familiar with the central government. Hu and Xi both had spent years in the core leadership group as CPSC members before they became General Secretary, allowing them to know what to expect as the highest leader of China. Xi visited the United States when he was still the vice president. The American side also understood that he was going to be the next leader, so they treated him as one. This demonstrates that this progressive leadership promotion system is not only beneficial for leaders themselves, but also for other countries, so that they get to know up-and-coming leaders along the way.

The process of leadership election is developing towards a more democratic way. As we have analyzed above, the voting system and competitive elections have improved in the past decade. Therefore, we are optimistic about the future of China's leadership system. It has been established over a long time of exploration and meets the conditions of China as "a super country with large population" (Hu 2013). It is also in the political logic of the evolution of the ruling history of the Party. It is not a Western nor traditional communist leadership system. The formation and existence of China's leadership system has passed the test of history and is moving in a more democratic and sophisticated direction.

Conclusion

The Chinese political leadership system is unique in that it has developed through the history of China and the CPC. The formation of new leadership has gone through Mao and Deng's eras, when personal influence dominated the transition process, to the current more institutionalized format. In Mao and Deng's time, the formation of new leaders depended on basically Mao and Deng. However, since Jiang took office, along with other leadership power, the influence of individual leader on successor nomination has decreased. Power transitions, as other policy decisions, depend on collective leadership. In other words, the highest leader himself has to compromise and cooperate with other elites in the CPSC and Central Politburo. The process of generating new leaders also went from direct appointment to the current institutionalized competitive election system. We have summarized two distinct features of the Chinese political system: formal and informal mechanisms and collective decision-making. Although the big trend is that the system is moving in an institutionalized direction, informal mechanisms still influence the actual nomination. We have to look at this transition system through the lenses of these two features. The Chinese political leadership system has its own merits by meeting Chinese current political and social conditions and ensuring policy consistency. It also provides opportunities for leaders to get their hands wet as they prepare to lead the country.

Notes

1. For more detailed power difference, see Figure 1 in Bachman, David (1992). "The Limits on Leadership in China," *Asian Survey*, 32, No. 11. pp. 1048.
2. For more information on CPSC, see Alice Miller (2011). "The Politburo Standing Committee under Hu Jintao," *China Leadership Monitor*, No. 35, http://media.hoover.org/sites/default/files/documents/CLM35AM.pdf.

References

Bachman, David (1992), "The Limits on Leadership in China," *Asian Survey*, 32, No. 11, pp. 1046–1062.

Bartke, Wolfgang and Peter Schier (1985), *China's New Party Leadership: Biographies and Analysis of the Twelfth Central Committee of the Chinese Communist Party*, Armonk, N.Y.: M.E. Sharpe.

Brown, Kerry (2009), *Friends and Enemies: The Past, Present and Future of the Communist Party of China*, London; New York: Anthem Press.

Cheng, E. J. Y. S. and Y. Zheng (2011), *Whither China's Democracy: Democratization in China Since the Tiananmen Incident*, City University of Hong Kong Press.

CPC Member Net [共产党员网] (2012), 《中国共产党党章》, http://www.12371.cn/2012/11/18/ARTI1353240237279676.shtml (Accessed on Sep. 12, 2013).

Deng, Xiaoping (1980), 《党和国家领导制度的改革》, http://zg.people.com.cn/BIG5/33839/34943/34944/34946/2617285.html (Accessed on Sep. 17, 2013).

Deng, Xiaoping, (1982), 《在中央顾问委员会第一次全体会议上的讲话》, http://cpc.people.com.cn/GB/69112/69113/69684/69696/4949906.html (Accessed on Sep.17, 2013).

Dittmer, L., H. Fukui and P. N. S. Lee. (2000), *Informal Politics in East Asia*, Cambridge University Press.

Guo, Yuzhen (2012), 《中共"九大"轶事》, http://cpc.people.com.cn/GB/68742/70427/70428/7335200.html (Accessed on Sep.22, 2013).

Hu, Angang [胡鞍钢] (2013), 《中国集体领导体制》, Beijing, China Renmin University Press.

Hu, Angang (2013), "Collective Leadership, China's Way," *Beijing Review*, http://www.bjreview.com.cn/nation/txt/2013-09/09/content_566699.htm (Accessed on Sep.17, 2013).

Hu, Angang (2012), "Spirit of Collective Leadership," *China Daily*, http://www.chinadaily.com.cn/opinion/2012-08/11/content_15664836.htm (Accessed on Sep. 18, 2013).

Kopstein, Jeffrey and Mark Irving Lichbach (2000), *Comparative Politics: Interests, Identities, and Institutions in a Changing Global Order*, Cambridge; New York: Cambridge University Press.

Kopstein, Jeffrey and Mark Irving Lichbach (2005), *Comparative Politics: Interests, Identities, and Institutions in a Changing Global Order*, New York: Cambridge University Press.

Lewis, John Wilson and University of London. Contemporary China Institute (1970), *Party Leadership and Rrevolutionary Power in China*, Cambridge Eng.: University Press.

Liu, Shaoqi (1969), "Training in Organization and Discipline," in *Collected Works of Liu Shaoqi: Before 1944*. Union Research Institute.

Miller, Alice (2011), "The Politburo Standing Committee under Hu Jintao," *China Leadership Monitor*, No. 35, http://media.hoover.org/sites/default/files/documents/CLM35AM.pdf (Accessed on Sep. 22, 2013).

People.com (1982), "Constitution of The People's Republic of China," http://english.people.com.cn/constitution/constitution.html (Accessed on Sep. 12, 2013).

People.com (2006), "16th Party Congress Report," http://english.cpc.people.com.cn/66739/4496615.html (Accessed on Sep. 12, 2013).

Song, Yijun (2013), 《邓小平为核心的中央领导集体形成始末》, http://dangshi.people.com.cn/n/2013/0608/c85037-21793779.html (Accessed on Sep.18, 2013).

Sullivan, Lawrence R. (1986–1987), "Leadership and Authority in the Chinese Communist Party: Perspectives from the 1950s," *Pacific Affairs*, 59, No. 4, pp. 605–633.

Tsou, Tang (1986), T*he Cultural Revolution and Post-Mao Reforms: A Historical Perspective*, Chicago: University of Chicago Press.

Wu, Bangguo (2011), "Work Report of NPC Standing Committee," *Chinese Government's official website*. http://english.gov.cn/official/2011-03/18/content_1827230_6.htm (Accessed on Sep. 12, 2013).

Xinhua News Agency (2013), "CPPCC's New Leader Vows not to Copy Western Political Systems," http://news.xinhuanet.com/english/china/2013-03/12/c_132226807.htm (Accessed on Sep.13, 2013).

Xinhua News Agency (2007), 《从书记到总书记中共中央最高领导称谓历史变迁》, http://news.xinhuanet.com/politics/2007-08/25/content_6601227.htm (Accessed on Sep. 15, 2013).

Xinhua News Agency (2012), "CPC Congress to Select Central Committee Members by Competitive Election: Spokesman," http://news.xinhuanet.com/english/special/18cpcnc/2012-11/07/c_131958095.htm (Accessed on Sep. 22, 2013).

Xinhua News Agency (2013), "Presidium Elected, Agenda Set for China's Landmark Parliamentary Session," http://news.xinhuanet.com/english/china/2013-03/04/c_132206014.htm (Accessed on Sep.15, 2013).

Yan, Changgui (2006), 《"四个伟大"是谁提出来的》, http://cpc.people.com.cn/GB/68742/69118/69662/4718717.html (Accessed on Sep. 18, 2013).

Chapter 7

What Makes Hereditary Politicians an Issue in Japan?

*Kwangwook Kim**

Introduction

The year 2012 witnessed the year when many new political leaders were inaugurated. In Northeast Asia, the sharp increases in political leaders' replacement came to an end through the elections in Japan and Korea. Shinzo Abe, Japanese Prime Minister from the Liberal Democratic Party of Japan (LDP), and Geun-hye Park, Korean President-elect from Saenuri Party, could be clear cases of hereditary succession since they both have fathers who were former political leaders. This gives implication of the political reversion to conservatism. Such afterimages of hereditary succession of political power seem to be formed when people long for the period that their nation was once prosperous or when people expect their country to be more stable.

No countries all over the world can completely break away from the hereditary succession of political power. Even the Democratic Party of Japan (DPJ) issued a manifesto to forbid hereditary succession of political power. But it fails to cut off all the candidates' hereditary succession of power, while setting a limit on new political candidates. One of the main reasons to forbid politicians' hereditary succession of power is to comply

* Kwangwook Kim, Lecturer, Department of Public Policy, Gifu Keizai University, Japan.

with the principle that outstanding people should be secured through free competition as they are equally given chances to participate in politics.

However, considering general social circumstances in Japan, it is clear that the folkways which sustained through the hereditary system in enterprise management or culture circles remained deep-rooted even in the political society. Two different concepts are as follows: one is to keep the hereditary system in order to preserve good things of the past and the other is to forbid hereditary succession in order to secure outstanding people. They seem contrary to each other, but they still in the same continuum to discover and preserve good factors.

As one of the common phenomena appearing in both elections in Korea and Japan in December, 2012, they appealed to nationalism while showing great expectations that their countries would be rich and powerful ones. The territorial issue between Korean and Japan was reflected in both countries' nationalism. It further deepened the antagonism and as a result both the peoples' distrusts toward the other country have come to the climax. If both countries put their national interests on the first priority and keep the counter-posing attitudes to each other without giving an inch of ground, what will be resulted in the international political situation and what will bring about in the relationship between Korea and Japan in the future?

It is true that President-elect Park's father, Jeong-hee Park, has been criticized as a developmental dictator although he played a great role in developing Korea after the military revolution. On the other hand, it should not be overlooked that he was the very person who successfully normalized the Korea-Japan relation that had been closed for almost 20 years. Japanese Prime Minister Abe's father, Abe Shinttaro, served as a Foreign Minister in succession through adopting diplomatic strategies that improved Japan's relations with Asian countries including Korea. At that time, the present Prime Minister Abe served as a secretary of the Foreign Minister. All the countries in Asia pay their attentions to how he will succeed to the diplomatic ties that can improve Japan's relations with other Asian countries.

Banning Hereditary Diet Seats Stated in the DPJ's Manifesto

On November 18, 2012, for the general election, DPJ set a manifesto policy that forbids the hereditary succession from the single-member constituency candidates based on an understanding that it should conform to its manifesto policy as an official approval. Then, the party requested all the candidates to sign on a written pledge in order to show the compliance with the manifesto policy. On the same day, Yoshihiko Noda, the Japanese Prime Minister at the time, declared in the press conference that "We should tear off hereditary succession and there is no exception to this regulation." While criticizing LDP by refusing the hereditary Diet seats, DPJ adopted an election strategy for the Japanese general election which is distinguished from LDP.

Because of this election strategy, DPJ did not acknowledge Yuichiro Hata, who was planning to run for the general election from Nagano District 3 as the minister of Land, Infrastructure, Transport, and Tourism, and was from the House of Councillors and the former Prime Minister, Tsutomu Hata's eldest son. Even in the manifesto set for the 2009 general election and the 2010 House of Councillors Election, DPJ stated the prohibition of hereditary succession of Diet seats.[1]

Out of all the policies from the manifesto set for the 2012 general election, DPJ announced five main ones. The fifth one was mainly about the prohibition of hereditary succession in order to provide the political reformation and regain people's trusts in politics. The following shows what it states.

With its internal rules, the policy continues to counter the so-called hereditary Diet seats by banning individuals from running for the same electoral district as a retiring Diet member to whom they are related with up to the third-degree kinship (Strict adherence to DPJ rules and regulations).

> When an incumbent parliament member is retired, DJP prohibits his or her family members or relatives (within the third-degree kinship) from running for an election in the same electoral district, so-called hereditary succession as its bylaw.[2]

As a result of the general election held in December 2012, it was found that out of all the 146 hereditary candidates,[3] 111 ones won the election while only 35 lost. The winning rate was 76%, out of which 23.1% was hereditary candidates for the very former parliament members. Out of the 89 hereditary candidates from LDP, 86 were elected, which

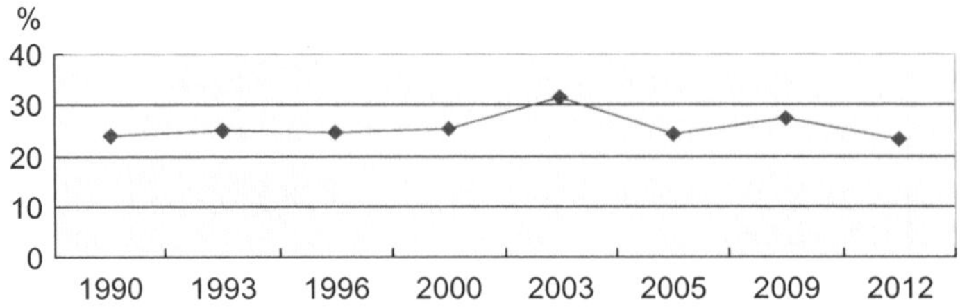

Figure 1. The Ratio of Hereditary Diet Seats after 1990.

accounted for 78.4% out of all the hereditary parliament-elects. Especially, LDP showed 96.6% in the winning rate of hereditary candidates and this was extremely high compared to other countries.

However, as a result of the 45th general election held in October 2009, the number of LDP member in the House of Representatives of Japan decreased from 296 to 119. Out of all the LDP members of the Japanese Parliament, the number of hereditary ones was 50, accounting for 42%, which showed an increase by 10%. LDP also sets the regulation on hereditary candidates in its manifesto for elections that when a retired parliament member's spouse or relatives up to the third-degree kinship run for an election in the same electoral district, LDP will not approve or recommend any of them starting from the following general election.[4] With regards to the selection of candidates, even the Regeneration Committee of LDP insisted that they should keep the election pledges related to the restriction on hereditary candidates after analyzing the causes of defeat in the election.

However, LDP set "Restriction on Hereditary Candidates" as its manifesto on the premise that they should have the support of LDP members through the primary election in Japanese prefectures before approving its candidates. Although the primary election is accepted, there still remains an issue on what standards it should be conducted. If the party considers the possibility of candidates being elected more, hereditary candidates will be more advantageous since their levels of public awareness are relatively high even for a general election.[5] As a result of the general election held in 2012, the so-called Hereditary Diet Seats were 111. The percentage of hereditary candidates being elected was 23.1% out of all members of the Diet Japan. LDP's Hereditary Diet Seats were

87, followed by nine members from the Japan Restoration Party. On the contrary, DPJ did not accept new hereditary candidates any more, resulting in six candidates being selected out of all the 22 former hereditary parliament members.[6]

There were only two Diet Seats that failed the general election among LDP's hereditary candidates. Tomu Tanikawa from Osaka District 19, whose father served as a secretary-general to the House of Councillors in succession, could not keep the silence of the wave of Japan Restoration Party, which made a good fight in Kansai electoral districts. Although Koichi Kato gained over 70,000 votes, he lost a parliamentary seat by 1,465 votes against Juichi Abe who insists on a shift in generation.

In Osaka electoral district 16, Kazuo Kitagawa, the former general secretary of New Komei Party (hereafter NKP), who once lost the 2009 general election, could win the following election by being recommended by LDP and Japan Restoration Party.

What makes the hereditary succession of Diet seat an issue in elections is the very system that prevents competent political candidates from entering the political society. It is said that three kinds of backgrounds are needed to win elections in Japan, and they are ground (地盤), signboard (看板), and bag (鞄): ground means local support groups; signboard means a level of public awareness; and bag means political funds respectively. Especially in single-member constituency system that depends more on an individual's popularity, hereditary candidates who have succeeded their parents' reputation, election camp organizations, and political funds are superior to others', and they certainly are able to lead an election in an extremely advantageous position.

Hereditary Politicians and Theory of Justice: Reflected on Rawls's Theory of Justice

In his theory of justice, John Rawls believes that justice should be defined as a source of ethical values and judgments sustaining the democracy. He defined justice as "effectiveness displayed by various social institutions as the first priority" that are "common adventurous designs demanding mutual profits". Besides, he said that profits created through social activities should be distributed, but social rules leading to the most reasonable and appropriate ways of distribution on each occasion will be the very principles of social justice. As a result, Rawls summarized people's thoughts of justice as two principles.

One is for everyone to have equal rights for fundamental freedom. In other words, when all people are given equal freedom, they have equal rights even for the most extensive freedom. The other one is that social and economic inequality must be resolved by meeting the following two conditions. One is to maximize profits for those in the most underprivileged circumstance (Difference Principle); and the other is to be incidental to positions or jobs open to everyone under the condition of equal opportunity (Principle of Equal Opportunity).

In other words, in order to realize true equality on the premise that backgrounds or talents can be social and accidental natures to everyone, it is necessary to understand the principles above. In order to realize justice through institutions, his theory puts emphasis on moral that the effect of such accidental nature should be minimized as much as possible.

In both the 2009 and 2012 general elections, DPJ emphasized justice through its manifesto. The justice emphasized by DPJ was concretized through equal opportunity, responsibility for the future, and the prohibition of free ride. One of the greatest policies was the very prohibition of hereditary parliament members. While leading election campaigns by applying the rule to all the candidates as a just institution, DPJ attempted to prevent a premium phenomenon from appearing to hereditary politicians. Particularly, prior to qualifying politicians' capabilities, the party tried to limit their competition based on the standard of fairness called as the prohibition of hereditary succession. DPJ even tried to realize justice in other political fields like welfare policies.

In July 2009, through Party Reform Execution Headquarters, LDP sent President Abe a reply regarding the party reform, parliament reform, and the reform of electoral institutions. Out of them, the party sets the conditions for approved candidates that they must go through a strict and open qualification process without a special treatment for hereditary candidates from electoral districts where incumbent parliament members are retired. The reply also stated that candidates succeeding to incumbent parliament members are forbidden to succeed to political funds as well as fund management organizations. However, due to strong opposition from hereditary parliament members in LDP and their sponsor organizations, the introduction of restrictions on hereditary candidates was put off till the general election after the following one.[7]

In contrast, DPJ puts emphasis on reformation by establishing an article regulating hereditary candidates in its manifesto for the 45th general election and this caused DPJ's headwind, the opposition DPJ defeated the ruling coalition between LDP and NKP.

DPJ tried to realize justice through the reform of social security institutions or employment policies from all the articles in its manifesto in 2009. Both its social security system and employment policies were public pledges to stabilize the lives of people. However, the problem was how to secure finances.

In the articles related to the social security system between LDP's and DPJ's manifestos in 2009, there were differences in some degree. But various social welfare dispensation policies were noticeable. DPJ increased the government's financial burden by proposing welfare policies dispending all the people from children to senior citizens. On the other hand, LDP tried to be differentiated from DPJ by expressing "Medium Welfare and Medium Burden". But, it still requires a financial burden in some degree. In both the parties' employment policies in their manifestos set in the same year, neither of them emphasized "the sustainability of employment". Particularly, DPJ suggested a policy in a form of directly paying those who were looking for jobs as much as 100,000 yen a month for employment training. Afterwards, since it was regarded as an idea of populism to receive more votes through various welfare dispensation institutions, the party ended up being criticized not to accomplish those absurd policies.[8]

LDP's manifesto published in 2012 emphasized strategies of growth. LDP appealed to the creation of wealth through growth, while criticizing DPJ aimed for distribution policies through minimized growth.[9]

Since the formation of a party in 1955, LDP has often handed over the reign of power, particularly to Hosokawa's administration and Hata's in the 1990s and to DPJ in 2009, but it has mostly remained as the ruling party for a long time. Then, how did LDP regain the position as the first party from the election held under the single-member constituency system in December 2012?

According to the survey conducted in March 2012, it was found that most voters thought the Japanese politics had not improved at all through the past turnover of political power.[10] Interestingly, the survey conducted in August 2012, about four months before the general election showed the unfavorable results to the ruling party. Likewise, the survey conducted by the mass media before August 2009 also showed the disadvantageous results to the ruling party, LDP at that time.

In other words, there were more voters who did not support Noda administration (64%) than ones who did (27%). For about the reason that they did not support Noda administration, the majority of respondents (40%) said that they did not support DPJ's policies, followed by factors related to Prime Minister Noda (16% for his leadership and 15% for distrust in him) and distrust in DPJ (15%).[11] For about the question which party they would cast votes for, 21% of them chose LDP while only 11% chose DPJ, and such a support trend sustained till December, the election month.

Why Forbidding only the Hereditary Succession in the Field of Politics?

Even parliament members selected through the elections were divided into cons and pros for the prohibition of hereditary succession in the same electoral district. As a matter of fact, hereditary succession has been handed down to the overall society in Japan. It is quite easy to find such cases in other various fields including manufacture, construction, publishing, school management, pharmaceutical products, and medical service, etc. This is why this study attempted to discover Japanese people's positive attitudes toward hereditary parliament members from their cultural points of view. On the contrary, their negative attitudes toward hereditary parliament members were based on the disqualification of hereditary succession of political power by the Japanese Constitution and other laws, and even ethical issues.[12]

What makes Japanese politicians' hereditary succession an issue is that predecessors are able to hand down political funds to their successors without tax. It differs from individuals or enterprises' cases where they have to pay inheritance tax depending on the size of wealth. Cases that political fund management organizations are handed down to successors are largely divided into two kinds. One is to succeed to political fund management organizations as they are, and the other one is to make a new political fund management organization and transfer all the funds. In either case, successors are non-taxable objects.[13] In other words, hereditary politicians are able to succeed to political funds as an advantageous means of election. Since such a fund flow leads to the succession of non-taxable money, rather than reaching an ideal objective of seeking and inviting qualified individuals, it sets barriers for non-hereditary candidates to participate in politics.

Another reason that they try to prohibit politicians from hereditarily succeeding to electoral district is to prevent lawmakers from depending on government officers with regards to policies. Hereditary parliament members have a relatively higher rate of being reelected than non-hereditary ones. It is because politicians spend most time on affairs for their local districts when they have lots of interests in success or failure for the following election. Then, they are behind the development of their capabilities for national policies, which finally becomes a negative factor for not politicians but government officers to lead the development of policies.

On the other hand, since non-hereditary parliament members should put efforts to establish local support groups and political fund management organizations, the rights and interests of their local districts may easily sway them. In this respect, hereditary parliament members do not have to be captured by the connections of their local districts because of their higher reelection.[14] They can concentrate their capabilities on central politics, which is a step far from their own local districts since they take an advantage from the hereditary succession of electoral district. But as pointed out earlier, they still cannot get away from the weak point that politicians' tension with government officers is being weakened. Moreover, since the ruling party has many political affairs which need to be handled through the cooperation with government officers, evaluations on lawmakers are also made by government officers. And these evaluations are part of the overall public evaluation on politicians as well.

Politicians carry out political activities in every party and in the Parliament which deals with the seniority system and competition system. In such a system, hereditary parliament members take an advantageous position in being selected as a leader. Although some non-hereditary parliament members seem to appear with high competitiveness, their average age is relatively low when they are newly elected. And they will get naturally behind other dimensional competitions and power struggles against hereditary parliament members who have been reelected many times and had important posts in the party and the Parliament.[15]

In compliance with the Japanese Public Official Election Act, any election campaigns can continue from the time when candidacy is accepted and when the election schedule is officially announced to the day before the Election. For the general election in Japan, 12 days are given as the period of election campaign, and during this period, new political faces are disadvantageous in informing and introducing them to voters compared to hereditary parliament members or other parliament members who have been elected for consecutive terms. Hereditary parliament members or the parliament members who served for many years carry out the practical election campaigns through their own sponsor organizations, which makes large differences in the aspect of public awareness.[16]

In 2009, Hatoyama appealed his plan for the following government through the DPJ manifesto, and his promises were presented as five principles and five policies. Out of which one theme is to break away from the existing bureaucratic government. Also, out of the five principles, the first one describes that the ruling party should take initiatives for all the political affairs rather than shifting the responsibility to government officers. In the past, policy-making, adjustment and decision were done by the section chief of Gakseong Office and permanent deputy-minister, but the three heads of State Affairs Committee, the first lord, vice lord and administrative official, should lead the process.[17]

Then, what is the political system of LDP like? Since 1955, LDP has mostly come to power for half a century, and thanks to the constant economic growth of Japan, the party could utilize the economic outcome as its financial funds affluently, which helped most Japanese people and naturally accepted LDP as their long-time ruling party. This political system is called, "55-year System", and particularly, this political system is formed through the symbolic mechanisms with government agencies. It functions to establish wide networks through the party and sponsor associations and it leads the policy-making process with decentralized colors,

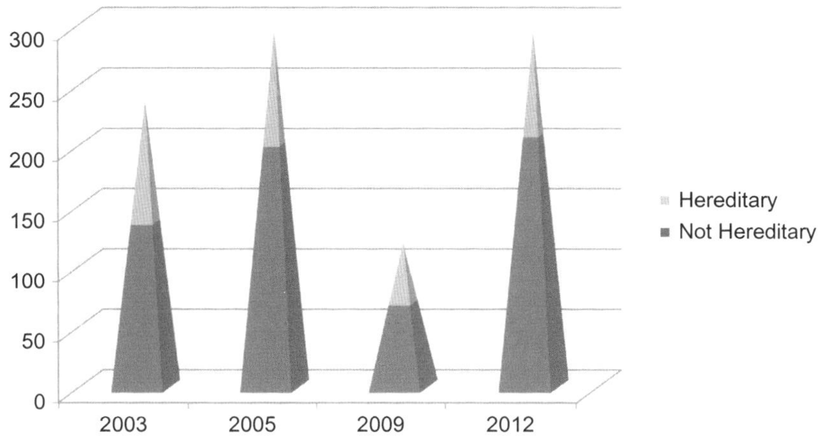

Figure 2. The Ratio of Hereditary and Non-Hereditary in LDP.

while valuing bottom-up agreements during the collection of opinions. Here, its close cooperation with the bureaucratic organizations is one of the most important characteristics this political system has.[18]

As Abe administration started in Dec. 2012, there were some changes between politicians and government officials. Instead of the three heads of State Affairs Committee, the symbol of DPJ's political initiative and post-bureaucracy, LDP valued cooperation between politicians and government officials. When DPJ came to power, the permanent deputy-general's press conference was banned since it might cause misunderstanding that government officials lead political affairs. Instead, DPJ decided its policy to let ministers who are also politicians lead press conferences. However, since LDP became the ruling party, vice-ministers' press conferences have been allowed because it is necessary to supplement ministers' press conferences.[19]

Meanwhile, what are actual circumstances of other fields far from the political one? According to some researches on the hereditary business management, when the management of a company is associated with the founder's blood relationship, or when any of the founder's family members or relatives simply succeeds to its management because he or she is a major shareholder, the company is more likely to suffer a loss. In other words, it is commonly recognized that when a hereditary executive gets involved in the management of a company, it weakens competition between competent people in the labor market, further damaging the company's value and reputation.[20]

In Korea, hereditary succession in churches became a social issue. The circumstances surrounding the hereditary succession in Korean churches are associated with the economic growth in Korea. In other words, as the economic growth in Korea had affected other social fields, Korean churches have been more influenced by the economic growth in Korea. Adversely, this constantly affected the atmosphere of large-sized churches with various cases of struggles for their interests including ministers. Facing the public criticism, Korean large-sized churches revised their regulations in order to prohibit hereditary succession of religious influences as a part of purifying themselves. In September 2012, the Korean Methodist Church, a denomination of Korean Christianity, revised its regulation in order to prohibit hereditary succession of church. Precisely speaking, the religious organization added an article to the existing regulation, "A minister or his spouse must not be constantly sent to a church where either of his parents is a minister. A minister or his spouse must not be sent to a church where either of his parents is an elder."[21]

When Korean churches suffered from financial difficulties, it was considered as a virtue instead of being criticized to hand down a father's church to his children. However, along with the economic growth in Korea, there appeared large-sized churches in the metropolitan areas, and the financial scale of churches became larger. Forbidding the hereditary succession in large-sized churches was originally to block the succession of wealth through religious authorities.

In the late 1990s, the issue of hereditary succession in large-scaled protestant churches in Korea turned into a social issue in addition to ministers' irregularities and adulteries and moreover spread out as an anti-Christianity movement. Therefore, religious leaders tried to regain public trusts from their church members by making their efforts on purifying the church while prohibiting the hereditary succession of religious power.

There are reasons why it is difficult to reflect pluralistic values on the policy-making process in a democratic way to hereditary parliament members. Securing pluralism in a democratic state is one of the processes of uniting its society, and members of the parliament should have such an attribute. However, since the parliament is composed of people who lean too much towards a particular social class, they will fail to speak for people's interests properly.

Hereditary Succession of Political Power and Nationalism

Due to the appearance of new political leaders in Japan and Korea, both countries showed the noticeable reinforcement of nationalism. Their reinforcement of nationalism will function to emphasize national interests so much that international tensions will be more intensified between Japan and China and between Japan and Korea.

Voters in both Japan and Korea value economic policies most of all even though they still have much expectations on foreign affairs and security policies. As a public pledge, the LDP tries to lessen internal tensions by establishing Territory and Sovereignty Issue Operation Headquarters (a tentative name) as a governmental agency while revising the Cabinet Department Establishment Act. The new administration established the Territory and Sovereignty Operation Planning & Coordination Office in the Cabinet Ministry of National Defense on February 5, 2013; and by letting the agency make connections with Ministry of Foreign Affairs and Northern Territory Operation Headquarters in the Cabinet, LDP allowed this agency to take a responsibility of investigating and verifying the present circumstances of Japanese territories and leading public opinions.[22]

In the meantime, Saenuri Party in Korea has proposed plans to protect the Korean territory and sovereignty by establishing the control tower which is called the National Security Center as a new foreign affairs and security policy.

For peace and stability in the East Asian region, it is important to maintain communication and international cooperation between related countries. Although new political leaders in Japan and Korea are chosen through elections, no one denies the fact that they are based on the hereditary succession of political power. What matters most, however, is whether such characteristics among them are helpful for national revival. They should realize that it is the time to show the leadership greatly enough in order to sustain peace in this region.

As one of the public pledges, the Japanese LDP is trying to reinforce the Japan-U.S. alliance and increase national interests based on its traditional security assurance theory. Besides, for the reinforcement of the function of Prime Minister as a conning tower, the party has established National Security Council (NSC) to effectively cope with all the critical situations in terms of security. Furthermore, LDP aimed to change the name of Japanese military troops from the Self-defense Forces to National Guards through the revision of constitution. Right before the general election in December 2012, all the parties that would become the ruling party, such as LDP, Party for All, Japan Restoration Party and NKP, including right wing-inclined parties, clarified their positions that they value the U.S. rather than other Asian countries, different from the views of DPJ and Communist Party, in regard to the election issue of security and diplomacy.[23]

The Japan-U.S. alliance has been reinforced through the process of changing the constitutional interpretation about exercising the right of self-defense into counterattacks when the U.S., a Japanese ally, is attacked by another country, as if Japan were invaded. According to the policy book of LDP, in order to improve its war deterrent force while coping with the U.S. new national defense strategies, the Japanese government is taking an action to reestablish guidelines. In contrast, DPJ made the practical public pledge for foreign affairs and the national defense policies while sustaining its long-time calmness and keeping its distance from LDP by emphasizing an exclusively defensive security policy. Recognizing the fact that the Japan-U.S. relation is important for their alliances, DPJ is seeking the way of reinforcing their relationship by participating in the U.S.-led Trans-Pacific Partnership (TPP) and through economic cooperation between Japan and the U.S.

Some Japanese voters support hereditary politicians because they admire political leaders as a solution to their complaints about the realistic politics. This forms their longing for old great politicians and even for the periods, and further makes them to look for politicians playing the pivotal role. Most hereditary politicians are consciously or unconsciously recognized to have pursued publicness as a server for the people, state and even the world thanks to their forefathers' good precedents, which makes them to remain in an advantageous position when receiving the support of voters. In other words, either education in politicians' families or expectation for their future political activities seems to have created such an orientation.[24]

Prime Minister Kishi, who was the present Prime Minister, Abe's grandfather on his mother side, signed the Japan-U.S. Security Treaty in 1960, and with regards to this issue, he had to face and overcome the spiral of anti-government and the anti-U.S. political situations caused by security-related struggles. Even in the process of normalizing the diplomatic relations between Korea and Japan, he was deeply engaged through his personal connections with Manchu. After Japanese diplomatic relation with Korea was normalized, he tried to keep political and economic cooperation through Japan-Korea Cooperation Committee.

Besides, in the 1950s, Prime Minister Kishi reestablished the Japan-U.S. relations in order to restore Japan by making a security treaty with the U.S. to lead an economic revival, and laid the Japanese national foundation by improving the diplomatic relations with other countries in Asia.[25] A half century after that period, Japanese people have recognized once again there were some problems related to the national security and the economic section, and it was Prime Minister Abe who made it as a main issue for the past general election.

Even if hereditary politicians and voters have the same objectives, there may be differences in some degree between them. According to the survey conducted on December 15, 2012, the day before the general election, there appeared some distances between nationalism-based candidates and Japanese voters. Such right-sided parties including LDP, Japan Restoration Party, and Your Party have established political items related to nationalism, out of which candidates were for the revision of constitution, the reinforcement of national defense capacity and the right of collective self-defense, while their supporters showed a rather neutral tendency toward those political pledges.[26]

Even in the election issues appearing through a survey conducted the week before the election, it is also associated with the fact that people pay more attention to the economy, stimulative measures, and social welfare than politics and diplomacy-related issues.[27]

In addition, NKP which participates in the conservative political group as a coalition party keeps its distance from LDP's policies related to nationalism, such as the revision of Japan Self-defense Forces Act and exercising the right of collective self-defense[28].

Prime Minister Abe explains his views of state and nationalism through his book. First of all, he points out that it is wrong to recognize Hinomaru as the symbol of militarism, and Kimigayo as the symbol of Japanese Emperor. Nevertheless, he does not assert that human beings with universal values should be fostered as a global citizen. Instead, he argues that it is natural to have local and national patriotism, and the Japanese bond with other countries can be naturally formed through the belongingness to home town and state. In this way, he appeals to people's local and national patriotism while being on the alert against a criticism that people's perceptional change of Hinomaru and Kimigayo will lead to a prejudiced nationalism.[29]

In the House of Representatives, Prime Minister Abe through the answers on the issue of marine territory with China, emphasized that Japanese diplomatic progress has come to a polite, quiet, however, when infringed on the sovereignty should be assertive stance on territorial disputes with its neighboring countries.[30]

In 2006, however, he already received a request from the economic circles that Abe administration's nationalism should not aggravate international diplomatic problems with Japanese neighboring countries, such as China and Korea, further worsening the economic relations with them. It has been still an appropriate recommendation for the present Abe administration, which makes him to take that much careful step.

Conclusions

When politicians have more experiences of being selected as a parliament member and serving more important official posts, they are more likely to be elected as the Japanese Prime Minister while it is difficult for others who do not take the position. Moreover, when they have more experiences of being elected as a parliament member, they are more likely to take important positions in the cabinet and party, naturally leading to higher possibility of serving as the Prime Minister in Japan. In the organizational culture of LDP which has been positioned as the ruling party for a long time in Japan, such an attribute is pervasive. With setting out a logical argument that the Japanese hereditary succession of political power weakens the democracy at the end, DPJ has criticized the nomination system of LDP since 2012 when it became an opposition party after the general election.

Not only when they are newly-elected as a lawmaker, but when they work for the cabinet and party, the hereditary parliament members have the superior competitiveness to those who are not hereditary politicians, and even the position of Prime Minister has become the competitive goal between hereditary parliament members. Although candidates are openly nominated in democratic ways, hereditary candidates are still in advantageous positions in Japan. Such a phenomenon does not appear only in Japan.

In addition to such criticism against the hereditary parliament members in Japan, the following question has been constantly raised that whether they are politicians with capabilities and competitiveness. The overall evaluation of their capabilities and competitiveness as a politician is made through elections and various different criteria including their popularity are applied to the evaluation. The political positions have been handed down from predecessors to successors. However, since they have been qualified through their competitiveness in parties and the parliament, they cannot be easily excluded from the political circles in Japan because of their identities as hereditary politicians. Even in non-hereditary parliament members who have served important posts as a politician have been elected for consecutive terms. If a similar phenomenon appears, how should it be explained? As a matter of fact, every party defines its retirement age as a parliament member. But it does not seem to be a measure to restrict hereditary politicians' terms.[31]

A fierce battle for hereditary parliament members in Japan started appearing when the 2009 general election was about to start. In the 2009 election, the criticism against hereditary parliament members became one of the great controversies which resulted in a chance for DPJ to hold the reigns of government. But in the 2012 election, the economic recovery was the greatest issue among voters and it further strengthened LDP hereditary parliament members again.

It was the required time for coordinating a policy that the Liberal Democratic Party had to wait for three years by change of power for re-regency.

Notes

1. http://www.dpj.or.jp/policies/manifesto2009.
2. http://www.dpj.or.jp/global/downloads/manifesto2012.pdf.
3. A hereditary politician is defined by the manifesto of DPJ and the standards of the Nihon Keizai Shimbun (17 December 2012), based on (1) who succeeded the constituency in the national or local from the parents or the relatives with the experienced legislators within third-degree kinship, and (2) who do not inherit the hereditary constituency, but one's parents are the lawmakers.
4. http://www.jimin.jp/policy/manifest/pdf/2009_yakusoku_a.pdf.
5. Takashi Uesugi (2009), p. 155.
6. JijiTsūshin, December 17, 2012; Nihon Keizai Shimbun, December 17, 2012.
7. Mainichi Shimbun, June 2, 2009.
8. Dongailbo, June 6, 2012.
9. http://jimin.ncss.nifty.com/pdf/j_file2012.pdf.
10. 53% of the voters evaluated that the transfer of power was a right thing to do, which is higher than 36% who do not think so. In addition, only 3% of the voters think that the transfer of power has led to a better political atmosphere, while 58% responded that it has remained almost the same, which indicates that most of the Japanese voters have made a harsh evaluation on DPJ. Yoshiaki Kobayashi (2012), p. 197.
11. Yomiuri Shimbun, August 13, 2012.
12. Satoshi Yoshikawa, "Senkyo to seshuseidonituite," Noriyuki Fujii, eds., (2010) pp. 303–304.
13. Uesugi, 65–75.
14. http://www.tkfd.or.jp/research/project/sub1.php?id=225.
15. Naoto Nonaka (2008), pp. 127–133.
16. Gerald L. Curtis (1971), pp. 153–178.
17. Kobayashi, 36.
18. Nonaka, 111–112, 201–202.
19. Asahi Shimbun, February 6, 2013.
20. Francisco Pérez-Gonz-lez (2006).
21. The rule of the prevention of heredity revised on September 25, 2012 is the 136th article of 3rd volume of Methodist Church of South Korea meeting regulation Chapter 2, Section 8.
22. Mainichi Shimbun, February 5, 2013.
23. Asahi Shimbun, December 15, 2012.
24. Ichikawa Taichi (1990).

25. Shinichi Kitaoka (1995).
26. Asahi Shimbun, January 28, 2013.
27. Asahi Shimbun, December 9, 2012.
28. Asahi Shimbun, January 30, 2013.
29. Shinzō Abe (2006).
30. Asahi Shimbun, February 8, 2013.
31. LDP defines its mandatory retirement system as 73 years old for members of the House of Representatives and 70 years old for members of the House of Council/ors. On the other hand, NKP has a regulation that the party shall not approve any of its members who will turn 66 during their service.

References

Atsushi Sugita (2013), *Seizitekisikou* [Political Thinking], Tokyo: Iwanamisyoten.

Francisco Pérez-Gonzlez (2006), "Inherited Control and Firm Performance?" American *Economic Review*, December 2006, Vol. 96, No. 5, pp. 1559–1588.

Gerald L.Curtis (1971), *Election Campaigning Japanese Style.* Tokyo: Kodansha, pp. 153–178.

Ichikawa Taichi (1990), *Seshudaigisi No Kenkyu* [The Research of Hereditary Diet Members]. Tokyo: Nikkei Inc., pp. 270–274.

Jiro Yamaguchi (2009), *Seikenkoutairon* [The Theory of Regime Change], Tokyo: Iwanamisyoten.

Koji Nakakita (2012), *Gendainihon No Seitou Democracy* [The Party Democracy in Contemporary Japan], Tokyo: Iwanamisyoten.

Naoto Nonaka (2008), *Jimintōseizi no owari* [The End of LDP Politics], Tokyo: ChikumaShobō.

Noriyuki Fujii, eds., (2010), *Nihon No Minsyutekikibankeisei No Tankyu* [The Pursuit of Democratic Base Formation of Japan], Kyoto: Houritsubunkasha.

Shigeru Inaida (2009), *Seshugiin* [The Hereditary Diet Members], Tokyo: Kodansha.

Shinichi Kitaoka (1995), *Jimintou* [Liberal Democratic Party of Japan], Tokyo: Yomiuri Shimbunsya, pp. 75–85.

Shinzō Abe (2006), *Utsukushiikunie* [Towards a Beautiful Nation], Tokyo: Bungeishunjū.

Takashi Uesugi (2009), *Seshugiin No Karakuri* [The Mechanism of Hereditary Diet Members], Tokyo: Bungeishunjū, pp. 65–75, 155.

Yoshiaki Kobayashi (2012), *Seikenkoutai* [Regime Change]. Tokyo: Chuokoron-Shinsha, 36, 197.

Chapter 8

Reassessing Incumbency Advantage in Korean Politics: An Evidence from Korean General Elections Since 2000

*Yeawon Kim**

Introduction

Many political scientists have argued that incumbency advantage in the U.S. congressional elections gives a substantial effect over challengers who want to defeat incumbents' seat. In particular, Mayhew (1974) observed the rapid increase in number of incumbents won by higher margins as the result of reelection seeking behavior. The argument supports a variety of different evidences and resources of incumbents to defend high-quality challengers, including perquisites of office, consequences of name recognition, higher constituency service, use of frank mail and the ability of incumbents to function as a voting cue.

The argument that incumbents are more likely to win elections than their challengers contrasts another argument that incumbency has not increased or negative effects on the electorate. Jacobson (1987) notes that members of Congress are no more likely to win safely because of new electoral institutional players such as PACs, polling and national party campaign committees. Plus, he indicates declining partisanship of candidates in a few

*Yeawon Kim, Ph.D Candidate in the Department of Political Science at Kyung Hee University, South Korea.

electoral cycles. Outside the U.S. congressional elections, many election scholars estimate that incumbency advantage engaged in rent-seeking activities frustrates electoral outcomes.

Although South Korea has single member district system since the 13th general election in 1988, the literature reviews on the voting outcomes in general elections have pointed to the evidences of voter's party preference rather than their attachment to individual candidates. However, they suggests that candidate factors are becoming more important. Empirical evidence from the Korean National election studies show how important candidate factors are in Korean congressional election. Among the respondents, 46.2% voted for their candidates after reviewing who they are and how many years they have served. This rate doubles two candidate's party label or other political issues.

The predominant wisdom that the candidate-centered voting pattern helps incumbent's electoral success presents under the single member constituency system. Then, does incumbency advantage increase in Korean politics under single member district system? It is often assumed that the incumbency advantage is eliminated in other countries with stronger political party systems and frequent party-line voting behavior. Then, have incumbency effect vanished margins in Korean electoral coordination? According to previous evidences on incumbency effects in developing countries, does Korea have negative incumbency effect and why? I challenge the existing assumptions on incumbency advantage in Korean politics, using legislative election data from the national election commission (NEC) in Republic of Korea.

Thus, this research analyzed whether parties' status in Korea National Assembly (KNA) affects South Korean incumbents and how incumbency advantage differs by region over a decade. I define that incumbency advantage does not have a direct relationship in candidate's district level within South Korean political environment, raising questions about the increase of incumbency advantage in Korean general elections as a means for making inferences about the reelection. This research has two important contributions. Firstly, it brings effective literature on the incumbency advantage to South Korean political context, showing that voter behavior theories and empirical finding on whether it is applicable in Korean political context, especially strong regional differentiation. Second, measured by the influence of political parties on the reelection rates of individual incumbents, the results re-evaluate how much incumbency advantage is driven by political structures and attributable to general patterns in development of democracy.

In this chapter, it is organized into four sections. The first section introduces the research topic, question and its significance. The second section studies the development of incumbency advantage and its consensus. The third section examines incumbency effect with a focus on whether there has been an increase. It also compares between percentage of incumbents and average vote percent of incumbents over parties and regions from 2000 to 2012. Other indicators of incumbency effect, sophomore surge, retirement slump and slurge, are presented here in this section as well. The fourth section addresses the reinterpretation of incumbency advantage trends and the implication of the assessment of Korean Politics.

Literature Reviews on Incumbency Advantage and Its Trends

1. Incumbency Advantage in the U.S. Congressional Election

American scholars have paid attention to find the factors why incumbents have their electoral advantages in congressional elections since the 1970s. Accordingly, there is much of the work why incumbents have an electoral effect. Fiorina (1977a) argues that incumbents can do constituency services that their challengers cannot. Incumbents have a chance to response constituent's opinion to the bureaucracy and negotiate with their constituents, but challengers cannot provide such services. Stokes and Miller (1966) claim that most incumbents have more name recognition than their challengers. Alford and Brady (1993) and Abramowitz (1975) also find which factors incumbent takes advantage of reelection. They claim the importance of incumbents' reputation, voters' evaluation toward incumbents' constituency service rather than name recognition.

However, scholars find another factor in partisanship. In American political context, especially, partisan voting has substantially declined while split-ticking voting has increased since 1970s (Converse 1976; Burnham 1965; Cummings 1966). Krostroski (1973) firstly showed that the importance of incumbency advantage increased while partisan influence had declined in post-war era. Fiorina (1977b) also demonstrates the decline of partisanship between voters and parties. He explains that such voting behavior substantially posited the rise of incumbency advantage. Since voters less attached to both parties: the Republican and Democrats, electoral results could be explained by personal activities like incumbent advantage (Wattenberg 1991; Brady, Cogan and Fiorina 2000; Jacobson 2001).

The favorable environment to incumbent is attributed to the increasing use of the perquisites of elected office such as staff, communication with constituents and frank mail. Fiorina (1981), Jacobson (1981) and Mayhew (1974) examine a significant effect on the incumbents benefits: advertising, credit claiming and position taking on issues. McAdams and Johannes (1983) further explain policy oriented voting behavior from electorates concentrates on incumbents who already fit well with electoral coordination.

Another factor of incumbent effect can be reviewed as political changes in incumbent situation such as a partisan secular realignment and Southern Democrats' religious attachment to the conservative party, GOP (Jacobson 2003; 2007; Polsby 2004; Brewer and Stonecash 2006; Ware 2006). Stonecash, Brewer and Mariani (2008) argued that the realignment generated an increased incumbency advantage, especially higher Republican incumbent seats. For example, the Democratic incumbents have little gain in South comparing to the past, because more Republican incumbents running in Southern district are likely to appeal to conservative voters through partisan realignment. Furthermore, Cox and Katz (2002) proved incumbency advantage with the value of a House seat for Republican incumbents. Since the value is lower, they often withdraw such seats when they think of better result. In contrast, Southern Democratic incumbents have proved the most advantageous in secular regional realignment (Hayes and McKee 2010). Eventually, the Republican incumbents have their safer vote percentage than Democratic incumbents.

Can the incumbent advantage explain outside of the U.S.? Scholars in other countries have not been well documented on incumbency effects. Cain, Ferejohn and Fiorina (1987) researched that British voters choose more incumbent members of Parliament than challengers. Comparing to factors in U.S. congressional election, there was a strong party effect in their findings while the party effect had declined in the U.S. Other scholars out of the U.S. focus on whether incumbent advantage exists in emerging democracies in African or Latin America. In contrast, McDonald (2014) finds that incumbent disadvantage in African countries is associated with voter's political information, poorer economic conditions and partisan structure. According to Titiunik (2002; 2004), there is a strong negative effect on incumbency advantage on both vote share and probability of reelection, and thus, institutional instability, political contexts and partisan weaknesses in Brazil supports negative incumbency effects in developing countries.

2. Korean Literatures on Incumbency Advantage

Many scholars examine that incumbents in the Korean general elections have increased their vote percentage in recent elections. The evidence, however, indicates that there has been no large improvement in electoral security of incumbents since 2000. The majority Party in Korea at present, Saenuri Party (Hannara Party in the past) has improved its electoral security. This research provides a very different interpretation on incumbent advantage. Firstly, Kim's research (1989) shows weak incumbent advantage in Korea. For example, the party dismissed 28 of the 86 incumbent local chapter chairmen (32.6%), while nominating 125 new individuals as candidates (Kim 1989). The Republican-Democratic Party in Korea (RDP), the major opposition party, fielded 202 candidates, including 41 incumbents. There were more newcomers than incumbents among the winners: 167 of 299 Assembly members, or 55.9% of the membership.

The prevailing consensus on incumbency advantage is that incumbency advantage in South Korean political context. The factors of incumbent effect on the general elections have been depending on the electoral coordination, partisan effect, regionalism and candidate abilities. In 2002, Hwang (2002) finds the influence of political factors by analyzing the vote margin in the general election. Park and Kim (2008)'s argument points out the underestimated role of incumbency advantage on the general elections from the previous research. Using the data from 2000 to 2008 Korean general elections, they find that incumbents are more likely to be reelected in Korean General elections, but their analysis is limited on the number of incumbents. Nor is the relationship between vote share and open seat outcomes in the three general elections. Kim and Eom (2013) show that high electoral competition leads to the decrease of reelection, but the finding has difficulties in generalization since it shows the 19th National Assembly Elections only.

I compare literature reviews of the increasing incumbency advantage in the vanishing marginals in Korean General election. Even when the incumbency effect is investigated at the party level in majoritarian systems as in Lee (2008), an incumbent party's interest in a district usually coincides with that party's legislators' interests in that district as incumbent legislators usually campaign for reelection. The previous research in the certain area of the political parties contribute to the success of the reelection is being given. On the other hand, belonging to a political party is a modification from the limited lands more reelected incumbents belonging to the ruling party in the next election are likely to succeed in this study. Hence, I deny the initial premise: there is no increase in the real incumbency advantage.

Researchers have difficulties in identifying casual effects between incumbency advantage and other factors with omitted variables. For example, when they use the incumbency advantage by a dependent variable, they nearly take into account the influence of South Korea's political parties or regionalism in voters' districts. That is, they test the causal relationship between electoral competitiveness, candidates' ability or political parties and reelection without examining correlation between the vote and seat shares based on a large number of factors such as political parties' electoral strategies and candidates competitiveness at district level. Furthermore, previous studies look at the incumbency advantage in a general election or merely analyze the patterns of incumbency advantage. Thus, I would expect this research to contribute to reduce selection bias and deepen future studies on an incumbency advantage.

Measuring Incumbency Advantage

1. Methods and Data

The experiment for reassessing incumbency advantage would be ideal in Korean political environment because it is not easier to account for selection bias than American Politics. For example, there are differences between numbers of congressional seats or electoral institutional system and changes among political parties by every four years. Recently, three hundred legislative members of Korean National Assembly have secured their seats since 2012. The South Korean National Assembly is composed of 246 members directly elected by constituents and 54 proportional representatives elected in FPTP-PR parallel voting system. Some former proportional representatives may have run for constituency seats after gaining congressional careers in KNA.

Even though electoral and congress studies in the U.S. accumulated the phenomenon of incumbency advantage for a long periods, scholars are attempted to solve methodological problems between causal effects and causation. From a theoretical point of view, they interpreted the positive relationship between incumbency status and reelection. Traditionally, the reelection rate was calculated by dividing the total number of legislators who won reelection by the total number of incumbents running for reelection (Hobgerg and Peterson 1998). Another calculation is average vote percentage of incumbents who get votes. Erikson (1971) found that sixty percent of incumbents increased their vote share through empirical test for the first time.

Furthermore, there are three sophisticated approaches when scholars measure incumbent effect. Erikson (1971) firstly uses the sophomore surge approach, attempting to reduce selection bias and identify whether a candidate is incumbent or non-incumbent. Levitt and Wolfram (1997) also use the approach, examining the difference of vote share (percentage) between first and second terms of congressional candidates. The sophomore surge may focus on the ability and constituency service of incumbents because they measure the increases of vote shares from initial election to successive election (Cover 1977; Cover and Mayhew 1977; Born 1979 and Collie 1981).

Another approach is retirement slump. Cover and Mayhew (1977), Payne (1980) and Ansolabehere and Snyder (2002) use the difference of vote share between incumbents in last election and newly-chosen candidates from incumbents' party. If a Republican incumbent receive 53 percent in his last election and a new GOP candidate won by 51 vote percentage, the slump in the district is two percentage points. Thus, retirement slump defines the decline in the partisan vote in a district when an incumbent leaves in the election.

The slurge consists of averaging the surge and slump estimate. Gelman and King (1990), Levitt and Wolfram (1997) and Cox and Katz (2002) produce the slurge estimate within a regression model, showing both democratic incumbents' status and partisan holding seats within the district. To analyze how South Korea' incumbency effect in general elections, I examined five measurements of incumbency effect. In this section, I reviewed several differences between incumbency effect, parties and regions along with my explanations for them. As a result, former proportional representatives may take advantages of being able to use electoral resources or partisan support, but this study does not include proportional representatives as incumbents for constituency seats.

2. Results on Incumbency Advantage

First and foremost, the results on the rate at which incumbents were re-elected indicated a measurement of the incumbency effect in Korean general elections. Among the incumbents, 60.7% of won their seats again in the 16th general election. In the next election, however, 1.5 percentage points lower than last election as shown below in Figure 2. The graph demonstrated increases of incumbents' winning in the next two elections.

Compared to Figure 2, the average percent of incumbents' vote share showed more fluctuations in fourtimes' general elections (See Figure 3).

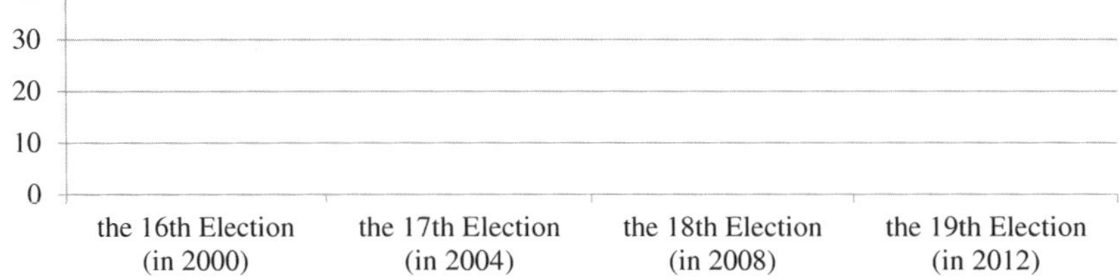

Figure 1. Percentages of Incumbents Who Pursued Reelection.

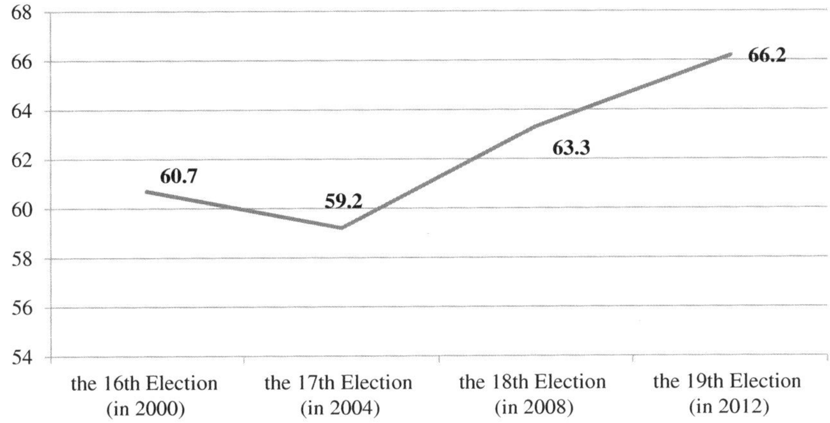

Figure 2. Percentages of the Number of Incumbents Who Won.

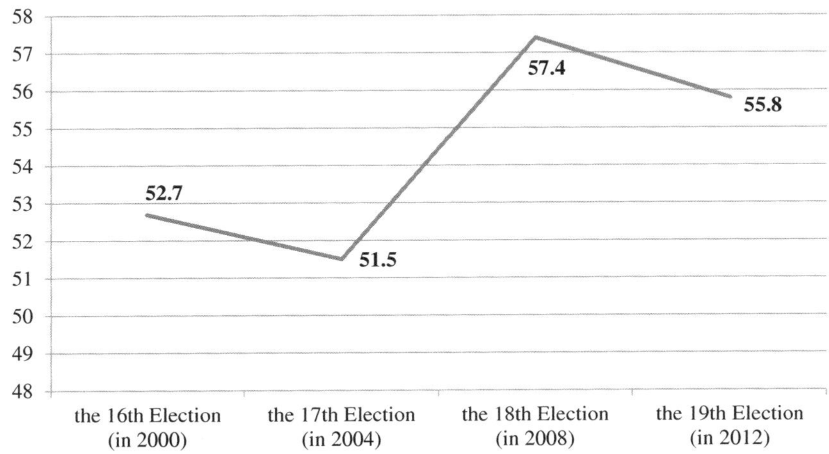

Figure 3. Average Percentages of Incumbents in the Elections.

There was a large increase between the 17th and the 18th general election. It can be seen that the Korean voters would choose the stability to solve economic problems because economic downturn became a major issue in 2008. Also, the 18th general election was caused by the coattail effect. The 18th general election periods overlapped with presidential honeymoon period.[1]

Compared to the percentage of incumbents who seek for reelection, about 23 percent of incumbents who had run for reelection were defeated against their challengers in 2000, whereas the gap between incumbents seeking the reelection and incumbent winners became lower about three to five percent in two other elections. We can find incumbents have some difficulties in the reelection in 2000. During the election periods in 2000, candidates had been pressed for disclosing their personal information. The manifesto campaign driven by civil society activists and NGOs requested voters not to choose disqualified candidates or incumbents. It dealt with a heavy blow to incumbents who had already exposed their personal information: whether they served in military camp, how much and frequently they paid taxes or whether they had criminal record. Thus, the gap ranked the highest among the other elections.

Although it declined 1.2 percent in 2004, it produced a larger increase in 2008. We can find the reason that Korean incumbents got lower percentage of votes in general elections is because of the plural partisan system. For example, one district in Seoul held a competitive election because incumbents had to defeat two qualified challengers from each party. The incumbent won the election by the least votes among reelected incumbents. The result points out the crucial problem in the incumbent percentage measurement because it can exclude incumbent who would not run and make statistics much less than the figure shows.

Other measurements such as sophomore surge, retirement slump and slurge can solve the problem. Figures 4, 5 and 6 show all of them. While

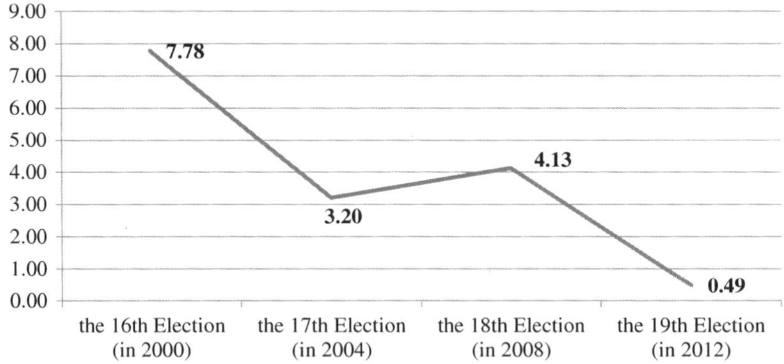

Figure 4. Sophomore Surges.

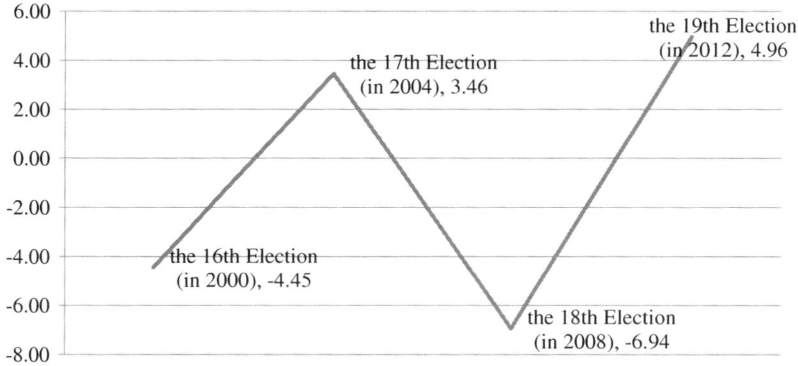

Figure 5. Retirement Slumps.

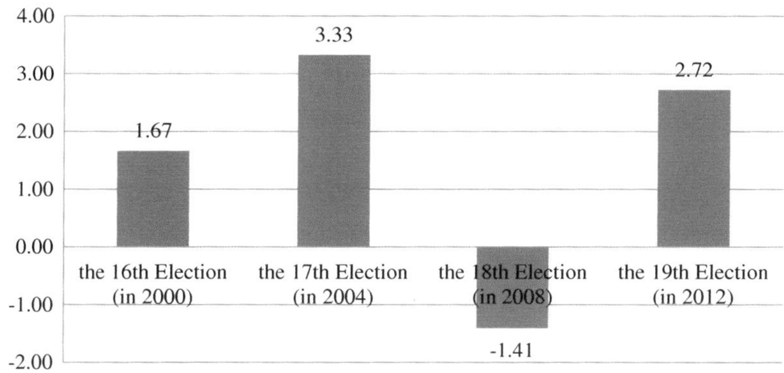

Figure 6. Slurges.

the 16th election had the highest sophomore surge in total, two elections in 2004 and 2008 had low sophomore surge rate. The reason of low sophomore surge in KNA was an impeachment trial of the President Roh Moo-Hyun by office holders produced antipathy among voters. Since then, incumbents who ran for their second term were reelected by close votes. However, average percentage of freshmen candidates did not experience retirement slump despite the open seat election. The incumbent suffered retirement slump only in the general election of 2004. The center line in Figure 6 shows the slurge. The results describe both incumbency and open seat were so competitive in the 17th general election.

Table 1 presents incumbency effect over regions in a series of Korean parliamentary elections since 2000. Overall, election outcome is

Table 1. Reelection Rate by Regions in South Korea.

	16th General Election	17th General Election	18th General Election	19th General Election	Total
Metropolitan Area (Including Seoul, Inchon and Kyunggi)	69% (49/71)	57.8% (41/71)	57.8% (48/83)	54.7% (35/64)	59.9% (173/289)
Jeolla Province	83% (15/18)	50% (11/22)	84.2% (16/19)	70% (15/20)	72.2% (57/79)
Kyungsang Province	83% (39/47)	81% (34/42)	83% (39/47)	94.4% (34/36)	84.9% (146/172)
Chungcheong Province	50% (8/16)	37.5% (6/16)	75% (15/20)	47.1% (8/17)	53.6% (67/169)
Jeju & Gangwon	45.5% (5/11)	16.7% (1/6)	70% (7/10)	57.1% (4/7)	50% (17/34)

characterized by stable regionalism during election periods. A specific region holding a majority of the incumbent seats could rule by voting in unison on legislative issues. Kyungsang province had the highest reelection rates among all regions. There was close congruent rate between Kyungsang and Jolla province, where Saenuri and Democratic party had been supportive. In contrast, Jeju and Gangwon had the lowest rate of incumbent advantage since seats in KNA consists of a legally prescribed minimum number of legislative members. The exact size and composition were decided by the population, but there were usually 17 members who were reelected on average.

The Saenuri Party, a major conservative political party in South Korea, had held a majority of seats in the Korean National Assembly. In the 2004 congressional election, however, it was defeated by the largest liberal party, Our Open Party (Yeollin Uri Party). The loss was recorded in Korean political party history for the first time. The Saenuri Party (New Frontier Party, NFP) used its former name as Hannara Party (the Grand National Party, 1997–2012). It was known as the Grand National Party before the 19th parliamentary election. Some literatures indicate that "Pro-Park coalition" differed from Saenuri party in both 2008 and 2009

Table 2. Reelection Rate by Political Parties in South Korea.

	16th Election	17th Election	18th Election	19th Election	Total
Saenuri Party	75% (63/84)	63.5% (54/85)	83.4% (56/68)	73.7% (56/76)	73.2% (229/313)
New Politics Alliance for Democracy Party	70.5% (43/61)	56.5% (35/62)	42% (37/88)	78.8% (37/47)	58.9% (152/258)
Liberty Forward Party	25% (8/32)	0% (0)	85.7% (6/7)	22.2% (2/9)	33.3% (16/48)
Others including UPP, Justice Party, and Independents	21.4% (3/14)	40% (4/10)	75% (12/16)	7.7% (1/13)	37.7% (20/53)

General Election. However, I saw candidates from "Pro-Park coalition" the same as from Saenuri party. There were two reasons on the setting. First, there were three incumbents in 2008 and one incumbent in 2012 from the coalition in the specific district around the North Kyungsang province and Daegu. Second, voters could not distinguish between the party and the coalition. They were more likely to consider the coalition a "faction" in Saenuri party.

The New Politics Alliance for Democracy (NPAD) merged from the Democratic Party and the minor New Political Vision Party in 2014. Previously, the party named Millennium Democratic Party in 2000. The party divided into two parties, Our Open party (Yeollin Uri Party) and Democratic party. Yet, they merged again in 2008. I add candidates from both parties by accounting for the temporary division in 2008. The Liberal Forward Party (LFP) was generated in 2008 by merging with the People First Party. The candidates from the party were supported from Chungcheong Province in the 16th and the 17th general election, but the party was completely defeated by the Democratic and Saenuri party in their districts.

Discussion and Conclusion

The analysis presented here various ways of looking at incumbency advantage in the general elections of Korea since 2000. Previous studies on incumbency advantage tend to depend on the percentage of incumbents who win, but my research is based on the in-depth analyses of generation through the comparison between Korean general elections. No matter for which congress they serve, incumbents face strong challengers and difficult situation. In addition, Korean politics has critical election which can be turning point of incumbency advantage. The KNA has important election in 2004. I study different changes in 2004 and 2006 elections. Focused on presidential coattail effects and economic downturn on general election, incumbency advantage can be linked with Rothenberg theory or presidential popularity research. Researchers need to re-examine the correlation between incumbent advantage and president popularity more closely. Future research should explore the larger effect of president factor in congressional elections.

This chapter estimates incumbency effects on electoral outcomes at the congressional election level in Korea, which has a mixed election system including district and proportional system. I find a small incumbency advantage on average in Korea by analyzing the vote percentage for each incumbent seat. This implies that the incumbency effect in Korea is not large. In this sense, it may be difficult to say that incumbency is an important determinant of the electoral outcome. The fluctuation of the incumbency advantage since 2000 can be attributed to partisan influence and subsequently changing voting behavior. However, the incumbent advantages between incumbent parties are much larger since incumbents from Saenuri Party relatively succeeded their next congressional term. Nonetheless, I find no ruling effect in total incumbency advantage.

The absence of a ruling pattern is more difficult to interpret. These factors may also have different weights in different institutional settings and the results may not be generalizable. Since there are factors that may cause advantages, such as resources, and other factors that may cause disadvantages, such as asymmetric voter reactions, the effects in opposite directions may be cancelled. However, I can replicate the traditional cost of ruling result in this data set using a conventional specification. It is directly linked to the incumbency of parties but not to the candidate's perquisite. If further research finds the correlation between candidate's perquisite and partisan campaign support is positive, we would expect that the study can contribute to an incumbency advantage in Korean political context. Investigating the mechanism and framework on incumbency effect in detail is an interesting question left for future research.

Notes

1. The President Lee Myung Bak was elected on December, 2007 and there was the next general election day on April, 2008.

References

Abramowitz, Alan I. (1975), "Name Familiarity, Reputation and Incumbency Effect in a Congressional Election," *The Western Political Quarterly* 28: 668–684.

Alford, J.R. and Brady, D.W. (1993), "Personal and Partisan Advantage in U.S. Congressional Elections," Dodd, L.C. and Oppenheimer, B.I., eds., *Congress Reconsidered.* Washington DC: CQ Press.

Ansolabehere, S. and J. Snyder (2002), "The Incumbency Advantage in U.S. Elections: An Analysis of State and Federal Office, 1942–2000," *Election Law Journal*, Vol. 1, No. 3: 315–338.

Born, Richard (1979), "Generational Replacement and the Growth of Incumbent Reelection Margins in the U.S. House," *American Political Science Review*, Vol. 73, No. 3: 811–817.

Brady, David W., John F. Cogan, and Morris P. Fiorina (2000), *Continuity and Change in House Elections*, Stanford, CA: Stanford University.

Brewer, Mark D. and Jeffrey M. Stonecash (2006), *Dynamics of American Political Parties*, New York: Cambridge University Press.

Burnham, Walter Dean (1965), "The Changing Shape of the American Political Universe," *American Political Science Review,* Vol. 59, No. 1: 7–28.

Cain, Bruce, John Ferejohn, and Morris Fiorina (1987), *The Personal Vote: Constituency Service and Electoral Independence*, Cambridge: Harvard University Press.

Collie, Melissa P. (1981), "Incumbency, Electoral Safety, and Turnover in the House of Representatives, 1972–1976," *American Political Science Review*, Vol. 75, No. 1: 119–131.

Converse, Philip E. (1976), *The Dynamics of Party Support*, Beverly Hills, CA: Sage.

Cover, Albert D. and David R. Mayhew (1977), "Congressional Dynamics and the Decline of Competitive Congressional Elections," in Lawrence C. Dodd and Bruce I. Oppenheimer, eds., *Congress Reconsidered*, Washington D.C: CQ Press: 62–82.

Cox, Gary W. and Jonathan N. Katz (2002), *Elbridge Gerry's Salamander: The Electoral Consequences of the Reapportionment Revolution*, Cambridge University Press.

Cummings, Milton C. (1966), *Congressmen and the Electorate*, New York: Free Press.

Erickson, Robert S. (1971), "The Advantage of Incumbency in Congressional Elections," *Polity*, Vol. 3, No. 3: 395–405.

Fiorina, Morris (1981), "Some Problems in Studying the Effects of Resource Allocation in Congressional Elections," *American Journal of Political Science*, Vol. 25, No. 3: 543–567.

Fiorina, Morris (1977b), "One Good Term Deserves Another: The Advantage of Incumbency in Congressional Elections," *American Journal of Political Science*, Vol. 21, 523–541.

Fiorina, Morris P. (1977a), *Congress: Keystone of the Washington Establishment,* 2nd edition, New Haven: Yale University Press.

Gelman, A. & King, G. (1990), "Estimating Incumbency Advantage without Bias," *American Journal of Political Science*, Vol. 34, 1142–1164.

Hayes Danny and Seth C. McKee (2010), "Sectional Change and the Variable Incumbency Advantage," paper presented at the annual meeting of the Midwest Political Science Association, Chicago, IL, April 2010.

Hwang, Ah-ran (2002), "The Incumbency Advantage in the 2010 Local Elections in Korea," *Local Administration Studies*, Vol. 25, No. 4: 3–26.

Jacobson, Gary C. (2012), *Politics of Congressional Elections*, 8th edition, New York: Pearson.

Jacobson, Gary C. (1987), "The Marginal Never Vanished: Incumbency and Competition in Elections to the U.S. House of Representatives," *American Journal of Political Science*, Vol. 31, 126–141.

Jacobson, Gary C. (2001), *The Politics of Congressional Elections*, 5th edition, New York: Longman.

Jacobson, Gary C. (2003), "Party Polarization in Presidential Support: The Electoral Connection," *Congress and the Presidency*, Vol. 30, No.1: 1–36.

Kim, Hong Nack (1989), "The 1988 Parliamentary Election in South Korea," *Asian Survey*, Vol. 29, No. 5: 480–495.

Kim, Sang Eun and Ki Hong Eom (2013), "The Effects of Electoral Competition on Vote Share and Reelection: Empirical Analyses of 19th National Assembly Elections of Korea," *Contemporary Politics*, Vol. 6, No. 2: 69–93.

Krostroski, Warren Lee (1973), "Party and Incumbency in Postwar Senate Elections: Trends, Patterns, and Models," *American Political Science Review*, 67: 1213–1234.

Levitt, S.D. & Wolfram, C.D. (1997), "Decomposing the Sources of Incumbency Advantage in the U.S. House, "*Legislative Studies Quarterly*, 22, 45–60.

Mayhew, David R. (1974), "The Electoral Connection and the Congress," in Mayhew, David R, eds., *Congress: The Electoral Connection*, New Haven, CT: Yale University Press.

McAdams, John C. and John R. Johannes (1988), "Congressmen, Perquisites, and Elections," *Journal of Politics*, Vol. 50, No. 12: 412–439.

McDaonald, Bobbie (2014), "Estimating Incumbency Advantages in African Politics: Regression Discontinuity Evidence from Zambian Parliamentary and Local Government Elections," *International Development Working Paper Series*, 14–151, April 2014.

Park, Myoung-Ho and Min-sun Kim (2008), "An Analysis of Incumbents Reelection in Korean General Elections," *Social Science Studies*, Vol. 15, No. 1: 161–175.

Payne, J.L. (1980), "The Personal Electoral Advantage of House Incumbents," *American Politics Quarterly*, 8, 375–398.

Polsby, Nelson W. (1968), "The Institutionalization of the U.S. House of Representatives," *American Political Science Review*, Vol. 62, No. 1: 144–168.

Republic of Korea National Election Commission, http://info.nec.go.kr.

Stokes, Donald E., and Warren E. Miller (1966), "Party Government and the Saliency of Congress," in Angus Campbell, Phillip E. Converse, Warren E. Miller, and Donald E. Stokes, eds., *Elections and the Political Order*, New York: John Wiley and Sons, Inc.

Stonecash, Jeffrey M., Mark D. Brewer, and Mack D. Mariani (2003), *Diverging Parties: Social Change, Realignment and Party Polarization*, Boulder, CO: Westview.

Titiunik, Rocio (2009), "Incumbency Advantage in Brazil: Evidence from Municipal Mayor Elections," *University of California-Berkeley, mimeo.*

Ware, Alan (2006), *The Democratic Party Moves North: 1877–1963*, New York: Cambridge University Press.

Wattenberg, Martin P. (1991), *The Rise of Candidate-Centered Politics: Presidential Elections of the 1980s*. Cambridge, MA: Harvard University Press.

Chapter 9

The Endurance of Political Family in the Philippines: Hereditary Election

*Yoko Yoshikawa**

Introduction

The Philippine has a history of electoral democracy for more than a century. The country is also well known for its restored democracy in 1986 which ushered in a sequence of Asian democratization after 13 years of the authoritarian regime. Subsequently the progressives, civil society and mass democracy emerged against the traditional elite politics. For them elections continue to be central political avenue for desired social changes, where dynasties and clans are the major political actors.

The political dynasties and clans continue to revive and prosper by taking advantage of the existing framework of the electoral system regardless of regime changes ranging from oligarchic democracy, authoritarian regime, or predatory regime (Kasuya and Quimpo 2010:49–53) to restored democracy. This basic trend has not been sufficiently reversed despite of the challenges attempted by the non-clan leaders and civil society, whose impact has remained limited. The significant result is that powerful political families are one of the major non-formal institutions that can influence the official decision making of the President (Brilliantes, Jr. and Amarles Illago 1994:117).

In the 1990s, scholars and journalists began to question the quality of the restored "democracy", and were motivated to revitalize interest in the

*Yoko Yoshikawa, former Professor, Faculty of Policy Studies, Nanzan University, Japan.

"Anarchy of Families" by analyzing the individual political family (McCoy 1994; Mojares 1994; Lacaba ed. 1995; Sidel 1999; Roces 2001; Parreno 2003) and the comprehensive studies on the elected officers (Gutierrez 1994; Coronel *et al.* 2004; Simbulan 2005; Rivera 2011). The puzzle may not be hard to answer. The Local Government Code of 1991 granted the local government units more authorities and responsibilities in formulating reforms and programs through decentralization and devolution from the national government which has increased local financial resources (Brilliantes, Jr. 1997:84–90). The local governments hitherto, because of their limited resources, were compelled to depend on the national government, essentially the Office of President. The Code renewed the opportunities for political families to vigorously seek local power (Rocamora 1995:xxv). This reasoning is viable after the 1990s but it does not explain the fundamental factors of persistence and prosperity of political family.

Electoral politics introduced in the American colonial era has been the main breeding ground, enabling the provincial land owning families to control the electoral constituencies by mobilizing the voters living within informal hereditary relationships since the members of the House are elected from a single member district. The local and national elections, being held every three years (every two years prior to 1972) grant them with the legitimate mandates of dominating the elective offices. With the same family name and the vast amount of political funds, the political families are capable of providing alternating human resources for the candidates who are equipped with the highest education and profession or business experience.

After 20 years of trial and error, an automated election system was introduced in 2010. Though it considerably curtailed various electoral frauds that prevailed in the past, it could not yet assure the weakening of political families as major political players in the local-national elections.

Defining the Political Dynasty

1. Deliberations Over the Anti-dynasty Provision of the Constitution

The 1987 Constitution unprecedentedly includes an anti-dynasty provision which prohibits political dynasties in the Declaration of Principles and the Basic Policies of State.[1] In the deliberation of the Constitutional

Commission of 1986, a progressive commissioner explained the rationale of the proposed provision which is "to widen the opportunities of competent, young and promising poor candidates" to work in the government, because most of present officials come from powerful clans with vast economic fortunes. Another commissioner criticized the system where "public office becomes inherited. Our government becomes monarchical in character ...." by depicting the prevailed practices in the Philippines as follows: (1) most of the public offices such as the seats in congress, the governorship, mayoralty, vice mayoralty, councillorship, and even the presidency are inherited by a local political family; (2) circulation and passing on of offices among the immediate members of kin and relatives; and (3) the candidacy of the offspring with full backing and patronage of the incumbents by every means ensuring that the younger family will be the successor but the incumbents still exercise moral and effective influence upon the son. Nine years later his father may return to the same office by election. The same commissioner even predicted the possibility that Benigno S. "Noynoy" C. Aquino III, one son of then incumbent President Cory C. Aquino, would succeed the Office of President (Bernas 1995:150). After 24 years, his prediction came true.

Opponents of the anti-dynasty provision argued that in a democratic system the voters should decide who should be elected and that the candidates should not be subject to any prior restriction. This stand of liberal democracy reflects the political realism of the Filipino elites who have benefited from retaining power. The Commission subsequently arrived at a compromise in such a way that the provision was adopted in the Constitution, provided that it did not define the circumstances under which political dynasties are prohibited and what political dynasties are, but that they "may be defined by law" by the Congress (Bernas 1995:148–149). As the Congress is the principal playground of political dynasties and clans that have entrenched themselves, any anti-dynasty law was viewed as "exhausting long in coming" or may not come (Bernas 1987:62). In the final analysis the Cory Constitution, without outright banning of dynasties, left room for the future assumption of Benigno "Noynoy" C. Aquino III to the presidency.

Yet in December 2013 in the 16th Congress, reacting to dynasty building by the incumbent President Aquino III, a consolidated Anti-Dynasty

Act of 2013 sponsored by the minority party-list representatives passed for the first time the House Committee on Suffrage and Electoral Reforms. As it is pending at the plenary session where the majority are the members of political families, the prospect for its future enactment is quite dim.

2. Defining Political Dynasty and Clan

The political family is variously referred to as political clan or dynasty, bossism with or without violence, or warlords with violence, according to the peculiarity of the family. Whatever term may be used, it is generally accepted that dynasties and clans are those families that retain political power for generations, with more than one member of family and kin holding multiple elective offices in their local and national constituencies in the past and present.[2]

The real difficulty, however, rests with definitions in terms of their legal and political implications. The Anti-Dynasty Act of 2013 (HB3587),[3] for example, defines political dynasties as follows: [it] refers to the concentration, consolidation or perpetuation of public office and political power by persons related to one another; a political dynasty exists when two or more individuals who are related within the second civil degree of consanguinity or affinity hold or run for national or local office in successive, simultaneous, overlapping terms (Section 3 (a)). The Act emphatically prohibits spouses and persons related to the incumbent within the second civil degree, whether legitimate or illegitimate, full blood or half-blood run as successor. It also prohibits more than one candidate among those candidates related to one another to run for national or local offices.

The foregoing prohibition reflects the reality of candidacy. The sphere of related family members who run for the offices is very inclusive. In the Philippines, inheriting political positions extends not only along vertical (lineal) but also along horizontal lines by intermarriages among political families in other regions to forge alliances for winning elections (Fegan:41, Gutierrez:17, Simbulan:140).[4]

Strategies for Perpetuating Powers

1. Establishing the Local-National Axis

The building of political dynasties is the effective strategy for perpetuating power in the local and national political arena (Bernas 1987:62). It is the outcomes of not only the election system but also the strong national legislative-executive power over the local government (Simbulan 2005:250). A lopsided distribution of power and resources between the central and local governments has compelled the local units to depend on the central government.

First, the strategy of dominating local offices, particularly governorships and mayoralties in the bailiwick is indispensable. Winning these offices is crucial as all Philippine elections are conducted by a simple plurality of votes, and by a single district system for the House except for the party-list members. Some appointive offices (government corporations and judges, etc.) in the local constituencies are also helpful.

Secondly, winning simultaneously more than one congressional district and the governorship in the bailiwick province is the most effective strategy for constructing the local and national flow in exchange for state and non-state resources and the delivery of local votes for national candidates. In other words, domination of the offices is retained by securing the interwoven local — national patronage system (Hutchcroft 2010:419). The system allows the candidates to take full advantage of the state institutions and resources such as government approval, public work projects, Internal Revenue Allotments (IRA), the Priority Development Assistance Fund (PDAF) formerly known as the County Development Fund (CDF), or the so-called pork barrel (budget) and other congressional initiative allocations. Therefore, for any local candidates wishing to win election, the backing of the national superiors (padrinos) is vital so that the local-national patronage flow will be politically assured in the eyes of the local voters.

Thirdly, although, the Philippine election has been characterized by "Guns, Goons, Gold" and the violent warlords with their private armed forces have become the exception rather than the rule, their presence is still real in several provinces (Acosta 2007). A recent example is the Ampatuan clan of Maguindanao province in Mindanao who committed the bloody massacre of the rival camp in 2009. The significance is that the Ampatuans has grown their violent power as a consequence of the patronization extended by the center, then incumbent President Macapagal-Arroyo in exchange for the illegally maneuvered vote deliveries in the elections.[5]

2. Circulating Among and Passing to Family Members

One of the strategic rules of the game of building dynasties is to engage in the "musical chair game" which means circulating elective or appointive offices among the family members. Once any elective office is obtained, it is to be rotated among the senior and junior family members to overcome the term limits imposed on reelection.[6] The family patriarch will allocate posts and assign who will run and what to run for.

The political family cannot afford to permit erosion by rival families as the Filipino voting behavior is highly volatile and heavily candidate-centered. More than 80 percent of voters have no specific political party to support (Yoshikawa 2011(b): 149–156). The incumbents need to capture the strategic posts to win the voters in the bailiwick including social network groups. For this, the typical strategy, as mentioned in Section 1, is to rotate the local and national offices among the same family members. The data show that 61 percent of all 228 representatives of the 12th Congress (2007–2010) have been in public office prior to their first election to Congress, and 81 percent of these previously-held public offices were local offices (Coronel *et al.*, 2004:16).

The transaction for vote delivery by the local candidates to particular national candidates happens in exchange for rewards such as state resources and access to the power center through the intervention of the national legislators. If this is smoothly accomplished among the same family members without much negotiation, the outcomes would benefit both parties and enhance the family reputation. For the most part, local voters choose candidates based on the personal assistance they extend and the completion of public work projects in their constituencies.

The term limit imposed on re-election was adopted primarily to open the democratic space for pluralistic legislative recruitment. In reality it brought about a Congress full of younger scions. The clans and dynasties went around the term limit by adapting countermeasures that accelerate the quick circulation of the position among various members of the family, particularly replacements from the younger generations. When an elder incumbent faces the term limit, any immediate family member such as spouses, siblings, children, grandchildren, and kin will be assigned to replace the vacated posts. They use the same family name, the same channels of campaign fund-raising, and patronage connections, all of which are benefits of the patrimonial heritages.

A campaign poster often carries two faces of the senior and the younger candidate indicating that the latter is the right descendant of the former in their family. For example, in 2013 Gerald Anthony (Samsam) Gullas, Jr., grandson and the descendant of a dominant political dynasties of the 1st district of Cebu, ran at age of 26 for Congress as a lone candidate, replacing his grandfather Eduardo R. Gullas, Sr.[7] His winning was perfectly assured when he claimed as follows:

> "If you vote for me, you get two people to represent you in Congress."
> "I know I am young but the most important thing is that I have my Papa Eddie (The elder Gullas)." (Ursal 2012)

He proudly admits that he is a mere substitute for "Papa Eddie". As usual, the vacating elder Eduardo ran for the mayor of Talisay, bailiwick town for the Gullases where Anthony's younger brother is a councilor, having been elected as the youngest at the age of 18. Three years later the elder Gullas Sr. will most surely return to his congressional seat (Ursal 2012). After more than 40 years of being a political family, the Gullases is now one of six established dynasties in Cebu (Cullinane 1994:179–181).[8]

Younger members of political families led to the fresh and younger representatives in Congress. Among the first four elections (1987, 1992, 1995, 1998) in the post democratized period, the 1998 election generated a Congress of "more youthful but still a family affair" in the 11th Congress (1998–2001). The new faces were 130 out of 220 full members. Its share has risen to 59% compared with 41% in the 9th (1992–1995) and 17 percent in the 10th (1995–1998) but then declined to 32 percent in the 12th (2001–2004). The congresses became far younger excluding the first 8th Congress (1987–1991). In the 11th Congress, one-fifth of 208 members excluding party list representatives were under 40 years old. Yet these "new faces" were not truly new. Most of them are the scions of political clans and dynasties (Tiglao 1998:23–24).[9] A truly new face that has emerged is Emmanuel Manny Pacquiao, the ex-world boxing champion and the incumbent representative of the lone district of Sarangani province. He has ventured into building his own family dynasty in his province where the Chiongbians has dominated for long (Aquiles 2012).[10]

Political Families as Social and Political Units

1. Bilateral Extended Kinship Translated to Political Power

The Filipino family has a bilateral extended kinship system which is similar to most Malay kinship systems. Unlike the paternal lineal kinship system in East Asian countries, bilateral family lineages extend equally both to paternal and maternal linages for generations along vertical and horizontal lines. It produces a more generational corporate group extending to second or third degree cousins. A large members of living relatives are embraced as “mga Kamag-anak”.

A Filipino ego is born embedded in the web of kinship networks where one learns belongingness, family loyalty, the reciprocal norm, and values like “utang na loob”, by building up the dyadic relations with the superior kin in apprenticeship (McCoy 1994:7). Furthermore, friends and buddies in social relations are treated as quasi-family including the Catholic ritual of standing as godfather, godmother (Kumpare and Kumare), godparents (Compadrazgo), and godchildren.

The extended bilateral kinship can be easily converted into mobilized coalitions. The candidates would mobilize the social networks linked by various cultural norms in election. The alliance is forged not only by the relatives of blood and intermarriage (consanguinity or affinity) but also by friends and people who are in the ritual or informal patron-client ties. The coalitions also provide the assets such as money, services, family name recall, political backing and connections with the big person (padrino, principalia, dakulang tao) (Simbulan 2005:171–186). The bigger the mobilizing coalitions are, the more favorable for transforming into stronger power (McCoy 1994: 9–10). Once he is elected, the power execution by the public office holder is not confined to his immediate family, but the benefits are to be shared with and extendable to the rest of kin and persons in social networks.

2. Family Solidarity and Loyalty Than Party Loyalty

A political scientist in the early 1960s noted that the Filipino family was the strongest unit of society, demanding the deepest loyalty of the belonging members (Grossholt 1964) than any mere social unit. Therefore one needs to understand the crucial role of the family and kinship in Filipino elective politics even after the country has developed and urbanized.

The Philippine Constitution protects the primacy of the family as the basic autonomous social institution and its foundation as a nation. The Constitution also strengthens family solidarity, reflecting the influence of the Catholic Church, a powerful social institution in the Philippines.[11] The voice of the Church was well represented in the Constitution.

This family solidarity extends to other realms, infiltrating into the political and economic, even to military realms. While the pattern of a family-run business is common worldwide except in a few developed countries (Suehiro 2006:9–12), in no other political arena in Asia do personal and family relationships play such a prominent role as they do among the Philippine elites who already occupy the pinnacle of political power (Pye 1985:302). Most Filipinos tend to participate in politics as a family member rather than as an independent individual. The family possesses the permanent identity and reputation as the named unit. These qualities are transferable from the senior member to the junior standard bearer through apprenticeship and identity as a member of the elite political family since childhood (Fegan 1994:50–51).

The informal power of political family undermines the development of a stable institutionalized party system in the Philippines. The present weak multiparty system does not provide clear-cut alternatives to basic public policies, manifesto and ideology. Political family finds no incentive to develop authentic party system in a long run. The ties and loyalty among kin are automatic and most enduring negating the volatile and fluid party loyalty which is activated only at election time. The alliance among political families as a corporate body is more workable than among political parties. The clientelistic politics based on the patron-client reciprocity require a lot of patronage, logistics, and services in exchange for maintaining such relationships.[12] In the Philippines, patronage is very important not only for election but also for legislative politics (Kasuya 2008:63–68). Yet most of national candidates and some of local candidates struggle to gain the approval of the official candidates from any national party largely for electoral expediency and benefits.

Unlike in a parliamentary system where party victory is absolutely important, what matters in the Philippine presidential system is the ultimate winning of an individual candidate whichever party he may be affiliated with. The priority is not the party's collective victory *per se* nor the winning of the running mates. The party of the president-elect would be the governing or administration party even if he is the minority president. Given the unstable multi-party system, the first concern of the prospective or incumbent president is how to secure control over the legislators and the local executives because neither party line voting nor party discipline is strictly imposed. Building administration coalitions by negotiation is a common strategy. This explains the massive party switching of congressmen, senators, and a sizable number of local politicians toward the party of the would-be or the incumbent president. They rampantly jump ship in order to seek administration patronages before filing their certificates of candidacy, and immediately after the elections, they lose no time in hitching themselves onto the presidential bandwagon.[13]

Many political parties are patrimonial parties founded by politicians which shine and wane after a while as the power center shifts due to the presidential bandwagon. If a popular star member of a political family decides to run for a national office like presidency or vice presidency, his new national party will be founded or old but inactive party will be reactivated in the guise of a national party.[14] Alliances and coalitions with local political families in different regions will be negotiated to organize them for the campaign and for machine-building to deliver the votes. When no powerful family dominates in a local electoral arena, constant negotiations among the non-dominant rival families will take place in every election (Florentino-Hofilena 1995). Raising campaign funds will mobilize all available kinship networks using family assets like money, the social relationships with friends and buddies, and those negotiated partners such as economic interests and religious affiliations.

With this unstable multi-party system and rampant party shift in every election, it is hard for the voters to connect the political party with the individual candidate who is supposed to be officially affiliated with it. The party-list parties are the exception. Some voters recognize political parties merely by the name of the presidential candidate and may refer to it the party as so and so's party.

Historic Origin of the Traditional Families and State Institutions

1. Colonial Origin of Traditional Political Family

Unlike historical dynasties in other Asian countries, the Philippines has never been politically centralized under one large scale dynasty before colonization. Some exclusive elite families emerged from the classes of the "principalia" and the "cacique" landed classes (caciquisim) during the 400 years under the Spanish and the American colonial eras. These economic elites (landlords and business interests) have retained the autonomy of their own economic base. While they were independent from state interference, they gained the most favorable benefits from state institutions. Tracing back to the late 19th century, the class of Illustrados and the Chinese mestizos gained tremendous wealth and political benefits as the appointed officers of the colonial local government. During the Philippine Revolution, President Emilio Aguinaldo of the first Philippine Republic in 1898 appointed members of prominent elite families to be his cabinet members and representatives of provinces of the first Malolos Congress. The American colonial government began to implant the direct electoral system of 29 provincial governors in 1906, 81 Philippine Assemblymen in 1907 and 24 Senators in 1916 as the colonial "democratic" institutions (Cullinane 2003). Since then, the traditional economic-political elite families had continued to control local and national offices and the law-making legislature throughout post-independence electoral politics (1946–1972).[15] One rent-seeking type of political oligarchy were the Lopezes of Iloilo province. Their main purpose for entering politics has consistently been to pursue and protect their family business interests by withholding the top political power from a weak Philippine state. The Lopezes fought many political and economic battles against the rivals and Presidents.[16]

2. The Aquinos-Cojuangcos Dynasties

Dynasty building by the President is the rule rather than the exception (Gutierrez 1994:57). Though the Marcos-Romualdez-Veloso dynasties of Ilocos Norte-Leyte provinces were notorious for their authoritarian dynastic rule during the martial law period, many of the past presidents necessarily developed their dynastic links with local clans seeking for support.[17]

However, among the 15 presidents since Emilio Aguinaldo in the 19th century Philippine Revolution to the incumbent President Benigno S. "Noynoy" C. Aquino, III (2010–2016), only two political families, the Aquinos-Cojuangcos and the Macapagals-Arroyos, produced two presidents in sequence of generations. The former had President Corazon C. Aquino (1986–1992) and the incumbent within 23 years in the post democracy era. The latter, then Vice-President Gloria Macapagal-Arroyo assumed the presidency (2001–2010), not by election, but by "People Power II" which ousted President Joseph E. "Erap" Estrada, forty years after her father, Diosdado Macapagal (1961–1965) became president.[18]

The fundamental factor responsible for such historic accomplishment of the Aquinos-Cojuangcos is that they are one of the traditional dynasties composed of a web of political and big business families. Being the descendant of two prominent political dynasties in Tarlac and the only son of the assassinated father, Senator Benigno "Ninoy" Aquino Jr. and the beloved mother, President Corazon "Cory" Cojuangco Aquino, the election of Senator Benigno S. "Noynoy" Cojuangco Aquino III to the presidency undoubtedly owes largely to his parents and the network of families, particularly to the image of clean and popular Cory.

The history of the Aquinos-Cojuangcos traces back to the Spanish and American colonial eras for 100 years. Noynoy is the fourth generation. His paternal lineage from Senator Benigno S. "Ninoy" Aquino Jr. originated from Servillano Aquino, landed gentry, a general of the Katipunan, and a representative of Tarlac in the Malolos Congress. His son, Benigno Q. Aquino Sr. was a member of the Philippine Legislature during the American colonial era and was the speaker of the National Assembly during the Japanese occupation period. His son, Senator Benigno S. "Ninoy" Aquino Jr., then secretary-general of the opposition Liberal Party, was arrested by President Marcos' martial law government in 1972. He was assassinated in 1983 by the Marcos military men.

Cory C. Aquino, widow of the senator, reluctantly ran for presidential election in 1986 for the sake of unity against the powerful incumbent President Ferdinand Marcos as the substitute for her assassinated husband. She was immensely popular for her reputation as an honest person and a devout Catholic. She became the symbol of the oppositions in the "People Power" uprising which eventually led to the ouster of the Marcoses.

Yet Cory's appointed cabinet members and the elected members of the 8th Congress (1987–1992) revealed the mixed faces of new progressive political elites and the return of the old political-economic elite families. Many were the same oligarchs of the pre-martial law period. Though many of the Aquinos have been long in politics, more Aquinos were visible during the Cory Presidency (1986–1992) to support her administration. The Aquino dynasty have a web of political families.[19]

Noynoy's maternal Cojuangco lineage from Corazon "Cory" Cojuangco originated from a Chinese migrant and sugar haciendero, Melencio (renamed "Jose") Cojuangco, grandfather of Cory, represented Tarlac in the first Philippine Legislature during the American colonial era. Cory was the daughter of his eldest son, Jose, Sr. During Cory administration, her younger brother, former Congressman Jose "Peping" Cojuangco Jr. took care of the ruling party (Laban, later the PDP-Laban and the Liberal Democratic Party) for a political Cory. His wife Tingting was Governor of Tarlac. The Cojuangcos have a big web of political families including three Cojuangcos.[20]

The Aquinos with Jose Cojuangcos, and the former Congressman Eduardo "Danding" Cojuangco, Cory's cousin and a close Marcos crony, have been torn apart due to suffering of the former caused by the Marcos martial law government. In 1992, Danding who is a powerful politician and wealthy business tycoon, and the Chairman of the San Miguel Corporation ran for presidency from a new party he founded, the Nationalist People's Coalition (NPC), but lost. To oppose him, President Cory C. Aquino endorsed her Secretary of National Defense Fidel Ramos, the general and cousin of Marcos who led the revolt against the Marcos dictatorship, who ran from his new party, Lakas-Tao.

A generation-long family feud between Danding Cojuangco and the Aquinos came to rapprochement in 2001 for rebuilding their dynasty under the patriarchal hand of Danding since all of younger generation of the Aquinos-Cojuangcos needed their respective constituencies and elective offices without conflicting to one another.[21]

Yet in the 2010 presidential election, the two candidates of the Aquinos-Cojuangcos dynasty, Gilbert E. G.C. Teodoro and Benigno S. Noynoy C. Aquino ran for the presidency. Former Congressman and National Defense Secretary Gilbert "Gibo" Eduardo G. Cojuangco Teodoro,

Danding's favorate nephew, resigned from his uncle's NPC and stood from President Macapagal-Arroyo's ruling party, Lakas-Kamp-Christian-Muslim-Democrats. This Gibo's action infuriated the uncle who withdrew his support. Teodoro was a brilliant bar topnotcher, competent and a reform-minded professional, but he came in 4th.[22] It is not surprising that among the four substantially winnable candidates (Table 1), the two, who have earned contrasting reputations, came from the same established traditional dynasty, the Aquinos-Cojuangcos.

The foregoing proves that backed up with their immense wealth, family name, and political dominance, the traditional dynasty with their big web of political-economic families was able to provide rich human resources for local and national leaders for a long time. Thus, incumbent President Aquino III was naturally anticipated to recruit some from the Aquinos-Cojuangcos to support his administration. This was confirmed in 2013 when Paolo Benigno "Bam" Aquino IV, his cousin, entered as a ruling Senator.

3. Between the Two Dynasties: The Choice of the LP Presidential Candidate

The Liberal Party (LP) is a middle-sized party, but stands out with some measure of party discipline and ideology of liberal democracy among the major parties (Coronel *et al.* 2004:69). As its legislative seats are minor than those of short-lived ruling administration parties, the LP takes the tactical strategy of allying with the administration coalitions in election and inside the House.

The Liberal Party (LP), a split wing of the Nacionalista, was founded by Manuel A. Roxas, the first President of the Republic of the Philippines, in 1946 that ushered the post-independent politics into a identical "bi-party" system. He was the grandfather of Senator Manuel Araneta "Mar" Roxas II, who has been preparing to run for the 2010 presidency for several years as the LP standard bearer. He assumed the majority leadership in the Congress at the age of 42. Being Secretary of Trade and Industry, he was elected as Senator in 2004 by his popular image of "Mr. Palengke" (public market) political advertisement. He has invested a lot in building up the party machine, the command votes, campaign organizations and political communication including his engagement with a TV news anchor.

Table 1. The Preferred Top Ranking Presidential Candidates (June 2009–April 2010) (Unit: %).

Candidate \ Date	2009 6/9*	2009 9/9*	2009 12/5	2009 12/27	2010 1/21	2010 2/24	2010 3/19	2010 3/28	2010 4/16
Aquino	—	60	46	44	42	36	37	37	38
Villar	33	37	27	33	35	34	28	29	26
Estrada	25	18	16	15	13	15	19	17	17
Teodoro	0.8	4	5	5	4	6	6	8	9

*The total percentage amounts to more than 100% as the respondents were asked to prefer up to three candidates.

Source: Social Weather Stations, Dec. 2009–April 2010 recomposed by Yoshikawa.

On the other hand, "Noynoy" C. Aquino III has been a poor figure as congressman and senator with no outstanding track record. He was totally unprepared to run for presidency.

The death of ex-President Cory Aquinoon August 1 2009 abruptly brought a change. The recurring telecast of his mother's funeral ceremony impressed Noynoy, only son and Cory's faithful heir. He suddenly surfaced to the top ranking among the winnable candidates in the various public opinion surveys and maintained it until the last (Table 1) owing to his beloved mother's popularity and the memory of his father's tragic assassination. Mar Roxas II, however, remained in the low rank. Mar's plan to become the second President from the Roxases-Aranetas lost momentum by the end of August, two months before the deadline for filing the official candidacy.[23] The LP house was divided over the final choice between the two, Senator "Mar" A. Roxas II, the descendant of the Roxases-Aranetas of Capiz in Visaya and Senator "Noynoy" C. Aquino III of the Aquinos-Cojuangcos of Tarlac in Luzon. Both came from wealthy traditional political families since Spanish period.

The great impact of opinion surveys on electing officials in the Philippines has been well acknowledged since 1992 election. The public opinion "polls" is part of standard vocabulary for anyone when choosing whom to support. National candidates therefore are extremely sensitive to the influence of survey findings which holds sway over the electoral outcomes (Miranda 2006:24).

The bottom line came down to who would be a winnable vote-getter between the two to defeat ex-president Estrada. After assessing winnability and the power of the machines, the command votes, the market votes generated by image and popularity from the findings of opinion surveys (Teehankee 2010), "Mar" Roxas II gave way to Noynoy. In inside talks with Noynoy and a few party leaders, and the two families, he offered to Noynoy C. Aquino III the LP presidential candidacy. Mar resigned himself to be Noynoy's running mate, a post unacceptable for a big shot (Hofilena and Go 2011: Chapter 13–76). Mar lost the vice presidency to Jejomar "Jojo" Binay, former Makati mayor and a long time ally of Cory C. Aquino, who has emerged as another dynasty-builder.

The Noy-Mar tandem was perceived as an alliance of scions of wealthy and influential dynasties by the civil society. The Akbayan, a moderate progressive party-list party, denounced Aquino's victory in 2010 as "KKK driven" and the 2013 victory as dynasty building.[24] The action of the incumbent President has aroused public concern over how far he would wield power to pursue dynasty-building during his presidency.

Statistical Analysis of Political Family

1. The Statistical Surveys on Political Family

The various studies reported the number and the share of the dominant political families in the local and national political arena. The figures vary depending on the scope of definition, electoral offices selected, the number of years, and the constitutional political system they dealt with. Therefore the reported figures should not be considered as the absolute number of political families.

These studies are roughly classified into two types: one is studies of political families dominating in the respective provinces in a long time range. Another is focusing either on the congressional legislators such as congressmen and senators, or local executives like governors in a relatively short time frame.

Simbulan's comprehensive study on political families in the post-independent years prior to the martial law came up with the list of a total of 167 families in 57 provinces from 294 representatives for 17 years between 1946 and 1963. He called them the "Modern Principalia" of the post-independence Philippines (Simbulan 2005). Applying a broad and inclusive concept, political families are defined as those whose members hold any multiple elected and appointed offices at the national and local levels at any time in the same period. The average numbers of political families per province vary from one to several. For comparison, it should be born in mind that the 1935 Constitution fixed the maximum number of congressional seats to 110 but it never reached that number.[25]

Another small survey on the representatives done by Yoshikawa (unpublished) as of 1970 identified 53 political families, whose family members simultaneously held more than one national offices (president, vice president, senator) and gubernatorial offices (below governorship was disregarded). Of 53 families, 18 held congressional and gubernatorial offices of the same province. Seven families held senatorial and congressional offices by a pair of family members.[26] One of dominant local dynasties was the Duranos-Calderons of Cebu who dominated Danao City and most of congressional districts in Cebu City. Even the Magsaysays-Diazes, the family of pro-mass President Ramon Magsaysay (1953–1957) dominated the province of Zambales.[27]

In the post democratized period (1987–2013) under the 1987 Constitution, the number of congressional seats were set at a maximum of 250 starting from 200 including 20 percent of seats allocated to party-list representatives. The number of provinces grew from 72 in 1988 to 80 in 2010.

Gutierrez surveyed the 199 representatives of the 9th Congress (1992–1995) by applying an extremely inclusive concept of political family. He classifies any representative who has any member of family and kin who holds or has held in the past elective and appointed offices since the prewar colonial era. He even includes those candidates who had aspired for elective offices. The survey focused on the relationships between political power and the wealth of these families. Their family backgrounds provide us with a picture of how elite families maximize power by interacting political power with economic wealth through a vertical and horizontal web of interlocking family inheritance involving business and professional connections.

One hundred forty-five or (73%) of the 199 congressmen are members of political families. Thirty (15%) come from the third or fourth generations who are descendants of national politicians since the prewar colonial era (the traditional families). Sixty-four (32%) are children of politicians who represented their province in the postwar era and their descendants continue to represent the same provinces (the old families).[28] Only one-fourth (25%) of the 199 are recruited from the best educated middle class (bureaucrats, professionals and entrepreneurs) or non-clan members who entered politics during the Martial Law regime and after (Gutierrez 1994:3–5; 18–31; Appendix A).

In *The Rule Makers*, Coronel *et al.* (2004) provides us with interesting statistical data on the members of four Congresses of the House and the Senate (1987–2004 excluding 1995–1998) who are hereditary generations. From Table 2, it is worth noting that the number of political clans are increasing from 122 in the 8th to 139 in the 12th as the House elective offices has increased in number. It is also confirmed that more than sixty percentage of the representatives are offsprings of political families. Though the share of the clan members in four Congresses are 62% by average,[29] the share increases to 66% in 2001 if the party-list representatives are excluded. Among the four generations, the second generation is the biggest group in share (46% by average) throughout four Congresses. The 3rd and 4th generations are gradually increasing in number and in share, by which the Congress is becoming younger.

The number of hereditary political clans in Table 2 are confined to the House. The local political clans that dominate only local offices like governors and mayors are not included.

2. Who Replaced Patrimonial Inheritance

The practice of circulating elective offices among the members of family as the patrimonial inheritance of this particular political family is also confirmed in the post democratized period. In Table 3, 81 representatives were surveyed who finished three consecutive terms (nine years) at the end of the 10th Congress (1995–1998). For the next 11th Congress, nearly half of them, 36 (44%), were replaced by their immediate kin; children (22%); spouses (12%); siblings (4%); nephews (5%); and father (1%). (Coronel *et al.* 2004:19 Tables 1.11 and 1.12). The share of replacement by all categories of political families was 70 percent vs 30 percent, the share of non-clan members.

Table 2. Hereditary Generations in the House (1992–2004).

Congress		8th (1987–1992)	9th (1992–1995)	11th (1998–2001)	12th (2001–2004)
Total no. of Reps		198	200	220	228
Total Clans		122	128	136	139
Share of Clans		62%	64%	62%	61%
Excluding Party-List Reps		62%	64%	65%	66%
Generation Break	1st	31 (26%)	32 (25%)	34 (25%)	37 (27%)
	2nd	66 (54%)	59 (46%)	59 (43%)	59 (42%)
	3rd	22 (18%)	34 (27%)	31 (23%)	32 (23%)
	4th	3 (2%)	3 (2%)	12 (9%)	11 (8%)

Source: Coronel *et al.* (2004: 48, Table 2.1, 60, Table 2.4). Data for the 10th Congress (1995–1998) is not available. The first generation with no families and kin in elective offices, by definition, are non-clan members, therefore they are not included in the figures.

Table 3. Replacements for Three-Termers in the Congress (the 11th and the 12th).

Congress	No. in 11th		No. in 12th	
Who replaced	No.	%	No.	%
Children	18	22	6	13
Spouses	10	12	6	13
Siblings	3	4	1	2
Nephews	4	5	0	0
Fathers	1	1	0	0
Total replaced by kin	36	44	13	28
Total Replaced by Other Political Families	21 (or 23)*	26	11	24
Total Replaced by Non-members of Clan	25	30	22	48
Total No. of Three-termers Replaced	81	100	46	100

Source: Coronel *et al.* (2004: 109, Table 2.10).
*Tiglao (1998).

At the end of the 11th Congress (1998–2001), 46 finished three consecutive terms. Of 46, the replacement by all categories of political family for the 12th Congress (2001–2004) was 24 (52%). However, out of 24, only 13 (28%) were replaced by immediate kin, and the rest, 11 (24%) were replaced by other political families, which indicate high competitiveness among the political families. Noteworthy is that those replaced by non-clan members reached nearly one half in number (22) and in share (48%). The performance seems impressive since the replacement ratio between the clan members and the non-clan members reached nearly 50–50.

The foregoing data of the 12th Congress is impressive. It needs to bear in mind that the impressive result seems more because of the peculiar nature of the 11th Congress when the massive replacement of the first three term timers (81) occurred. In 12th, while number of three term timers was reduced to only one half, the representatives from the all clan families and those replaced by their immediate kin have drastically declined in share, but they remained slightly more than those replaced by the non-clan members. In the 13th Congress (2004–2007), among 212 district representatives excluding party list members, 74 first termers (new faces) were the immediate kin of former representatives up to the 11th (Co *et al.* 2005:11–13 Table 3; the Philippine Panorama, August 22, 2004). It is premature to say that this diminishing trend of replacements by the clan members and immediate kin will continue due to the limited data available.

Co *et al.* (2004) identifies a total of 224 "politically prominent" families in 79 provinces, the biggest number among all of the studies. "Politically prominent" families are liberally included because of the nature of data drawn from the GMA News Research for the 2004 election.[30]

3. Winning Congressional-Gubernatorial Scheme

The latest study for the post democratized period was conducted by Rivera who examined the co-relations between the existence of the dominant political family and the extent of the Human Development Index in respective provinces based on the eight elections from 1987 to 2010. The study is a contribution to comprehend the national-local scheme as crucial strategies employed by political families.

Rivera defined the political families precisely by applying three yardsticks: (1) Those families and kin (e.g. up to third degree of consanguinity) whose at least two members won congressional and/or gubernatorial seats respectively; (2) an individual who has been elected at least three times as a representative and/or a governor in the same period; (3) and those elected who have family members who had ever served as president, vice-president, senator, representative or governor in the postwar years, 1946–2010 (Rivera 2011:68). The last yardstick permits us to gauge the continuity of political family from a longer-range perspective.

The result confirmed the resilience of political family even in the post democratized period. The study found a total of 178 dominant political families in 77 provinces (excluding depopulated provinces) for 23 years. Of 178 families, 100 (56%) are the old families and 78 (44%) are the new.[31] The old families since the postwar periods, some from colonial period, continue to overwhelm the new in number and in share. Seventy-two (94%) provinces have 2.3 political families per province on the average and 14 (18%) provinces have four to seven families.

Rivera is right to argue that defining political family by concentrating on those who win simultaneously congressional and gubernatorial offices enables us to identify the most powerful political family (Rivera 2011:61). 59 (33%) families in 46 provinces (60%) hold and held both the gubernatorial and congressional offices of the same province at various time between 1987 and 2010 (Rivera 2011:68 Table 12). For instance, in 2010, 34 (44%) provinces elected simultaneously the governor and at least one district representative from the same political family (Rivera 2011:69, Table 13). These 34 families are all included in the 59 political families previously mentioned except for province of Masbate. In 2013, however, nine of 34 families surprisingly lost either of two strategic posts.[32] As shown in Table 4, the dominant political families seem to be reduced in number to 25 in 2013 from 34 in 2010 though eight more families, mostly lone district provinces won both gubernatorial and congressional offices. A single dominant political family has ruled governorship in six provinces for 18 years between 1992 and 2010. Furthermore, a single political family has dominated 19 congressional offices for 23 years of the democratized period (Rivera 2011: 66–67 Table 10 and Table 11).[33]

With electronic voting introduced nationwide in the 2010 election, a transmitting, counting, and consolidating system was relatively successful in eliminating frauds. However, whether or not the effect of the electronic modernization facilitates any changes in election results, such as the winning of hereditary clan members and the voting behavior, remains to be seen.

Table 4. Political Families with Gubernatorial and Congressional Offices in 2010 and 2013 Elections by Province.

Province	Family 2010	Family 2013	Province	Family 2010	Family 2013	Added Provs. 2013*	Added Family 2013
1. Ilocos Norte	Marcos	Marcos	18. Antique	Javier	Javier	1. Apayao (lone)	Bulut
2. Ilocos Sur	Singson	Singson (R2)	19. Negros Occidentl	Mara & Ntilde, On	Mara & Ntilde On	2. Nueva Viscaya (lone)	Padilla
3. La Union	Ortega	Ortega	20. Siquijor	Fua	Pernes (R)/Villa (G)	3. Marinduque (lone)	Reyes
4. Isabela	Dy	Dy	21. Cebu	Garcia	Garcia (R)/Davide (G)	4. Palawan	Alvarez
5. Quirino	Cua	Cua	22. Biliran	Espina	Espina	5. Bukindonon	Zubiri
6. Bataan	Garcia	Garcia	23. S. Leyte	Mercado	Mercado	6. Magindanao	Manguda-datu
7. Tarlac	Yap	Yap	24. Leyte	Petilla	Petilla (G)	7. Tawi-tawi (lone)	Sahali
8. Aurora	Angara-Castillo	Angara (R)	25. N. Samar	Daza	Ong (R) (G)	8. Western Samar	Tan
9. Bulacan	Sy-Alvarado	Sy-Alvarado	26. Zamboanga del Sur	Cerilles	Cerilles	33 provinces/families	
10. Nueva Ecija	Umali	Umali	27. Camiguin	Romualdo	Romualdo		
11. Cavite	Remulla	Remulla (R2)	28. Lanao del Norte	Dimapolo	Dimapolo (G) (R2)		

12. Quezon	Suarez	Suarez	29. Davao del Sur	Cagas	Cagas (R)
13. Oriental Mindoro	Umali	Umali	30. Davao del Norte	Del Rosario	Del Rosario
14. Camarines Sur	Villafuerte	Villafuerte (G)	31. Sultan Kudarat	Manguda-datu	Manguda-datu (G) (A)
15. Masbate	Seachon-Lanete	Lanete	32. Agusan del Norte	Amante	Amante
16. Guimaras	Nava	Nava (R)	33. Agusan del Sur	Plaza	Plaza
17. Iloilo	Defensor	Defensor	34. Surigao del Norte	Matugas	Matugas
			34 Provinces/Families		25 Provinces/Families

Source: Rivera 2011: 69, Table 13. The 2013 election data were added by this writer.

(R): those won the district representatives but lost governorships

(G): those won governorships but lost district representatives

(A): the Assemblyman of the ARMM

*including provinces with small populations.

4. Increasing the Emerged Governors (1998–2007)

Gladstone focused on the governors of local clans in the four elections between 1998 and 2007 which allow us to assess the effect of the Local Government Code of 1991.

Among Gladstone's three categories of the traditional, new and emerged clans,[34] noteworthy fact is that the emerged clans are growing in local and national politics after democratization. Despite being fresh entries as non-clan members when they were first elected, the non-clan governors eventually transform themselves to become local or national clans after experiencing successive reelections. The trend of former non-clan families rising up as emerging clans may be called "clanization" process.[35] Table 5 shows the trend that the winning governors of clans are gradually increasing in number and in share in the four elections from 50 (64%) in 1998 to 63 (80%) in 2004, followed by a slight decline (55, 76%) in 2007 (Gladstone 2007, Table 1 and Table 2) while the non-clan governors declined in number and in share from 28 (36%) to 16 (21%) and 17 (23%) in the same period. Without incremental growth, non-clan governors remain one fourth of the total governors except in the 1998 election.

Those emerged politicians who entered politics after People Power democratization transformed themselves into the emerged local clans in ten years. The clan distribution by the three types in winning governorships in 2007 confirms that the share and the winning rate of the emerged (39% and 53%) is higher than the new (15% and 52%) and the traditional (22% and 41%) in the governorship (Gladstone 2007, Table 3). The new

Table 5. Number and Share of Clans and Non-clans in the Elected Governors (1998–2007).

Governor \ Year of Election	1998	2001	2004	2007*
Clan Member	50 (64%)	61 (79%)	63 (80%)	55 (76%)
Non-Clan Member	28 (36%)	16 (21%)	16 (20%)	17 (23%)
Total Number	78	77	79	72*

*All gubernatorial posts are 81 as of 2007. The data is incomplete as only 72 provinces were surveyed. 55 (76%) could be considerably underestimated.

Source: Gladstone 2007.

and the emerged clans, particularly the latter, filled the political vacuum vacated by the traditional clans. Intense political battles for winning the governorship among the three types of clans may explain why the share and the winning rate of non-clan governors remains low (23% and 22%).

Concluding Summary

The statistics on political families reported in the foregoing seven studies are summarized in Table 6. The figures vary depending on the political

Table 6. Summary of Numbers of Political Families in the Seven Studies.

Surveyed by	Political Family	Years Covered	Repres. Covered*	Provinces Covered**	Offices Covered
Simbulan	167	17 1946–1963	98~105	45~57	local, national, elected and appointed
Yoshikawa	53	1 as of 1970	108	67	multiple hold repres., governors, senators, president & v-president
Gutierrez	145	1 as of 1992	199 (200)		district representatives and candidates aspired for House
Coronel *et al.*	122~139	17 1987~2004	196~214 (214)	72~79	district representatives in the Congress
Co *et al.*	224	1 as of 2004	209 (214)	79	elected and appointed in the national and local offices
Rivera	178	23 1987–2010	198~222 (222)	77*** (72–81)	District representative, governor, senator, president, vice president
Rivera	59	23 1987–2010	222	46~77 (72–81)	hold or held both repres. and governor at various times
Gladstone	50–63	9 1998–2007	—	77~79 (78–81)	governor won in four elections

*Excluding party-list representatives whose elections are based on political party and group from national constituency.

**Including Regions: the National Capital Region (NCR), the Autonomous Region of Muslim Mindanao (ARMIM) and the Cordillera Autonomous Regions (CAR).

***The official number of provinces is 81. The numbers in brackets indicate the official number of district representative seats.

regime and period, the number of offices, and years that they were surveyed.[36]

1. When we compared the latest data of Rivera's 178 with Simbulan's 167 of the post independent years, the absolute number of political families in the post democratized period has increased by 1.06 times. However, considering the longer years that the former surveyed, more than doubled House seats in number and the number of provinces which increased by 1.4 times, it is fair to say that the political families in the post democratized period approached approximately the same extent in number or relative decline in relations to the increased number of national and local elective offices. Coronel *et al.* survey for the same 17 years came up with 139 families, a decrease by –0.8 times. Gutierrez's 145 and 224 of Co *et al.* are inadequate for comparison due to their very inclusive categories of political family.
2. The relative decline in number, however, does not imply the waning of the power of political families in the post democratized period. The intensity of their influence could be reinforced by the rapid turn of the family members. The overall political families up to the 4th hereditary generations including the traditional, the old, the new, and the emerging remain the majority in the Congress in share (around 61%–64%) than those from the non-clan families.
3. Because of the term-limit provided in the 1987 Constitution contributed to younger but more hereditary Congress. The 3rd and the 4th generations from the traditional and the old political families constitute nearly one third of the representatives who owe to their family inheritance of national and local offices. The 2nd generation constitute the largest group (more than 40%) in the Congress because of "clanization" that some of the first generation representatives and governors from the non-clans who filled the political vacuum left by the traditional or old families, in a same manner venture into their own clan buildings after successive reelections.
4. Approximately 41–44% of provinces are dominated by a dominant political family (a total of 59) who hold or held the two strategic offices: gubernatorial and district representative offices in their bailiwick provinces to reinforce the local-national relations.

5. As the consequence of the Local Government Code of 1991 which was effective in 1992, the provincial clan governors gradually increased in number and in share (76%–80%) versus the non-clan governors. The emerging clan won the governorship more in share and in the rate of winning than the new and the traditional clans.

The foregoing statistical analysis of the prevailed political families illustrates limited informal channels of recruitment for national and local leaders in the Philippines. However, the studies in number do not automatically allow us to relate with the qualitative analysis of the elected officials regardless of their origin of birth. Further scrutiny is necessary to find out whether or not a candidate won the competitive electoral races primarily on his/her own competence, quality of leadership and his commitment to essential public policies, or by the power of family inheritance, vast wealth or the patronage connection. A good example was the late former Mayor and Secretary of Interior Jesse Robredo of Naga City, Camarines Sur who came from a powerful political family.[37] His twice reelection for three consecutive terms (1988–2010 excluding one term) was undoubtedly achieved for his remarkable performances in the city governance.[38]

The resilience of the electoral inheritance by political families in the Philippines is inherently rooted in the social values and the election system of heavily candidate centered, in which the political elites and the voters at large are embedded, and of which political and economic elites can take advantage. Even if any constitutional banning or an Anti-Dynasty Law were ultimately enacted, its execution and effective enforcement in the foreseeable future may be illusive by the loopholes. Meanwhile, comprehensive electoral reforms and improvement in electoral governance are vital to constrain the further endurance of political family and to facilitate the change in voting behavior (Yoshikawa (a) (b) 2010).[39]

Notes

1. Article 2, Section 26. "State shall guarantee equal access to opportunities for public services, and prohibit political dynasties as may be defined by law."
2. Coronel and *et al.* (2004:47) take the minimalist definition. A representative who has at least one relative (up to second cousin) who had been elected to

public offices such as district representative, governor and vice governor, city and municipality mayor, vice mayor and councillors. People tend to look to their district representatives more as their local politicians.

3. Formal title is The Act of Prohibiting Establishment of Political Dynasties (HB3587 of 2013) pending at the plenary session as of August 2014.
4. The political families of Japan whose incumbents are referred as "Seshu Giin" (hereditary legislative member) of the national Diet are characterized more by the lineal ascendant than the Philippines. One leading newspaper defines as: (1) The members of the national Diet within the third degree of consanguinity including ex-and former members; (2) The Diet members who succeeded the electoral constituency, partial or entire; (3) Even without succeeded constituency, the Diet member whose either of parents was once the member of the Diet (Nihon Keizai Shinbun July 5 2013).
5. The Ampatuans and their private armies led by Governor Andal Ampatuan Sr. killed 57 journalists and political rivals in connection with a rival filing his candidacy in the 2010 election.
6. The Constitutional limit on consecutive terms is: One term, six years for the president; two terms, 12 years for vice president and senators; three terms, nine years for House of Representatives and all of the local officers. But one is allowed to run for the same office again after one full term has passed.
7. Though his father Paulino Gullas was politician in prewar era, Eduardo R. Gullas Sr., lawyer and owner of University of Visaya was first handpicked by President Marcos as "a fresh face" in late 1960s, to oppose the dominant dynasty, the Duranos. His son, Jose was congressman from 2001–2004.
8. Cullinane listed the other five as the Garcias, the Osmenas, the Duranos, the Kintanars and the Martinezes, but did not include the Cuencos, who also have been a traditional political family of Cebu. In 2013, the Garcias lost their governorship to a "new" face, Hilario Davide III, son of former Chief Justice of the Supreme Court, Hilario Davide Jr. whom President Cory C. Aquino appointed.
9. Included among the scions with their age and generation as of 1998 (11th Congress) are: Manuel Mar Roxas II (41; 3rd gen.), Benigno Noynoy Aquino III (38; 4th gen.), Maria Imelda Marcos (42; 3rd gen.), Alfred Cojuangco (36; 4th gen.), Carlos O. Cojuangco (35; 4th gen), Eduardo Cojuangco (3rd gen.), Ranjit Shahani (36; 3rd gen. nephew of ex-President Fidel Ramos), Juan Ponce "Jack" Enrile, Jr. (40; 3rd gen. son of Senator Enrile), Robert Arce Barbers (29; 2nd gen. son of Senator Robert Barbers), Allen Peter Cayetano (27; 2nd gen. son of Senator Renato Cayetano), Neptali Gonzales II (35; 2nd gen. son of former Senator Neptali Gonzales), Rodolfo Albano III (31; 3rd gen.

son of ex-Congressman Rodolfo Albano). In the 12th Congress (2001–2004) and the 13th (2004–2007), more new scions joined: Gilbert Cojuangco Teodoro (the 4th gen. nephew of) and Mark Cojuangco, the 4th gen. son of Eduardo Cojuangco), Felix William Fuentebella (4th gen.), Maria Milagros Magsaysay (3rd gen. of President Magsaysay), Conrado M. Estrella III (3rd gen.), Lorenzo R. Tanada III, (3rd gen. of Senator Tanada), Joseph H. Durano (3rd gen. of Ramon Durano), Joseph Emilio Aguinaldo Abaya (2nd gen. son of Abayas of the Aguinaldos), Rossano Rufino B. Biazon (2nd gen. son of Senator Biazon), Franscis Joseph G. Escudero (4th gen.), Jose Miguel Zubiri (2nd gen.), Raul T. Gonzalez, Jr. (2nd gen.), (Coronel *et al.* p. 19 added by Yoshikawa).

10. In 2013, Pacquiao's wife was elected as vice governor of Sarangani. His youngest brother ran for representative of South Cotabato. Pacquiao's People Champ Movement (PCM) was allied with Jejomar Binay's coalitions, the United Nationalist Alliance (UNA), candidate for Vice President, who defeated Manuel "Mar" Roxas II, running mate of Incumbent President "Noynoy" Aquino III.
11. The Philippine Civil Code (Article 216 and 219) and the 1987 Constitution Article II Section 12 and Article XV, Section 11. The Constitutional Commissioners who were pro-Catholic Church proposed the provision to be included in the Constitution.
12. The relationship requires continuous reciprocal behavior conducted by both parties between the resourceful political patrons (ang malakas, padrino, patron, backer) and the clients in exchange for unequal benefits such as providing resources in need, act of patronage, pay-off, and benefits, if the ephemeral party loyalty or party coalition is to be maintained.
13. For the presidential bandwagon framework, see Kasuya 2008:31–42. Most of the existing major national political parties except for the Liberal Party and the oldest Nacionalista were founded during the Martial Law period and the post democratized era for the leaders' own presidential candidacy before the elections. The Kilusang Bagong Lipunan (KBL) of the Marcos-Romualdezes, the Laban and the PDP-Laban of the Aquinos — Cojuangcos, now led by Jejomar Binay, the Liberal Democratic Party (LDP) now led by Senator Edgardo J. Angara, the National People Coalitions of Danding Cojuangco, the Lakas-NUCD of Fidel Ramos, the Puwersang Masang Pilipino of the Estradas, and the KAMPI of the Macapagals-Arroyos. The Nacionalista Party was revitalized by the Laurels, and later by Senator Manuel Villar for his candidacy in 2010. About 200 political parties (national, regional and local) are accredited with the Commission on Election. Most are local parties founded by local politicians.

14. The seminal studies done by Carl Lande (1965) and Mary Hollensteiner (1964) found that the semblance of competitive bi-party system (the Nacionalista and the Liberal Party) was in fact inherently power struggle between two or three influential families and factions allied in the vehicles of competing two national parties.
15. Some of the prominent "politica de familia" are the Lopezes of Iloilo, the Cuencos of Cebu, the Osmenas of Cebu, the Velosos of Leyte, the Cojuangcos of Tarlac, the Ortegas of La Union and the Laurels of Batangas, among others. Most of these old political families have maintained locally linked dynastic power for three or four generations.
16. The Chinese-Filipino business interests and wealthy sugar planter. The Lopezes intermarried with the Montelibanos, another big sugar planter and political family. The Lopezes were against President Diosdado Macapagal and President Marcos as his vice president before and during the martial law. The power of the Lopezes was wiped out by President Marcos but their economic power came back owing to the restored democracy. The economic battle was renewed over the control of the Manila Electric Company owned by the Lopezes against President Macapagal-Arroyo (2001–2009) and First Gentleman Mike Arroyo. The Lopezes' battle against the Arroyos in Iloilo dates back to the prewar time (McCoy 1994:429–536: Rushford 2009).
17. Exception may be President Fidel Ramos, military general by profession. Though he is the 2nd generation of political family, no children entered politics except for his sister, Senator Shahani and her son, Ranjit Shahani. He endorsed a young reform-minded congressman for governorship of Pangasinan, his bailiwick province as opposed to his nephew (Florentino-Hofilena 1995).
18. The power of the Macapagals was vastly weakened during the martial law regime. President Gloria Macapagals-Arroyos, resorted to dynasty-rebuilding during her administration primarily for inhibiting impeachment against her for alleged electoral fraud and corruption. Her two sons (the eldest led a dubious party-list group) and a brother in-law all became congressmen as protecting agencies of President Arroyo. In 2010, at the end of her presidency, President herself ran for the post of representative in her bailiwick Pampanga and won to avoid arrest.
19. Ninoy's brother, Agapito "Butz" Aquino and his sister, Teresa "Tessie" Aquino-Oreta became senators. Other political families related are: the Oretas (Malabon), the Guanzons (Bacolod City).
20. From Melencio' four sons, there are three Cojuangcos (Jose, Antonio, Eduardo). Other political families related are the Sumulongs (Rizal), the

Tanjuatcos (Tanay), the Yabuts, the Onsiakos (Nueva Ecija), the Reyeses (Marinduqe), the Jaworskis and actor "Ramon Rivera" (Jose Bautista).

21. Of two nephews of Danding, Noynoy Aquino held the 2nd district of Tarlac and Gilbert E. 'G.C.' Teodoro, a son of Danding's sister who was once an Assemblywoman, held the 1st district. Noynoy's uncle Jesli Aquino Lapus held the 3rd district. Danding's two sons Carlos and Marcos, went out to the 5th district of Pangasinan and Negros Occidental respectively to avoid conflicts where Danding has his business and the vast agribusiness landholdings (Gutierrez 1994:56; Coronel *et al.*: 54–55 96–97).
22. The disadvantages of "Gibo" Cojuangco Tedoro were his aversion to play nonsense media events, a relatively unknown family name, the official candidate of the ruling party endorsed by very unpopular incumbent President Arroyo and the limited campaign funding. He wanted to change the prevailing electoral culture and the system of populism (Hofilena and Go, see Chapter 4:2011).
23. His mother came from the Aranetas-Lopezes of Iloilo, wealthiest sugar landowners, industrial business and political families. His father was Senator Gerardo M.Sr. Roxas, President of the LP and his brother, Congressman Gerardo Jr. died in 1993.
24. KKK is abbreviation of Kaibigan, Kaklase, Kabarilan (friends, classmates and shooting buddies) which implies the Kamag-Anak Inc. (family kindred company). The Akbayan criticized President Aquino's dynasty-building in 2013 when he drafted Paolo Benigno "Bam" Aquino IV, his cousin, to join the administration senatorial race (Salvaverria 2012).
25. The actual seats of the House reached only 108 in 1970 from 97 in 1946. The number of provinces has increased to 67 in 1970 from 45 in 1946. The elections were held every two years.
26. The pair of father and son, husband and wife, siblings, in-laws, uncles and nephews, cousins, and cousins in-law simultaneously held multiple offices.
27. The Duranos are Ramon Sr. (1st district, Cebu), his wife (mayor of Danao City), nephew (3rd district), another nephew (4th district), son-in-law (5th district) and another son-in-law (7th district). The Magsaysays were a senator, two representatives and the governor of Zambales in 1970.
28. 45 have 60 siblings who hold or held or aspired for any offices ranging from the councilors to senators. 64 have 70 parents and 30 have grandparents who hold or held 33 offices. 23 have spouses hold or held or aspired for 25 offices. 21 have the children who are politicians who hold or held 24 offices. 55 have close blood-relatives who hold and held 98 offices. 32 have in-laws who hold

and held 45 offices (Gutierrez 1994 see the lists of Appendix Table A1-Table 7: 315–327).

29. This percentage will be a little higher if the party-list representatives were excluded in the total congressional seats as the party-list seats shifted from appointive to elective offices in 1998.
30. The list shows some defects. It omits some political families e.g. the Magsaysays while it includes the less qualified, e.g. the Cunetas of Pasay City.
31. Rivera categorized political families into the old and the new. The old are those whose political power base are traced to the postwar electoral politics, and some to the colonial era. The new are those who emerged after the restoration of democratic election in 1987 (Rivera 2011:68). Rivera's new family is practically the same with the emerged clans of Gladstone 2007.
32. For example, the Angaras of Aurora, the Remullas of Cavite, the Garcias of Cebu, the Villafuertes of Camarines Sur, the Petillas of Leyte, the Dazas of Northern Samar, and the Cagases of Davao del Sur and others.
33. For example, the Ortegas-Orosas ruled the province of La Union in Northern Luzon with no turnover. Twenty provinces experienced only single turnovers.
34. The new are those who gained prominence during the martial law regime (1972–1986) and still continues to be influential. The emerged are those who entered politics after the post democratized period since 1986 which corresponds to Rivera's new political families.
35. The word "clanization" here is created by this writer.
36. For example, the maximum number of House district seats under the 1935 Constitution was 120 but the actual number never reached beyond 110. The number has grown from 98 in 1946 to 108 in 1969. Under the 1987 Constitution, they grew from 196 in 1987 to 222 in 2010.
37. Jesse Robredo was the 2nd generation and a member of the influential Villafuertes of Camarines Sur. He was elected as the mayor at age 29 with the backing of his uncle and patron, Governor Luis Villafuerte., but he parted away with Luis after he assumed the mayoralty.
38. His reforms ranged from police personnel, bureaucracy, fiscal and economic policies, to the urban poor policy, the transparency policy, and the NGO and the civil society participation. When he faced with the term limits in 1998, he did not rotate his office to his family member but endorsed Sulpicio Roco Jr., son of Senator Raul Roco, another political family of Naga City.
39. Abolish the simultaneous conduct of local and national elections in one day to inhibit national and local interwoven relationship and to alleviate the heavy burdens on the voters' preference of the candidates from President to

local councilors (the total of 18,000 public offices in 2010 to be voted out). Empower the Commission on Election (Comelec) by granting more authority and the manpower vs. politicians for upgrading electoral governance and strict law enforcement. Curtail extremely lengthy campaign period and expense for image selling political advertisement. Strict law enforcement against the overspending campaign fund and rampart vote-buying. Reform the voting behavior candidate-centered toward performance-centered (Norris 2004:233; Yoshikawa (b) 2010:159) by requiring articulated manifesto and policy commitment. Remove various restrictions of the present party list system to be proportional representation system.

References

Acosta, Roy (2007), "Comelec, PNP Set Stage for Hope Honest, Orderly Peaceful Elections," *Graphic* (May 14), p. 14.

Aquiles, Zonio (2012), "Is Pacquiao Building a Dynasty?" *Philippine Daily Inquirer* (October 3). http://newsinfo.inquirer.net/281760/is-pacquiao-building-a-dynasty (Accessed on September 30, 2013).

Bernas, Joaquin G.S.J. (1988), *The Constitution of the Republic of the Philippines: A Commentary* (Vol. II), Manila: Rex Book Shop.

Bernas, Joaquin G.S.J. (1995), *The Intent of the 1986 Constitutional Writers*, Manila: Rex Book Shop.

Brilliantes, Alex B. Jr. (1997), "Local Governments in a Democratizing Polity: Trends and Prospects," in Felipe B. Miranda ed., *Democratization: Philippine Perspectives*, Diliman: University of the Philippine Press, pp. 83–113.

Brilliantes, Alex B. Jr. and Beienvenida, M. Amarles-Illago (1994), *1898–1992: The Philippine Presidency*. Quezon City: University of the Philippines.

Cantilero, M.J.O and Reyan L. Arinto (2012), "Congresssmen, Senator, Local Official Add to Senate Wanna-bets," *Business World on line* (October 4). http://www.bworldonline.com/content.php?section=nation&title (Accessed on September 30, 2013).

Co, Edna E.A., Jorge V. Tigno, Maria Elissa, Jaime Lao and Margarita A. Sayo (2005), *Philippine Democracy Assessment: Free and Fair Election and the Democratic Role of Political Parties*, Quezon City: Friedrich-Ebert-Stiftung and National College of Public Administration and Governance, University of the Philippines.

Coronel, Sheila S., Yvonne T. Chua, Luz Rimban and Booma B. Cruz (2004), *The Rulemakers: How the Wealthy and Well-born Dominate Congress*, Quezon City: Philippine Center for Investigative Journalism.

Cullinane, Michael (1994), "Patron as Clients: Warlord Politics and the Duranos of Danao," in McCoy ed., *An Anarchy of Families: State and Family in the Philippines*, Quezon City: Ateneo de Manila University Press, pp. 163–242.

Fegan, Brian (1994), "Entrepreneurs in Voters and Violence: Three Generations of a Peasant Political Family," in McCoy, ed., *An Anarchy of Families: State and Family in the Philippines*, Quezon City: Ateneo de Manila University Press, pp. 33–108.

Gladstone, Cuarteros (2007), "Political Clan Increases Monopoly of Local Power," Institute of Peoples Democracy. www.IPD.Org.Ph (Accessed on September 30, 2013).

Gutierrez, Eric (1994), *The Ties that Bind: A Guide to Family, Business and Other Interests in the Ninth House of Representative*, Quezon City: Philippine Center for Investigative Journalism and Institute for Popular Democracy.

Hofilena, F. Chay (1995), "Pangasinan: The President Tribal Grounds," in Lacaba, Jose F. ed., *Boss: 5 Case Studies of Local Politics in the Philippines*, Quezon City: Philippine Center for Investigative Journalism and Institute for Popular Democracy.

Hofilena, Chay F. and Miriam Grace A. Go (2011), *Ambition Destiny Victory: Stories from a Presidential Election*, Mandaluyong: Cacho Publishing House.

Hollensteiner, Mary R. (1964), *The Dynamics of Power in a Philippine Municipality*, Quezon City: Community Development Research Council, University of the Philippines.

Hutchcroft, Paul D. (2010), "Dreams of Redemption: The Localist Strategies of Political Reform in the Philippines," in Kasuya Yuko and Nathan Gilbert Quimpo, eds., *The Political Changes in the Philippines*, Pasig City: Anvil Publishing, Inc.

Kasuya, Yuko (2008), *Presidential Bandwagon: Parties and Party Systems in the Philippines*, Tokyo: Keio University Press.

Kasuya, Yuko and Nathan Gilbert Quimpo, eds. (2010), *The Political Changes in the Philippines*, Pasig City: Anvil Publishing, Inc.

Lacaba, Jose F. ed. (1995), *Boss: 5 Case Studies of Local Politics in the Philippines*, Quezon City: Philippine Center for Investigative Journalism and Institute for Popular Democracy.

McCoy, Alfred W. ed. (1994), *An Anarchy of Families: State and Family in the Philippines*, Quezon City: Ateneo de Manila University Press.

McCoy, Alfred W. ed. (1994), "Rent Seeking Families and the Philippine State: A History of the Lopez Family," in McCoy, ed., *An Anarchy of Families: State and Family in the Philippines*, Quezon City: Ateneo de Manila University Press, pp. 429–536.

Miranda, Felipe B. (2006), "Public Opinion and Democratic Governance," in Noel M. Morada and Teresa S.E. Tadem, eds., *Philippine Politics and Governance: An Introduction*, Diliman: The Department of Political Sciences, University of the Philippines, pp. 13–27.

Mojares, Resil B. (1994), "The Dream Goes On and On: Three Generations of the Osmenas, 1906–1990," in McCoy, ed., *An Anarchy of Families: State and Family in the Philippines*, Quezon City: Ateneo de Manila University Press, pp. 311–346.

Nihon Keizai Shinbun (2013), "Sesyu Koho," July 5.

Norris, Pippa (2004), *Electoral Engineering: Voting Rules and Political Behavior*, Cambridge: Cambridge University Press.

Parreno, Earl G. (2003), *Boss Danding*, Quezon City: The First Quarter Storm Foundation, Inc.

Pye, Lucian W. (1985), *Asian Power and Politics: The Cultural Dimensions of Authority*, Cambridge and London: The Belknap Press of Harvard University Press.

Rivera, Temario C. (2011), "In Search of Credible Elections and Parties: The Philippine Paradox," in Felipe Miranda, Malaya Ronas and Ronald Holmes eds., *Chasing the Wind: Assessing Philippine Democracy*, Manila: United Nations Development Programs, pp. 46–89.

Rocamora, Joel (1995), "Introduction: Class, Bosses, Goons and Guns," in Lacaba, Jose F. ed., *Boss: 5 Case Studies of Local Politics in the Philippines*, Quezon City: Philippine Center for Investigative Journalism and Institute for Popular Democracy, pp. vii–xxxi.

Roces, Mina (2001), *Kinship Politics in Postwar Philippines: The Lopez Family, 1946–2000*, Quezon City: Ateneo de Manila University Press.

Salvaverria, Lelia B. and Michael Lim Ubac (2012), "Another Aquino, Another Dynasty — Militants," *Philippine Daily Inquirer* (July 3). http://.newsinfo.inquirer.net/222235/another-aquino-another (Accessed on September 30, 2013).

Sidel, John T. (1999), *Bossism, Capital, Coercion, and Crime: Bossism in the Philippines*, Stanford: Stanford University Press.

Simbulan, Dante, C. (2005), *The Modern Principalia: The Historical Evolution of the Philippine Ruling Oligarchy*, Quezon City: The University of the Philippines Press.

Suehiro, Akira (2006), *Famiri-Bijinesu Ron: Kohatsu Kogyo Kokka no Ninaite [Studies of Family Business: The Agencies of the Late Industrialized Countries]*, Nagoya: Nagoya University Press.

Teehankee, Julio C. (2010), "Image, Issue and Machinaries: Presidential Campaigns in post-1986 Philippines," in Kasuya Yuko and Nathan Gilbert

Quimpo, eds., *The Political Changes in the Philippines*, Pasig City: Anvil Publishing, Inc., pp. 114–161.

The Philippine Panorama (2004), "House of Representatives 13th Congress of the Philippines 2004–2007," *Sunday Magazines of Manila Bulletin* (August 22).

Tiglao, Rigoberto (1998), "The Young Ones: Congress Is More Youthful — But Still a Family Affairs," *Far Eastern Economic Review* (August 27), pp. 23–24.

Ursal, Charisse (2012), "Clan Seek as Power Transfer from Grandpa to Grandchild," *Philippine Daily Inquirer Visaya*. (June 27). http://newsinfo.inquierer.net/219439/clan-seeks-power-transfer-from-grandpa-to-grandchild (Accessed on September 30, 2013).

Yoshikawa, Yoko (2010a), "Filipin-jin no Minsyusyugi-kan to Senkyo-kan" [Filipino Perception of Democracy and Election], in Yoshikawa Yoko ed., *Minsyuka-katei no Senkyo [Elections in Democratization Process]*, Otsu City: Koro-sha, pp. 111–139.

Yoshikawa, Yoko (2010b), "Filipin no Minsyusei: Seito Shijinashi Tohyosha to Kohosha Senko Tohyo" [Philippine Democracy: The Nonpartisan Voters and Candidate-centered Voting Behavior], in Yoshikawa Yoko, ed., *Minsyuka-katei no Senkyo [Elections in Democratization Process]*, Otsu City: Koro-sha, pp. 141–172.

East Asian Cultural Identity, History, and Norms

Chapter 10

The Construction of Cultural Identity in East Asia and Confucianism

*Bao Xiaqin**

The construction of "East Asian Community" requires making progress in politics, economy, culture and many other aspects simultaneously. In other words, it is made up of the following three indispensable parts: building cooperation institution and system in politics, promoting liberalization in economy, encouraging mutual identity and reliance in culture. However, the status quo indicates that although economic integration has yielded good results and mechanisms like "10 + 3" and East Asia Summit have been set up politically, cultural identity and political reliance are still confronted with great challenges.

The topic of this chapter is the construction of cultural identity in East Asia from social and cultural perspectives, and identity and reliance are the most crucial thing among all. The chapter presents some my studies from three aspects on the topic of "The Construction of cultural identity in East Asia and Confucianism".

What Happened to Confucianism and Japan's Choice

Japan's development strategy in modern times was to learn from the west, as it implemented the strategy of "Departing Asia for Europe/America",

---

* Bao Xiaqin, Associate Professor, School of International Relations and Public Affairs, Fudan University, China.

which in essence was "Desinicization" and "Deconfusization". As the famous Japanese Enlightenment thinker Fukuzawa Yoshi put it in *Leaving Asia Theory*: Confucianism does not fit in the trend of times, and it is the rooted reason for stagnation and adversary of modern China. In his view, Japan must criticize as well as get rid of the impact of Confucianism, while absorbing Western culture is the only way to avoid decline. Therefore, in modern times, there were two features about Japan's assessments on Confucianism: (1) from criticism perspective; (2) from Western perspective.

However, numerous countries and regions in East Asia such as Japan and the Four Asian Tigers enjoyed a boom in economic development in 1970s. The outcome of the high-speed economic development, as many people of insights pointed out, was due to the cultural background of "New Confucianism" which has been inherited for thousands of years. Such cultural background includes common spirits like education emphasizing, commitment, social harmony, tolerance and open-mindedness. Michio Morishima, a Japanese scholar, put forward the concept of "New Confucianism" in his book *On the Road to Success: The Spirit of Japan and Technology of West (1980s)*, and stated that harmonious interpersonal relationship and stable society are foundations of economic success. Many other scholars also believes that the modernization of Asia should not be equalized with westernization but based on Asian culture, and an unique Asian development model is in desperate need. In this way, Confucianism, an indispensable part of Eastern culture, received attention again and was carried forward in many Asian countries and regions.

In the post cold war years, along with the globalization and regionalization, the speed of regional cooperation in East Asia was accelerated and the establishment of East Asian Community served as the common goal for East Asian countries. Can Confucianism be the cultural power to unit East Asian countries once again? Such question concerned with the construction of "East Asian Community" became a hot topic in academia of China, Japan and South Korea. All these discussions were positive and meaningful with no doubt. It helped East Asian countries in forming a collective consensus on their Asian identity as well as strengthening their mutual closeness and cohesion.

The so-called "Modern Disease" also contributes to the retrieval of attention to Confucianism apart from the rapid development and economic prosperity of East Asian countries. Such "Modern Disease" is mainly displayed in the following three aspects: firstly, the greed for capital irritates people's unstrained pursuit of material wealth, resulting in the devastation of natural environment and ecological imbalance; secondly, the expansion of individualism creates a society dominated by utilitarianism with no moralities or social rules; thirdly, the increasing amount of social products and the expansion of social structures render people immersed in material life and even transform them into social tools for material wealth. All these aspects deprive people of their original subjectivity, self-value and even the whole spiritual homeland. The emergence of the "Modern Disease" has seriously threatened social stability and world peace.

How to dispel "Modern Disease"? Growing number of people turned to Eastern culture and Confucianism for remedy. The status of Confucius was raised to an unprecedented level worldwide after the rediscovery of the value of Confucianism. The resolution passed by the U.S. House of Representatives to celebrate the 2560th birthday of Confucius is a case in point. It follows that whether the defects of material culture from the west can be compensated in eastern culture, especially Confucianism, provides opportunity for the revival of Confucianism.

In that case, how can Japan, a country which has been westernized for hundreds of years, successfully blend into the big family of East Asian Community? Does it need to make transformation in terms of both identification and cultural recognition or strive to form closeness and common sense of a destiny community with other East Asian countries? Heated discussions were also aroused in the academia of Japan and it was these discussions that reflected Japanese's sense of urgency and loss in the process of the East Asian integration, as well as some insightful Japanese people strategic considerations about Japan's future development.

Some Japanese scholars hold the belief that Japan must grasp the opportunity of the development of East Asia and share the benefits created in the economic development via creating such East Asian Community, and they even go further in considering this as the "only solution to cure Japan". The emergence of opinions alike exactly illustrates the anxiety of Japan to go back to Asia.

It follows that the rapid economic development of Asia has become a huge impetus for building East Asian Community, and the cultural community is the ultimate linkage. After all, no community can be developed without the cultural environment or the ideological foundation.

Cultivating the "East Asian Culture" Based on Confucianism

As the birthplace of Confucianism, China has an antique culture with thousand years' history. Yet one thing to emphasize is that Confucianism is not equal to Chinese traditional culture although it is the foundation for Chinese culture. As a matter of fact, Confucianism itself has experienced a developing process. Especially since the "May 4th Movement", the reform of modern and contemporary Chinese society has gone through a process which included three stages: departing Confucianism, seeking and rebuilding a new Chinese spirit.

In the early 20th century, the success of "the Revolution of 1911" to overthrow feudalism and the emergence of "the May 4th Movement" made a fundamental change to the Chinese culture. And the vigorous western culture formed a stark contrast with the outdated/hackneyed Confucianism. At that time, the incoming western culture, including the idea of Liberal Democracy, Marxism and Socialism from USSR, became the culture mainstream in China. While on the other hand, considered as an "outdated and conservative culture", Confucianism was forced to retreat center stage of the cultural movement. Most of the frontier thinkers in China during that period advocated learning from Europe, USA and Russia. In their opinion, China must abandon Confucianism and make a fresh start in terms of cultural construction. Hu Shi, one of the distinguished thinkers of that time, advocated a total "Westernization". And Lu Xun treated Confucianism as a culture of "eating people". Similarly, Chen Duxiu encouraged democracy and science while objecting to Confucianism and the old ethics. Obviously, Confucianism was faced with opposition from the representatives of various ideological groups in China at that time. Yet one thing we cannot negate is that in essence, Confucianism serves as the philosophy and moral pursuit in agricultural society as well as the ideology to rule people. On the other hand, Confucianism is not without severe defects as it emphasizes moral perfectness while despising business spirit and ignoring the spirit of democracy and freedom.

However, Chinese culture has been raised to a higher status since 1980s, with the implementation of reform and opening policy as well as the rapid economic development. Confucianism, as the essential cultural resource in the process of Chinese modernization, has become the spiritual impetus and natural bond of development. In the meantime, Confucianism was rephrased and restored new vitality with the infusion of new elements.

It can be seen that Confucianism had experienced a booming-falling-rebirth process. Such process was not a simple repetition but advancement. Every single culture has two sides, with both essence and dregs. Therefore, we must select the knowledge and wisdom which fit in the modern society from the resourceful material of Confucianism. Besides, trying to figure out the universal value accepted worldwide and adjusting the traditional culture to meet the demand of the times are the starting points of our research into Confucianism.

Furthermore, it is unquestionable that Confucianism has exerted huge impacts on other countries in East Asia. However, different countries with distinct characteristics chose to develop in various ways. To the extent of my observation, the cultural foundation of future "East Asian Community" is not Confucianism, but the Eastern Asian culture which arose from Confucianism. And such East Asian culture is known for tolerance and modernism since it emphasizes the respect for various cultures and traditional customs in different countries.

Since recent period, the East Asian culture has experienced a fundamental change. The influx of western cultures presented new reference to East Asian countries, making them reach consensus, namely, the necessity of modernization. Besides, with the reference of western culture, the East Asian countries reflected on their own local cultures. For instance, China criticized all the utterance and thoughts in Confucianism classics that were not in conformity to modern spirits.

Currently, the cultivation of "East Asian Culture" calls for strengthening the collective identity of East Asian countries. Constructivists point out that the regionalization, to a great extent, is a social process to arouse collective cultural recognition. "Recognition is a cognitive process, in which the boundary of self-other becomes more obscure and eventually transcend at the surface while self is combined into other." Common awareness not only serves as the original impetus to form regionalism, but also represents subject consciousness of East Asia. Apart from this, the existence of stakeholders in this area is the basis for collective recognition. Driven by market, the mutual dependence between countries in the region will be enhanced and gradually the interest community will be formed facilitating the formation of the public awareness of the region.

However, the cultivation and development of "East Asian Culture" are still faced with great challenges.

First of all, numerous Asian countries have found their own ways of development since modern times, as they have adopted political systems and democratic models of various kinds based on their featured national conditions, historical and cultural backgrounds. And all these choices exactly prove the unique vitality of the countries. On the other hand, it is also the enlarging differences in the ways of development, cultures, religions and values between these Asian countries, which posed potential threat to the regional integration. As it did in the case of Japan, the implementation of the "Departing Asia" policy gave rise to a self-identity dilemma for the country which soon found itself hard to play a constructive role in the East Asian international system. That is why Japan lacked the passion for taking part in regional cooperation. Subsequently, regaining the sense of "Belonging to East Asia" and acceptance to regional cooperation might be a serious problem for Japan. Worse still, historical disputes also set huge obstacles in the cooperation process. If Japan fails to treat its history of invasion responsibly, or at least in a sensible way that other East Asian countries can accept, the mutual trust as well as the eventual regional integration will remains to be an illusion.

Secondly, the lack of trust and the surge of nationalism are both great challenges for building the "East Asian Community".

How to bring these East Asian countries close to each other is one of the biggest problems in constructing "East Asian Community". Above all, the political mutual distrust should be removed. In the post cold war years, the ideology which once took precedence died away while cultural diversity became more widespread. Despite this, barriers between countries haven't been put down and national conflicts between countries turned out to be tenser than ever before. In terms of political security, how to promote the mutual understanding and reliance as well as how to avoid regional conflict for territory are both severe problems. Furthermore, the sense of identity should be established on the mutual acceptance, understanding and trust among different countries and nations. Politicians in all these countries ought to take responsibility to treasure and guard such harmonious and cooperative situation, especially after all these years of wars, hot or cold. The Japanese scholar Tajima Eiichi (田岛英一) holds the point that the dilemma is caused by the nationalism among the general public and the future development of Sino-Japan relation is determined by "Supranationalism". East Asia should enhance communication and cooperation especially that among the general public, and get rid of the meaningless nationalistic disputes as soon as possible.

Confrontations and conflicts among East Asian countries remain to be solved. One essential factor contributing to the establishment of the European Community was the integration among European countries, laying the foundation for regionally recognized behavior codes and institutions. Because of this, the term "Europe" is far beyond a single geographical concept, as it also refers to a community built on similar views and culture. By contrast, although major East Asian countries also share similarities in culture to some extent, a common value system along with other behavioral codes and institutions has not been formed. For the time being, most East Asian countries are still suffering from a status of division and national unification problems that stand out among all. The conflict between South Korea and North Korea is just the case. Hence, there is no easy way for East Asian countries to solve their historical issues in a short time like the EU, let alone a more closely-related political, economical and cultural community.

Harmony in Diversity: An Innovative Integration of East Asian Culture Community

The construction of East Asian Community is not built in a day. How to make various nations, countries and regions develop, remain attractive to each other and create a culture community with global perspective while maintaining differences? "Harmony in diversity" might work as the code to deal with various cultural relationships in the future. Foreseeably, the establishment of the East Asian Community will be a consortium of nation. All these nations have developed their own striking characteristics and continuously seek "harmony" and "similarities" via communications while respecting each other.

As Wu Yin, vice dean of Chinese Social Institute, points out, China, Japan and Korea all belong to the East Asian culture circle which is typical of the coexistence of universality and particularity. Phenomena such as "K Pop, "Jap Lover" and "China Hot" rightly certify the dialectical unity of cultural university and specialty. In her opinion, "Harmony in diversity" can be treated as the code for handling with relations in various cultural backgrounds. Chinese culture, in general, has at least three positive effects for people in 21st century: the concept that "a just cause enjoys abundant support while an unjust cause finds little" can serve as a general principle in the area of international relations; "universal love and mutual benefit" are one of the goals in dealing with complex global economic problems; and "admiring nature" is a sensible way of living in harmony with nature.

Above all, by the principle of "Harmony in diversity", East Asian countries should discover the sense of identity for common culture via communication and interaction. "K Pop", "Jap Lover" and "China Hot" are just the beginning yet they represent a rosy future trend. Such pop cultures are extremely popular among teenagers. For instance, many famous foreign pop singers and TV stars have thousands of fans in China, and so do Chinese singers and actors. Japanese cartoon culture exerts a substantial influence on the whole Asia and even make worldwide fans infatuated. Apart from those, teenagers in China, Japan and South Korea concern more for each other and an increasing attention on learning neighboring language is a case in point.

Furthermore, we are supposed to interact with different cultures and change the original thoughts, always emphasizing the differences with other countries. Due to the ideological confrontations during cold war years and bad historical memories like wars, the unintegrated East Asian culture became more segmented than ever before, not to mention reaching regional culture recognition in a broader area. In order to break such cultural segregation, we should cultivate a sense of self-identity as "East

Asians" and keep updating our perspectives. After all, the mutual identity should keep pace with reality too.

Thirdly, a reconfirmation of the traditional identity is needed. The Japanese scholar Yokoyama Hiroak (横山宏章) claims that Japanese never resist traditional Chinese culture although they might not hold a positive attitude towards China in modern times. As a matter of fact, plenty of Japanese people feel it easy to accept Chinese culture, as is indicated by the popularity of "The Three Kingdoms" and "Outlaws of the Marsh". Therefore, such reconfirmation of identity can bring East Asian people closer to each other, at least mentally.

In conclusion, the construction of "East Asian Cultural Community" will be a long-term process. China, Japan and South Korea should strengthen their own sense of nationalism and simultaneously develop regional awareness and cultural identity based on "civil awareness" simultaneously. Confucianism will prove its unique value again in the process of building such "East Asian Cultural Community". It is hopeful that by transforming and spreading, Confucianism will be an indispensable part of the "East Asian Cultural Community" in the near future, contributing to the formation of the new East Asian Culture and achieving a creative integration of East Asian Cultural Community eventually.

Chapter 11

Do ICTs Change Citizenship Norms? Technological Determinism vs. Social Determinism[1]

*Seongyi Yun**

Introduction

Ever since the early period of widespread Internet use, online political participation has been very active in South Korea. This online political participation has been evolving in two directions: the supplier-centric model in which the existing representative democracy uses the internet to supplement its present actions, and the demander-centric model in which the citizens pursue a new type of participatory democracy. In South Korea, this demander-centric online participation model has been vitalized, while the supplier-centric model has been inactive. That is to say, Information and Communication Technologies (ICTs) have been effective tools for people resisting institutional politics, rather than been supplements to representative democracy. Though the South Korean government has tried to adopt the online politics in institutional political areas, the efforts have not been very successful. In South Korea, online political activities such as information sharing, discussions, and actual mobilizations have occurred

* Seongyi Yun, Professor, Department of Political Science, Kyung Hee University, South Korea.

on portal sites, personal blogs, online communities, and social media sites like Twitter, rather than on government-run websites.

On the other hand, many western governments have been successful in adopting ICTs to improve functions of political institutions. Bellamy and Raab (1999) analyzed the democratic significance of ICTs, using a four-rung "ladder of informatization" of politics based on parliamentary institutions. They concluded that the application of ICTs to government could well improve the parliamentary procedures and bring representative institutions closer to the public. This prompts the questions of why, contrary to their conclusion, the spread of ICTs in South Korea has boosted only non-institutional online participation and actually threatened institutional politics, rather than supplementing the representative democratic government.

Contemporary democracy moves between the competing themes of representation and participation. With the birth of larger democratic nation-state in democracies, the political process had to be adjusted in order to serve the citizens. This is due to the fact that in larger democracies, direct participation by citizens has become difficult and implausible. As a result, legislative and policy execution rights are entrusted to the representatives the people elect (Campbell 1980). Representative democracy tends to focus on the effectiveness of the output side of the political process and relies upon institutional devices such as Parliament, parties, and elections. Schumpeter (1975) argued that democracy refers to an institutional device through which citizens select representatives who will rule them rather than a political system in which they freely participate in the decision-making process. In line with the Schumpeterian thesis, representative democracy has mainly been developed as an elite-centered and top-down political process that provides political services.

The contrary perspective, which emphasizes participation, views democracy as a process in which self-governing citizens of a community directly participate in the formation of the community rules that concern them (Kramer 1972). Participatory democracy focuses on enhancing the efficiency of inputs to the political process, both through conventional methods such as participation in elections and through un-conventional methods such as petitions, demonstrations, and organized citizen activities. Supported by the Rousseauian thesis that democracy is the achievement of self-realization by active participation in policy-making (Kweit and Kweit 1981), participatory democracy has developed as a citizen-centered and bottom-up political process.

The impact of ICTs on the two contending trends of democracy in the age of information has been explored and discussed. Discussions on electronic democracy center on whether the political use of ICTs will favor representation or participation. There are two contradictory perspectives explaining social-political consequences of technology: social determinism and technological determinism. Social determinism views new technologies and their usage as consequences of social factors, such as the desires and concerns of a given social context. On the other hand, technological determinism views technologies as causal agents entering societies as active forces of change that humans have little power against (Baym 2010:44). Some scholars argue that the truth lies somewhere in between, and that these two philosophies are "interrelated nodes in constantly changing sociotechnical networks, which constitute the forms and uses of technology differently in different times and places for different groups" (Lievrouw 2006:250).

In order to explain explosive bottom-up online participation and inactive top-down online participation in South Korea, this study follows a synthetic perspective in which social consequences of a new technology are determined by the interaction of technology and social context. In other words, the question of whether online political processes supported by ICTs will mainly be the tools of "political suppliers" (the political elite) that supplement representative democracy or will be the tools of "political consumers" (citizens) that promote participatory democracy is closely related to both technological and social factors. In addition, the interaction of technology and social context should be analyzed distinctively at the macro (societal) and micro (individual) level. The combination of technology/social context and macro/micro framework provides four dimensions, which explain the background of explosive demander-centric online political participation in South Korea.

ICTs and Political Process

1. ICTs and Power Shift: Supplier-centric vs. Demander-centric

Historically, the development of communication technologies has promoted changes in human ways of life and power relationships within society. The invention of printing, which can be viewed as the pre-modern ancestor of today's information and communication revolution, has facilitated the replication of information, altered the means of communication, and destroyed the monopoly of information once enjoyed by groups in power. The mass media has contributed to individuals' ability to mobilize, the formation of communities with large number of people, and the formation of the modern nation-state. Meanwhile, contemporary new media have facilitated citizens' political participation — against which the existing political elites have responded with more effectiveness — by disrupting the existing structure of communication and promoting bi-directional interactions through networks. In such various ways, the communication system and the power structure are engaged in a close relationship marked by mutual support and competition.

Given such historical precedents, what can be said about the role of ICTs in providing directions for the restructuring of the political process? Which side will the development of ICTs strengthen in the political process: representation or participation? As for the future of political process in online space, there are two competing models as shown in Table 1: the "supplier-centric model" and the "demander-centric model". The two models differ in the selection of the actor that plays the leading role in agenda setting and decision-making in the political process (Norris 2001:95–111; Kim Yong-cheol and Yun Seong-yi 2005:21–33). Agenda setting, which is the first gateway of the political process, refers to the process of establishing policy priorities among social issues. Social issues that are excluded from the agenda are neglected. Therefore, agenda setting determines whose interests and what values are socially important (Cobb and Elder 1983). Policy-making, on the other hand, is a process of creating outputs based on the coordination of factional interests surrounding the selected agenda. Characteristics of the outputs differ based on the scope of participants and the rules that distribute their rights (Lindblom and Woodhouse 1993).

The supplier-centric online political process model is characterized by the mobilization of citizens by privileged groups such as the government, political parties, and the media. In this model, the leadership of agenda setting and policy decisions belongs to the political elites, whereas only customary and limited forms of participation are allowed to

Table 1. Online Political Process Model.

	Supplier Centered	User Centered
Actor	Government, parties, political elite	Citizens
Method	Top-down	Bottom-up
Characteristic	Output-centered/Strengthening of the political elite	Input centered/Self-mobilization of citizens
Strength	Promotion of responsibility and efficiency	Enhance the effectiveness of participation
Result	Concentration of power	Diffusion of power

citizens (INVOLVE 2005:20). The strength of this model lies in that it can institutionalize the political process in a stable manner and promote political responsibility and efficiency. In this model, however, citizens remain passive consumers who respond to the agenda as policies are imposed on them (OECD 2003:29–30). Therefore, Sclove (1995) argues that this top-down model alone is inadequate for strengthening democracy.

In contrast, the demander-centric online political process model is characterized by the formation of diverse discussion forums and the open and voluntary participation of citizens. The strength of this model lies in that citizens, who are active producers of issues and policies, enhance the dynamism of the political process (OECD 2003:30). In this respect, ICTs are technologies that encourage citizens' participation and interaction, and the bottom-up model effectively reflects such strengths of the ICTs (Shapiro, 1999). A shortcoming of the model is that citizens can degenerate into irresponsible and noisy participants. Therefore, Bauman (1996) warns that democracy can fragment under the bottom-up model.

Ultimately, both models are related to the structure of power. In the supplier-centric online political process model, the elites maintain the concentration of power and pursue effective rule. In this model, ICTs are considered as tools available to the government and political parties as they try to co-opt and mobilize as efficiently as possible. In contrast, the demander-centric online political process model seeks a decentralization of power to empower citizens and allow for their effective intervention.

In this model, ICTs are perceived as tools that enable citizens to participate in agenda setting and decision-making by bypassing the gate keeping carried out by the government, political parties, and the media. Therefore, the political use of ICTs has the potential to strengthen or redistribute the existing power.

In South Korea, online bottom-up politics has been especially impressive in the areas of electoral campaigns, social movements, and public deliberation. South Korea's online bottom-up politics is not confined to transferring patterns of citizens' participation to the online space or increasing the quantity of citizens' participation. The "power shift" from the elites to the citizens in the political process is the more essential aspect of politics in the online space. This power shift is an example of the challenges of participatory democracy to South Korea's shaky representative democracy.

2. Technological Determinism vs. Social Determinism

There is a long-running debate about the nature of technology and the role it plays in social, economic, and political life. There are two competing perspectives of the causal relationship between technology and society: technological determinism and social determinism. Technological determinism views technologies as causal agents that enter societies as active forces of change, which humans have little power to resist. Technologies are conceptualized as an external agent that acts upon and changes society (Baym 2010:24).

Technological determinism argues that "technology develops as the sole result of an internal dynamics and then, unmediated by any other influence, molds society to fit its patterns" (Winner 1988:35). New technologies for communication have ushered in a society which differs fundamentally from the societal orders of the past (Webster 2002). Christopher May argued that certain technologies "embody specific norms" (May 2002:25). It has been claimed that the Internet embodies values like freedom, community, equality, altruism, and democracy. Work by Rheingold (1993), Negroponte (1995), Grossman (1996) and Rash (1997) extolled the seemingly limitless possibilities of the Internet for forging new and stronger forms of political engagement by citizens. These early works on e-democracy tried to prove an "equalization" thesis. They argued that as Internet use disseminates and becomes a tool of political participation, more opportunities would be given to the citizens to express their opinions and eventually narrow the power gap between the elites and the masses. However, it has been argued that the Internet embodies values like social control, discipline, and hierarchy. Whatever the content, the key idea is that technology has its own inherent properties and that these are beyond the scope of human intervention (Chadwick 2006:18).

On the other hand, the social determinism perspective argues that people are the primary sources of change in both technology and society (Baym 2010:24). By social determinism, technologies are neutral tools, and non-technological forces such as social class, political power, or even individual personalities each has an independent effect on how technologies are designed and controlled (Chadwick 2006:18). This perspective presumes that specific technologies do not matter much in themselves at all. Using the example of the Internet, the social determinist argues that it is nothing particularly distinctive or new and that we can make sense of its effects by referring to preexisting models of social and political change (Chadwick 2006:19).

According to social determinism, a society's adoption of a specific online political process model depends firstly on the construction of the society. Furthermore, it depends on which group has the greater will to use ICTs strategically and actively. ICTs are new political resources and opportunities provided to political actors in the age of information. The online space created by ICTs is an arena of competition where social forces are engaged in hegemonic struggles to establish new values, norms, and order. Although exclusive domination of this space by a specific group is impossible, groups that use it strategically can enjoy greater benefits (Chang Woo-young 2006:143). To use the expression coined by Rheingold (2003), the Internet is "the great equalizer". Any group that establishes a larger number of linkages in the network grasps a greater number of rights in the new system of power that is being created in cyberspace.

The mode of adoption also reflects multi-dimensional social conditions and environments. As is the case with existing political institutions; ideas, practices, and outputs do not exist independently from their contexts. More specifically, all social outputs are created path-dependently under the influence of diverse factors. These factors encompass political, economic, and cultural dimensions and create complex and specific contexts. Moreover, the outputs are strong and durable enough to withstand

Table 2. Determinants of Patterns of Online Political Participation.

	Macro-societal Level	Micro-individual Level
Technological factors	Process of informatization	Individuals' use of ICTs
Social factors	Trust of representative democracy	Individuals' political capacity

any internal or external shocks (Krasner 1984). The establishment of the dominant political process model in online space can be understood from such a perspective. Once established, the model is frozen until it faces strong internal contradiction or external pressure that can trigger changes.

In addition to the contradictory perspectives, there is a view of synthesis on the causal relationship between technology and society. Katz and Aakhus (2002) argue that technologies have "logic" that influences but does not determine use. Douglas also contends that even though machines do not make history by themselves, they help make different kinds of histories and different kinds of people. That is to say, machines "can and do accelerate certain trends, magnify cultural weaknesses, and fortify certain social structures while eroding others" (Douglas 1999:20). In sum, the synthetic perspective asserts that people, technologies, and institutions all have power to influence the development and subsequent use of technology (Lievrouw 2006:250). That is to say, social consequences of a new technology are determined by the interaction of technology and social context.

This study, concurring with the synthetic perspective, argues that a specific configuration of online politics in South Korea, which is characterized by explosive bottom-up online participation and inactive top-down online politics is a consequence of both social and technological determinants. It also contends that the impact of both technology and social context should be analyzed at the two distinct dimensions of macro-societal and micro-individual level.

How is Bottom-up Online Politics Uprising?: Contextual and Macro Level Backgrounds

1. Social Factors: Shaky Representative Democracy

Currently, South Korea is categorized as a consolidated democracy by many indices of democracy, such as Freedom House, The Economist,

Polity IV, and the World Bank. For example, according to The Economist's index (2011), South Korea attained an overall score of 8.06 and was classified as a "full democracy" country (http://www.eiu.com). Polity IV (2011) evaluates quality of democracy with indicators of competitiveness and openness of executive recruitment, executive constraints, and competitiveness of political participation; using a scale from −10 to 10, Polity IV gave South Korean democracy an 8 (http://www.systemicpeace.org). In the case of the World Bank Governance Index (2010), South Korea achieved 0.72 in the range of −2.5 to +2.5 (http://www.govindicators.org).

South Korea has also been quite successful in the growth economy. The national per capita income has continually increased, from US$3,420 in 1987 to US$6,153 in 1991 and US$19,162 in 2008. Democracy indices and per capita GDP in South Korea prove that there is little doubt about democratic consolidation in South Korea. Despite this, the South Korean people have a deep mistrust of their government. This means that democratic consolidation does not fully synchronize with peoples' satisfaction with the functioning of democracy. Figure 1 shows that public trust in political institutions is declining continuously. In 1996, 49% of the people answered that they trusted the National Assembly, but the figure dropped to 9% in the 2006 survey. The trust level of political parties had also drastically declined from 39% in 1996 to 7% in 2006.

A steep decline between 1996 and 1997 may be explained as an influence of the financial crisis in 1997. But even after the mid-2000s, distrust of political institutions has increased steadily. This means that peoples' distrust is not simply fluctuating with the success or failure of government performance.

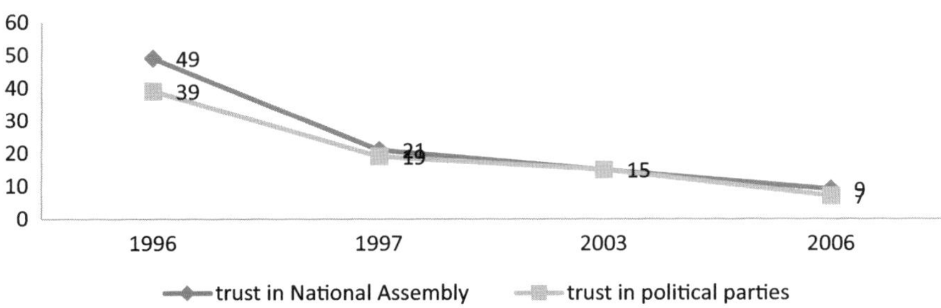

Figure 1. Trends of Public Trust in Political Institutions (%).
Source: KDB surveys (1996, 1997) and EAB surveys (2003, 2006).

Since the transition to democracy, civic movements demanding political reform have erupted. The surge is related to the characteristics of the democratic transition in South Korea and the low level of trust in the government and the National Assembly. Democratization in South Korea was based on a pact between the military and moderates in the opposition. Therefore, the transition did not lead to a complete break with the political practices of the past. Furthermore, the ability to cure deeply embedded and destructive political practices could not be easily recovered. A political system based on regionalism and built on a divisive political culture worsened the crisis of representation. In this context, a weakening of trust in the government and Parliament was inevitable. Explosion of online bottom-up politics primarily stemmed from a mistrust of representation.

Peoples' attitudes towards political institutions have a critical impact on the pattern of political participation. Voter turnout has been falling steadily over 29 years of parliamentary elections. On the other hand, unconventional participation has shown cyclical fluctuations. Since democratic transition in 1987, the rate of political protest had decreased until 2000, but then rose rapidly since the arrival of the Roh Moo-hyun government. A steady decline in voter turnout and a rapid increase of protest can be read as a warning sign for the healthy functioning of democracy.

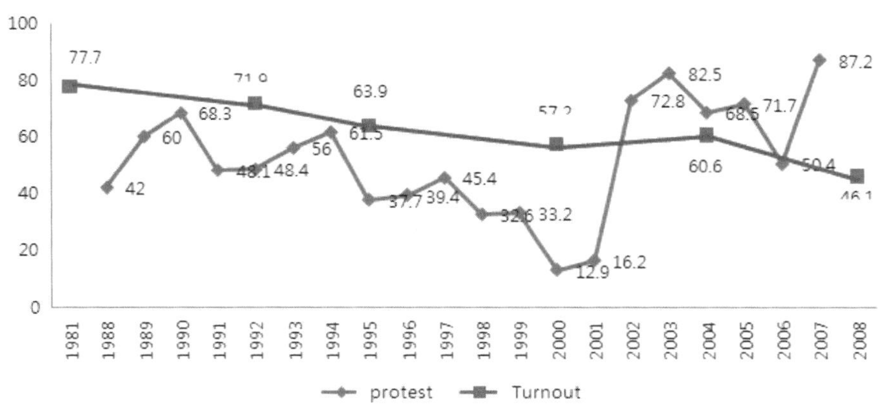

Figure 2. Protests and Turnout (1981–2008) (%).

Source: EAI (1988–2007)[2], National Election Commission (1981–2008).

2. Technological Factors: Process of Informatization

Then, what are the technological factors that contributed to the promotion of bottom-up online politics in South Korea? What factors led the demander-centric political process to become the dominant form in South Korea's online space? In this section, these questions will be answered from a macro perspective that focuses on government's informatization policy.

First, in the realm of policies, the government-led strategy succeeded in rapidly establishing the physical foundation for online political participation. In South Korea, informatization began in 1997, when the government and public organizations began to establish networks. The financial crisis of 1997, which was the most serious national crisis since the Korean War, accelerated the process of informatization that had progressed slowly in the previous 10 years. Threatened by the financial crisis that culminated in the country's management by the IMF, the government chose the IT industry as the core growth industry that would determine the future of the nation (The Ministry of Information and Communication 2000). Supported by government policies, the number of IT companies increased rapidly from 5,840 in 1994 to 9,400 in 1997. In 2001, there were 15,100 IT companies in South Korea. From 1998 to 2001, the annual average increase of added value in the IT industry was 16.4%, which was four times that of the annual rate of economic growth during the same period. Similarly, the share of the added value of the IT industry in GDP increased from 8.6% in 1997 to 13.4% in 2001 (Korea Information Society Development Institute 2005:43–62).

In particular, South Korea's unique geographic condition and organization of residential areas facilitated the establishment of broadband network. In South Korea, one-fourth of the population lives in Seoul, and most residential areas consist of apartment complexes or heavily populated regions. Therefore, a broadband network in South Korea could be established cost efficiently in urban and heavily populated areas. Consequently, an optical cable network that links 80 major cities throughout the country was established as early as 1997. In the early 2000s, all-directional social communication infrastructure, including a national information super highway and a public network, was completed. Therefore, it became possible to use the Internet in all schools and public organizations without payment of fees (Chang Woo-young 2006:150).

Moreover, from 1996 to 1998, the government directed a lowering of communication charges. Thanks to lowered costs, demands for communication services in public organizations were successfully generated. This in turn increased the revenue of communication service providers. The virtuous circle led to the rapid expansion of the information and communication market and facilitated the lowering of Internet access fees in the private sector. In South Korea, unlimited Internet access is available for just USD 25 a month in virtually all households. In the case of Internet cafes, the hourly charge in South Korea is just USD 1, which is much lower than the USD 7 in the United Kingdom, USD 5 in the United States, and USD 4.3 in Canada (Koreanclick 2005). Internet cafes, which appeared at the end of 1990s, increased rapidly, and there were 35,000 Internet cafes in 2007. Based on a solid network infrastructure and access/usage environment, Korea saw impressive achievements. As of 2007, 38 million users out of the total population of 47 million enjoy broadband Internet access. There are 14 million users of wireless Internet, and 79.6% of households have PCs. The weekly average of Internet usage is 134.7 hours, and there are 5.4 million Internet hosts. In sum, Korea is a leader in the area of informatization (National Information-Society Agency 2007).

How is Bottom-up Online Politics Uprising?: Individual and Micro Level Analysis

1. Political Trust and Political Efficacy

In South Korea, it is noteworthy that individuals' political efficacy is continuously growing, despite the high level of political distrust and low voter turnout. Political efficacy refers to political self-confidence or the effectiveness of an individual. Therefore, the trend means that people do not trust their government and have strong confidence in influencing political process. Peoples' distrust of government is related to the output of the political system, and political efficacy has to do with the input system. The former refers to affective satisfaction with the process and the outcome of political systems, and the latter concerns cognition, or the belief that their political behaviors affect the government (Erikson and Tedin 1995).

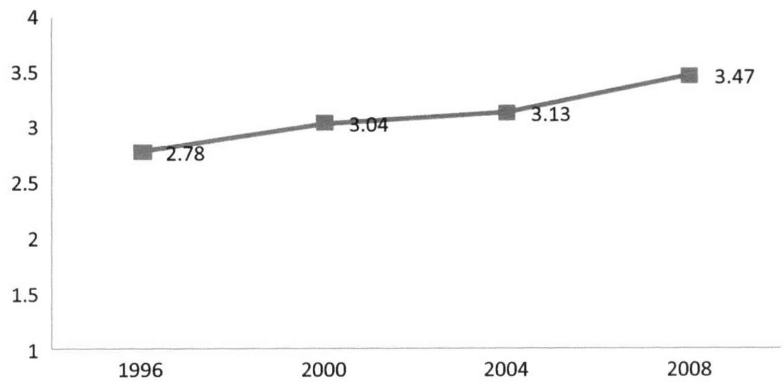

Figure 3. Mean Level of 4-point Political Efficacy Scale.

Source: Korean Social Science Data Center (KSDC), Surveys on voters' awareness in the National Assembly Election.

As discussed above, public trust in political institutions is continuously decreasing, while political efficacy of individuals is steadily increasing. This results in an imbalance between the input and output of the political system. It means that there exists a discrepancy between individuals' political capacity or demand for democracy and the performance of democratic governance. Under this circumstances, people have a perception of democratic deficit. Though the democracy is consolidated, it is still immature and unstable in that it cannot satisfy the people. The problem is that the discrepancy between the peoples' expectation and the performance of political institutions has grown in the last decade or so.

For an empirical analysis of a clash between Social Network Service (SNS) politics and representative democracy in South Korea, we surveyed 1,052 people between November 11 and 16, 2011. The survey data confirmed a direct relationship between individuals' political efficacy and their trust in political institutions. As shown in Figure 5, individuals of high political efficacy showed a low level of public trust in the National Assembly and political parties. As discussed above, public trust in political institutions is continuously decreasing, while political efficacy of individuals is steadily increasing. It was also stated that this kind of imbalance resulted in distrust of the representative democracy. The trend of negative correlations between political efficacy and public trust in political institutions was confirmed by the survey data.

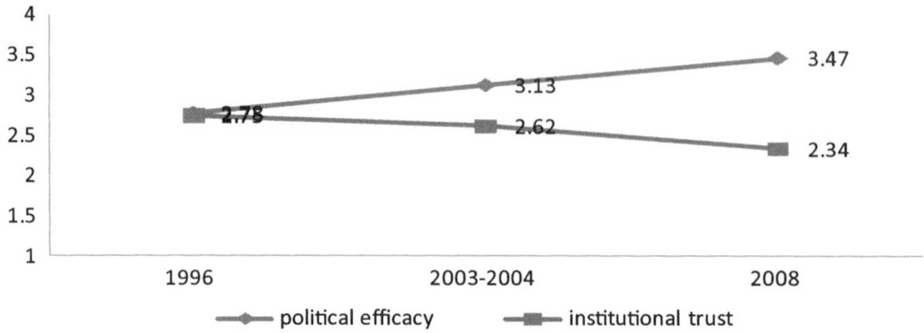

Figure 4. Discrepancy b/w Political Efficacy and Trust in Political Institutions.
Source: Korean Social Science Data Center (KSDC), ABS (1996–2008).

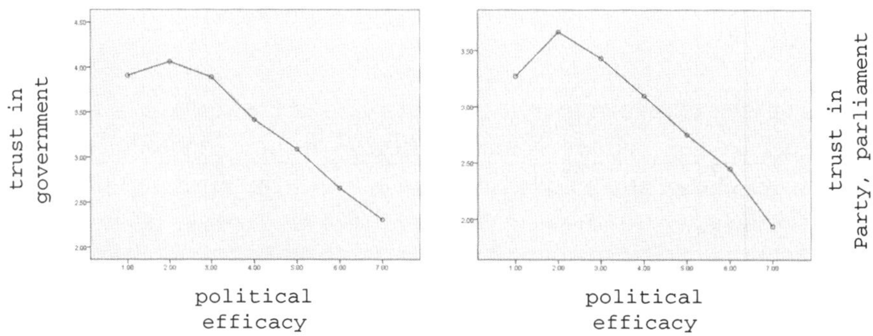

Figure 5. Relationship of Political Efficacy and Public Trust in Political Institutions.
$p = 0.000^{**}$ ($^{**}p < 0.01$) $p = 0.000^{**}$ ($^{**}p < 0.01$)

Peoples' attitudes towards political institutions have a critical impact on the pattern of political participation. Voter turnout has been falling steadily over 29 years of parliamentary elections. On the other hand, unconventional participation has shown cyclical fluctuations. After democratic transition in 1987, the rate of political protest decreased until 2000, but then rose rapidly since the arrival of the Roh Moo-hyun government. A steady decline in voter turnout and a rapid increase of protest can be read as a warning sign of an unhealthy and dysfunctional democracy.

The increase of unconventional participation turned out to have a close relationship with political efficacy and the level of public trust at the individual level. Individuals who have high level of political efficacy are

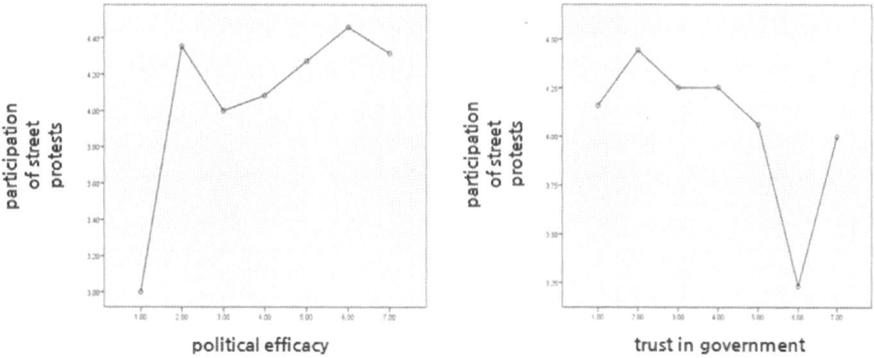

Figure 6. Relationship of Unconventional Participation and Political Efficacy and Public trust.

$p = 0.005^{**}$ ($^{**}p < 0.01$) $p = 0.000^{**}$ ($^{**}p < 0.01$)

more eager to participate in the political process. If they have a low level of trust in political institutions, they prefer unconventional participation such as street demonstrations, candlelight vigils, and strikes over participation in the institutional process. It is highly possible that citizens' dissatisfaction with the current democracy will lead to political instability when the unsatisfied citizens are equipped with the political wills and skills to participate.

In sum, at the micro/individual level, the explosion of bottom-up political participation resulting in unhealthy representative democracy in South Korea can be explained by continuous increase of individuals' political efficacy and steady decrease of public trust in political institutions.

2. SNS and Citizenship Change

As mentioned above, there are two contradictory perspectives explaining social consequences of technologies: social determinism and technological determinism. In this part, we will see how technology stimulates changes in political society based on technological determinism.

The survey data proved that political efficacy and the degree of SNS use have a significant positive relationship. When we divided the respondents into three groups of active, medium, and passive users of SNS, their levels of political efficacy turned out significantly different. While the

Table 3. SNS Impact on Political Information and Political Efficacy.

		Political Information	Political Efficacy
Degree of SNS use	Passive user	4.64 (1.44)	4.94 (1.56)
	Medium user	5.02 (1.22)	4.87 (1.43)
	Active user	5.23 (1.45)	5.34 (1.55)
	(df, F)	(2, 15.128) p = .000***	(2, 8.094) p = .000***

Note: Mean value (standard deviation) $*p < 0.1$, $**p < 0.05$, $***p < 0.01$.

Table 4. SNS Impact on Public Trust.

		Trust in Government	Trust in Political Party and National Assembly
Degree of SNS use	Passive user	3.10 (1.30)	2.66 (1.17)
	Medium user	3.11 (1.22)	2.81 (1.22)
	Active user	2.89 (1.29)	2.69 (1.33)
	(df, F)	(2, 2.614) p = .074*	(2, 2.468) p = .085*

Note: Mean value (standard deviation) $*p < 0.1$, $**p < 0.05$, $***p < 0.01$.

group who actively used SNS had political efficacy of 5.34 points (7-point scale), those who passively used SNS showed a much lower political efficacy of 4.94. In sum, if individuals use SNS more actively, they are likely to have a high level of political efficacy and political information. Use of SNS, in turn, indirectly has a negative impact on the stability of representative democracy through its impact on the increase of citizens' political efficacy.

Citizens' degrees of SNS use also turned out to have a significant correlation with their levels of public trust in government, political parties, and parliament. While medium users of SNS scored 3.11 of government trust, active users showed much lower score of 2.89. Active users of SNS also showed lower level of trust in political party and the National Assembly than medium user group. In other words, active users of SNS have stronger distrust in the representative democracy compared with other groups.

Use of SNS made a distinct difference in patterns of political participation. Active users of SNS preferred direct and unconventional

Table 5. SNS Impact on Political Behavior.

		Protest, Candlelight Vigil	Participation in Policy Making
Degree of SNS use	Passive user	4.01 (1.54)	2.38 (0.83)
	Medium user	4.29 (1.37)	2.57 (0.76)
	Active user	4.45 (1.52)	2.59 (0.74)
	(df, F)	(2, 7.067) p = .001***	(2, 7.324) p = .001***

Note: Mean value (standard deviation) $^{**}p < 0.05$, $^{***}p < 0.01$.

Table 6. Correlation Coefficient of SNS Use.

		Sex	Age	Protest	Trust in Gov.	Trust in Party and Parliament	Political Efficacy	Political Information	Ideology	Participation in Policy Making
SNS use	Pearson coefficient	−.044	−.297**	.124**	−.066*	−.020	.096**	.175**	.224**	.107**
	Significance	.149	.000	.000	.033	.515	.002	.000	.000	.001
	N	1052	1052	1052	1052	1052	1052	1052	1052	1052

participation such as street protests and candlelight vigils to institutional participation. While the active SNS use group scored 4.45 on asking preference of direct participation, the passive group scored only 4.01. The active SNS use group also showed stronger intention to directly participate than the passive users in the public policy making process, rather than leaving it to the hands of the representatives.

Table 6 presents correlations between SNS use and socioeconomic variables, political perceptions and political behaviors. As we expected, SNS use turns out to have a strong correlation with age (–0.297, p = 0.000) and ideology (–0.224, p = 0.000). Younger generations and liberals are more likely to use SNS actively. SNS use also has a close correlation with acquisition of political information (0.175, p = 0.000) and participation of street protest (–0.124, p = 0.000). As people use SNS more actively, they are more likely to acquire political information and to participate in the street demonstrations. In addition, SNS use has a modest relationship with trust in government (–0.066, p = 0.033), even though it has no significant correlation with trust in political party and parliament

Table 7. SNS impact on Desire for Participation within Same Age Groups (mean, SD).

age	SNS Use (N)	Desire for Participating Protest (mean, SD)	
20s	Passive user (41)	3.71 (1.75)	(1, 3.067) $p = .082^{*}$
	Active user (92)	4.23 (1.51)	
30s	Passive user (52)	4.31 (1.53)	(1, 4.037) $p = .047^{**}$
	Active user (49)	4.90 (1.42)	
40s	Passive user (73)	4.21 (1.32)	(1, 4.908) $p = .029^{**}$
	Active user (28)	4.86 (1.33)	
50s	Passive user (54)	4.04 (1.50)	(1, 3.191) $p = .079^{*}$
	Active user (15)	4.87 (1.88)	
Over 60s	Passive user (78)	3.65 (1.67)	(1, 0.201) $p = .655$
	Active user (10)	3.40 (1.78)	

$^{*}p < 0.1$, $^{**}p < 0.05$.

(–0.020, $p = 0.515$). This means that active users of SNS tend to more distrust their government and prefer to directly participate in the policy making process rather than leaving it at the hands of the representatives.

SNS users are currently concentrated in younger generations; however, it is necessary to confirm whether the different patterns of political perception and political behaviors among SNS user groups are caused by age effect or by pure SNS impact. To confirm the answer to this puzzle, we compared the desire for participating in street demonstrations among different SNS use groups within same age groups. As shown in Table 7, peoples within same age groups, except age of over 60s, revealed different level of desire for participating in street protest depending on their strength of SNS use. Particularly, active SNS users in their 50s showed a stronger participation need compared with passive SNS users in younger generations. This means that strength of SNS use make a certain impact on the behavior of political participation regardless of age.

Representative democracies are based on rule by the representatives. That is to say, under this system, the choices of the representatives are more beneficial to society than direct participation by the people. This is because the elitist democrats do not trust peoples' capacity to make reasonable and effective decisions on delicate political issues. However, the critical democracy theorists are suspicious of the authority of the

Table 8. Predictors of Participation Needs.

	Non-standardized B	Standard Deviation	Standardized β	t-value	Significance
sex	1.634	0.045	0.197	6.912	.000***
age	–0.311	0.015	–0.159	–4.986	.000***
ideology	0.061	0.019	0.097	3.289	.001***
education	–0.029	0.016	–0.056	–1.837	.066*
income	–0.029	0.012	–0.069	–2.383	.017**
Political efficacy	0.104	0.015	0.200	6.831	.000***
SNS use	0.110	0.047	0.070	2.362	.018**
Adjusted R^2 = .026, F = 6.549**, N = 1052					

*$p < 0.1$, **$p < 0.05$, ***$p < 0.01$.

representatives. They believe that democratic legitimacy can be better achieved by placing full confidence in the capacity of the people and involving the alienated people in the political process. In order to explore the factors influencing individuals' participation need, we performed linear regression analysis with seven independent variables. As shown in Table 9, sex ($\beta = 0.197, p = 0.000$), age ($\beta = -0.159, p = 0.000$), and political efficacy ($\beta = 0.200$, $p = 0.000$) turned out to be critical determinants of participation need. Again, if people are female, younger, liberal, lower income, higher education, or active SNS users, then there is a higher probability of perceiving participation needs. Above all, it is noteworthy that strength of SNS use ($\beta = 0.070$, $p = 0.018$) has independent impact on participation needs.

Individuals can acquire more political information, easily exchange political opinions with others, and be connected with more people due to SNS properties of interactivity, openness, and connectivity. Naturally, these activities increase the political efficacy of individuals and the desire for representing themselves, rather than depending on representatives. Figure 7 shows a logical path through which SNS politics clash with the representative democracy. As mentioned before, if people have higher political efficacy and more desire for political participation, they are more likely to distrust the government and political institutions. In addition, active use of SNS showed a close relationship with individuals' political efficacy, acquisition of political information, and participation needs.

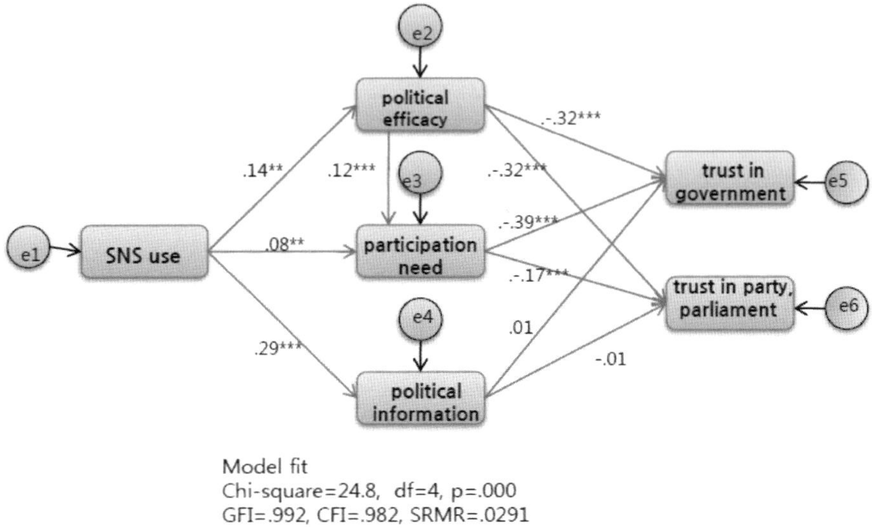

Figure 7. Path Analysis of SNS Impact on Public Trust.

Eventually, active use of SNS increases political efficacy and participation needs, which, in turn, leads to the distrust for government, political party, and the National Assembly, and ultimately to the conflict with the representative democracy.

Conclusion

The emergence of online bottom = up politics in South Korea can be understood as a complex interaction of social and technological factors. Furthermore, diverse macro contexts and micro factors have contributed to the emergence of the demander-centric online political process as the dominant pattern in South Korea. In other words, the shaky representative democracy, rapid informatization led by the government, rapid growth of the civil society after democratization, and active SNS politics have all contributed to the demander-centric political process.

In particular, SNS has been a revolutionary channel of participation for citizens. Taking advantage of participatory properties of SNS such as interactivity, openness, and connectivity, citizens have pursued agenda setting, public opinion formation, and political mobilization. Participatory properties of ICTs, especially SNS, contributed to the strengthening of individuals' political capacity representing themselves, rather than depending on the representatives. However, this does not mean that the active use SNS always leads to the challenge to representation. In South Korea, the macro context of shaky representative democracy causes the SNS politics to clash with the incumbent democracy, rather than complementing it.

For online bottom-up politics to contribute significantly to the consolidation of democracy in South Korea, responsible participation beyond the challenge to representation is necessary. This is because consolidation of democracy is only completed when democratic values and culture are internalized beyond the establishment of democratic institutions and procedures. In other words, rational citizens, tolerant rules, and communitarian trust are necessary conditions for the consolidation of democracy (Valenzuela 1992; Cohen 1997).

Because representation and participation are important and compatible values, democracy in the age of information can become healthier when the appropriate tension and balance between them are achieved. It is in this spirit that the OECD Report (2001) argues the following: "bringing together of the top-down and bottom-up approaches can enable a strong partnership of the government-citizen relationship leading to a strengthening of democracy". In the end, bottom-up and top-town political process models should be engaged in a harmonious relationship so that online political participation equips itself with not only effectiveness of participation, but also responsibility and efficiency of participation.

Notes

1. This work was supported by the National Research Foundation of Korea Grant funded by the Korean Government (NRF-2011-413-B00006).
2. Rate of protest means the proportion of street protests among total protests that had occurred between 1988 and 2007.

References

Bauman, Z. (1995), *Life in Fragments: Essays in Postmodern Morality*, Oxford, Cambridge, Mass: Blackwell.

Baym, Nancy K. (2010), *Personal Connections in the Digital Age*, Cambridge, UK: Polity.

Bellamy, C. and Raab, C. (1999), "Wiring-Up the Deck-Chairs?" *Parliamentary Affairs*, 52(3), 518–534.

Campbell, Ballard C. (1980), *Representative Democracy: Public Policy and Midwestern Legislatures in the Late Nineteenth Century*, Cambridge, Mass: Harvard University Press.

Chadwick (2006), *Internet Politics: States, Citizens and New Communication Technologies*, Oxford University Press.

Chang Woo-young (2006), "Jeonghcijel giwhigujowha sawhoiwondong" [Political Opportunity Structure and Social Movements: With a Focus on Cyberactivism of Civic Alliance for the 2000 General Election and Nosamo], *Jeongbowha Jeongchaek [Informatization Policies]*, 13(3).

Cobb, Roger W. and Charles D. Elder (1983), P*articipation in American Politics: The Dynamics of Agenda-Building*, Baltimore: The Johns Hopkins University Press.

Cohen, J. (1997), "Procedure and Substance in Deliberative Democracy," in James Bohnan and William Regh, eds., *Deliberative Democracy: Essays on Reason and Politics*, Cambridge, Massachusetts: The MIT Press.

Danziger, J., Dutton, W., Kling, R., and Kraemer, K. (1982), *Computers and Politics*, New York: Columbia University Press.

Douglas, S. (1999), *Listening In: Radio and the American Imagination*, Minneapolis, MN: University of Minnesota Press.

Erikson, R.S. and Kent L. Tedin (1995), *American Public Opinion*, New York: Allyn and Bacon.

Grossman, Lawrence K. (1996), *The Electronic Republic: Reshaping Democracy in the Information Age*, Penguin Books.

INVOLVE (2005), *People and Participation: How to Put Citizens at the Heart of Decision-making*, London: Involve.

Katz, J.E. and Aspden, P. (1997), *Perpetual Contact: Mobile Communication, Private Talk, Public Performance*, Cambridge: Cambridge University Press.

Kim Yong-cheol and Yun Seong-yi (2005), *Jeongja Minjujueui [Electronic Democracy]*, Seoul: Oreum.

Korea Information Society Development Institute (2005), *Jeongbosawhiwa Jeongbowha Jeongchaek [Information Society and Informatization Policy]*, Seoul: Bakyeongsa.

Kramer, D. (1972), *Participatory Democracy*, Cambridge: Schenkman Publishing.

Krasner, Stephen D. (1984), "Approaches to the State: Alternative Conceptions and Historical Dynamics," *Comparative Politics*, 16.

Kweit, M. and Kweit, R. (1981), *Implementing Citizen Participation in a Bureaucratic Society*, New York: Praeger.

Lievrouw, L.A. (2006), "New Media Design and Development: Diffusion of Innovations v Social Shaping of Technology," in L.A. Lievrouw and S. Livingston, eds., *The Handbook of New Media, Updated Student Edition*, London: Sage, pp. 246–265.

Lindblom, Charles E. and Woodhouse, Edward J. (1993), *The Policy-Making Process*, Englewood Cliffs: Prentice Hall.

National Information-Society Agency (2007), 2007 *Kukkwa JeongwhaBaekseo [2007 National Informatization Whitepaper]*, Seoul: National Information-Society Agency.

Negroponte, Nicholas (1995), *Being Digital*, Alfred A Knopf, Inc: New York.

Norris, P. (2001), *Digital Divide: Civic Engagement, Information Poverty, and The Internet Worldwide*, Cambridge: Cambridge Univ. Press.

OECD (2003), *Promise and Problems of E-Democracy: Challenges of Online Citizen Engagement*, France: OECD Publication Service.

Rash, Wayne (1997), *Politics on the Nets: Wining the Political Process*, W.H. Freeman & Co: New York.

Rheingold, H. (2003), *Smart Mobs: The Next Social Revolution*, Cambridge: Perseus Publications.

Schumpeter, J. (1950), *Capitalism, Socialism and Democracy*, New York: Harper and Brothers.

Sclove, R. (1995), *Democracy and Technology*, NY: Guildford Press.

Shapiro, Andrew L. (1999), *The Control Revolution*, NY: A Century Foundation Books.

The Ministry of Information and Communication (2000), *Jeongbotongsinbunya Jeongchaekseongkwa Vision [Policy Outputs and Vision in the Field of IT]*, Seoul: The Ministry of Information and Communication.

Valenzuela, J. Samuel (1992), "Democratic Consolidation in Post-Transitional Setting: Notions, Process and Facilitating Conditions," in Scott Mainwaring, Cuillemo O'Donell, and J.S. Valenzuela, eds., *Issues in South American Democracies in Comparative Perspective, Notre Dame*, Indiana: University of Notre Dame Press.

Webster, Frank (2002), *Theories of the Information Society*, Routledge: New York.

Winner, Langdon (1988), *The Whale and the Reactor: A Search for Limits in an Age of High Technology*, The University of Chicago Press: London.

Internet Sites:

National Election Commission (http://www.nec.go.kr)
Korean Statistical Information Service (http://kosis.kr)
The Economist (http://www.eiu.com)
The Center for Systemic Peace
(http://www.systemicpeace.org)
World Wide Governance Indicators
(http://www.govindicators.org)

Chapter 12

Functional Cooperation and Japan's Cultural Diplomacy: A Case Study of the Preservation of Angkor

*He Ping**

Introduction

Since its name became inscribed on the World Heritage List in 1992, the relics of Angkor, the grandeur of which has been largely restored, are protected as an Endangered UNESCO World Heritage Site. The project of restoring and protecting of Angkor has received considerable international attention and support, among which Japan's contributory part is of particular interest to researchers on Japan's cultural diplomacy.

In 1993, the first inter-governmental conference on Angkor was held in Tokyo as a vital step towards assisting peace restoration and construction of Cambodia. At the Tokyo Conference, the Tokyo Manifesto was issued, and an International Coordinating Committee (ICC) for safeguarding and development of the Angkor site was appointed to coordinate technical and financial support from the international community. The Plenary Session of the ICC convenes annually to examine general policies, determine central priorities

---

* He Ping, Associate Professor, Center for Japanese Studies, Fudan University, China. This work has been financed through the generous support of National Social Science Fund (13CGJ029) and Key Projects of Philosophy and Social Sciences' Research, Ministry of Education. An earlier Chinese version was published in Japanese Research, Vol. 28, No. 4, 2014, pp. 18–26.

and to approve new project proposals. The Technical Committee of the ICC also holds an annual meeting for the follow-up of the various projects, activities and researches being carried out by operators intervening at the site of Angkor. Co-chaired by Japan and France, the ICC was working alongside United Nations Educational, Scientific, and Cultural Organization (UNESCO) for protection and promotion of the region. Since 1993, UNESCO has also ensured the Standing Secretariat of the International Coordinating Committee for the Safeguarding and Development of the Historical Site of Angkor. In 1995, the Authority for the Protection and Management of Angkor and the Region of Siem Reap (APSARA) was established in Cambodia, which has been in close collaboration with countries around the world in making collective efforts to better preserve the Angkor's relics.

Japan has been playing a positive and significant role in the international cooperation in this regard, and its unique contribution has been collectively made by a number of national organizations and institutions, including Japanese Government Team for Safeguarding Angkor (JSA), Sophia University Team, Nara Research Institute for Cultural Properties and Tokyo Research Institute for Culture Properties. In July 1993, the Agency for Cultural Affairs, Government of Japan established a Consultative Committee for the Collective Research on the Cultural Heritage of Angkor to organize and supervise conservation and research work on the heritage site. Japan's unswerving efforts to preserve and restore these ancient relics not only have helped maintain the outstanding universal value of the World Heritage site, but have also reaped substantial benefits in improving Japan's diplomatic relations with Southeast Asian countries. A closer look at the concerted initiative taken by the Japanese institutions over the past two decades may offer some clues for a better understanding of the country's cultural diplomacy.

Japanese Government Team for Safeguarding Angkor (JSA)

Since its first step taken towards restoring its international status by joining UNESCO in 1951, Japan has been making continuous efforts to the preservation of cultural heritage and the promotion of cultural activities in the international arena. One of the significant symbolic gestures was the Japanese Funds-in-Trust for the Preservation of the World Cultural

Table 1. Angkor Preservation and Restoration Projects Funded by UNESCO/Japan Trust Fund for the Preservation of the World Cultural Heritage.[1]

Project	Scheduled Time Span
Conservation and Restoration	1994–
Cambodia Royal University of Fine Arts training program	1997–2007
Study on stone tablet inscriptions	1997–2007
Organizing ICC-Angkor meetings and other international conferences	1990–
Providing technical support for Angkor Conservation Office (ACO)	1992–1998

Heritage, deposited with UNESCO by the Japanese government in 1989. By 2012, Japan has financed 40 projects of restoration and preservation of historical relics in 41 countries, with total funding of 63.07 million U.S. dollars. Listed as one of the prioritized project supported by the Funds-in-Trust (see Table 1), Angkor has been receiving generous financial aid from Japan to safeguard its historical relics in danger. Another significant contributor in protection of the Angkor site is the JSA, which is led by Director General Professor Nakagawa of Waseda University.

JSA's participation in the program for safeguarding Angkor can be divided into three distinct phases. The first phase lasted for four and a half years, from November 1994 to April 1999; and the second phase lasted for six years, from May 1999 to April 2005. Before the second phase was completed, a total of more than 700 Japanese experts had been engaged in the conservation and restoration activities in Angkor in cooperation with approximately 180 Cambodian staff members. The third phase lasted for five years, from January 2006 to December 2010. Apart from conducting regular restoration activities, JSA is also involved in the transfer of techniques to local staff and human resources development to facilitate localizing preservation work in Cambodia. Besides, the joint framework of JSA-APSARA Safeguarding Angkor (JASA) is implemented in cooperation with the APSATA. All the above mentioned projects are mainly funded by the UNESCO/Japan Trust Fund. According to the released data from APSARA, a total of 70 experts in Cambodia have been collaborating with JSA in conducting researches and preservation activities in Angkor. The projects they are jointly running are going smoothly, including restoration of the southern and northern libraries of the Bayon, study of the structural stability of the central tower of the Bayon, organizing of the international symposiums on the preservation of the Bayon Temple, issuing the "The Bayon Charter", and publishing of "The Master Plan for the Conservation and Restoration of the Bayon Complex" and resources on the restoration and research in this regard. Currently, the ongoing project on the restoration of the southern tower of the Bayon is progressing steadily.[2]

Since 1995, reports and maps have been published annually by JSA in its recordings and make the conservation activities and scientific research more readily available to experts from the outset of the project, thus making a unique contribution to the dissemination of information and sharing of resources.[3] International symposiums on the preservation of the Bayon Temple have been held annually since 1996.[4] Based on the Venice Charter (International Charter for the Conservation and Restoration of Monuments and Sites) (1964) and the Nara Document of Authenticity (1994), "The Bayon Charter", which was drafted over the 2005 symposium, lays out the guidelines for practices in safeguarding the historical site of Angkor, with main focus on the Bayon Temple.

The restoration activities and data collected in the scientific research made public by JSA by means of its symposiums, reports and websites, provide valuable resources to international experts and also help keep the public updated on the ongoing preservation project. In July 2002, JSA Project Office by UNESCO was set up by UNESCO/Japan Trust Funds. In addition to day-to-day affairs, the office is also in charge of the organization of international conferences, symposiums and workshops, as well as the undertaking of cultural exchange activities. To publicly present their research findings and materials on conservation and restoration, JSA has also built a Bayon Temple showroom for tourists to get to know about its accomplishments, future plans as well as project reports.

Three Major Japanese Participants in the International Cooperation on Cultural Heritage Conservation in Angkor

Apart from JSA, three other Japanese participants, Sophia University Team, Nara Research Institute for Cultural Properties and National Research Institute for Cultural Properties, Tokyo, have also substantially contributed to the conservation and preservation of the Angkor relics in various ways.

1. Sophia University Team

The history of Sophia University Team can be traced back to 1980 when the Institute of Asian Culture Studies in Sophia University received the sincere invitation from the Cambodian government to undertake research and restoration work over the relics of Angkor, despite the fact that Japan had not yet established diplomatic relations with the country by then. In 1985, Sophia University held an international symposium on the conservation of the Angkor relics and made the *Sophia Appeal*,[5] aiming for better protection of the endangered cultural heritage. By the year 1998, Sophia University had already sent four research teams for preliminary investigation and 21 teams for formal research, producing a number of publications including Cambodia's Cultural Renaissance. With Sophia University playing a leading role, Sophia University Team actually consists of members from several universities and research institutes in Japan.[6]

One of the notable accomplishments so far achieved by Sophia University Team is its assistance to APSARA in introducing ISO14001.[7] Introduction of the international standard on environmental management helped better planning of the Angkor region. The 24 villages surrounding, with a population of approximately 23,000, are largely dependent on agricultural activities and produce large volumes of waste every year. Moreover, popularity of the historical site among tourists also presents multiple challenges to the preservation of the culturally invaluable ruins. With the soaring number of tourists from 5,500 in 1995 to 600,000 in 2004, the number of hotels around the site rose from 15 in 1995 to 65 in 2005. In view of the growing threats against preservation of the historical relics, Sophia Asia Center for Research and Human Development has collaborated with Japan Quality Assurance (JQA), International Standard Research Institute (ISRI), Japan Quality Assurance Institute (JQAI) and other consortia and enterprises in a three-year plan to offer assistance to APSARA. With the help from Japan, APSARA set up the Environmental Management System (EMS) unit to assume a vital role in more effective management of the region, to assist proper preservation of the relics and promote healthy and eco-friendly living of local residents, aiming for harmonious and sustainable coexistence among "nature, temple and villages" and balance among "environment, culture and community".[8]

To this end, Sophia University Team lends great support to Cambodia in its cultural heritage preservation in two major aspects. First of all, it helps with the training of specialists in environmental protection for APSARA, while preparing local experts to deal with various issues concerning environmental improvement, including waste disposal, water purification, forest protection, maintenance of historical sites, etc. This is mainly achieved by means of admitting Cambodian students in postgraduate programs in Japan and sending home researchers to Cambodia. Since the adoption of ISO14001, various attempts have been successfully made to make local government and residents more environmentally aware. These attempts include encouraging stores to cut down on waste, installing garbage cans, entrusting non-state enterprises with the garbage collection service, and launching education campaigns among primary school students on reducing waste. Moreover, Sophia University arranged a series of visiting programs named "Green Lectures", in which university and high school students were sent to Cambodia on an educational tour during which they exposed themselves to the unique Cambodian culture while actively engaging in the garbage collecting and cleaning work of the relics.[9] In virtue of the team's efforts over three years, APSARA earned the certification of ISO14001 in April 2006.

2. National Research Institute for Cultural Properties, Tokyo

Born as The Institute of Art in 1930, National Research Institute for Cultural Properties, Tokyo became an independent administrative institution in 2001. It is widely involved in international cooperation on the preservation of cultural heritage with Asian countries as well as many countries in other parts of the world.[10] One of its focuses of attention is on the deterioration and historical relics in Southeast Asia, and the conservation and restoration thereof, with Cambodia being one of its major cooperators and partners.

In 1990, National Research Institute for Cultural Properties, Tokyo established its research center for cultural properties in Asia, which, after a number of readjustments, became the Japan Center for International Cooperation in Conservation in 2006. This center has been collaborating with APSARA to conduct research on the protection of sandstone used for Ta Nei Temple, especially in protection against the potent biological effect. That is, investigations are carried out to examine the specific effects of the various types of lichens, mosses, ferns, and trees, which constituted the flourishing vegetation inside the Angkor temples, before taking appropriate protection measures against the possible decay and cleaning the relics with the slightest damage. To this end, National Research Institute for Cultural Properties, Tokyo has also been working in close cooperation with the research team from Blaise Pascal University in France, in the exchange of information and sharing of resources.[11] In collaboration with Japan's National Museum of Nature and Science, it has so far identified eight genera and nine species of mosses, one genus and two species of liverworts, and 20 genera and 22 species of lichens in the Ta Nei Temple relics, and carried out observation and studies on the living conditions for various species.[12]

3. Nara National Research Institute for Cultural Properties

Another major cultural institution in the international cooperation for cultural properties preservation is Nara National Research Institute for Cultural Properties, which was set up in 1953 and transformed into an independent administrative institution for cultural property in 2007. In virtue of its geographical priority, and its rich experience gained in long-term investigation on the relics of imperial palaces in Heizei, Asuka and Fujiwara, this institute specializes in study on ancient capitals. Shortly after the signing of the Paris Peace Agreements for Cambodia in 1991, it has started to play an active role in promoting protection of and research on the Angkor relics under the guidance of the Agency for Cultural Affairs since 1993. In its signed agreement with APSARA, Nara National Research Institute for Cultural Properties clarified six research fields of common interest, namely archaeological excavations, decay of the relics, decay of architecture made of sandstone, exploration of relics, science of restoration and conservation, and upgrading of large-scale relics. In comparison with other institutes, it focuses on and specializes in the excavation and preservation of pottery kilns.[13]

Working in close collaboration with research teams from Waseda University and Sophia University, Nara National Research Institute for

Cultural Properties started its cooperation with APSARA since 2002, focusing on safeguarding Western Prasat Top in Angkor. The first two phases of the international program, each scheduled for five years, were finished in 2010, and a following new phase of the program ensued from 2011.[14] Since 2010, it has furthered its archaeological excavations on Cambodian ancient cities of the post-Angkor Era such as Longvek and Oudong.[15]

International Cooperation in Cultural Heritage Conservation: A Regional Public Goods Approach

In terms of regional public goods, the Japan's contribution in safeguarding Angkor can serve as a typical case for its seeking functional cooperation and supply of regional public goods in East Asia. Following a time-honored "weighted summation" pattern in regional public goods supply, which, on basis of the sum of total contributions, assigns different weights to different countries, Japan has taken a similar approach in safeguarding the Angkor relics.

For one thing, the above Japanese institutions, with their own specialties and obligations, often work in close collaboration with each other. In addition to Japan's strong support, a number of international organizations also play a conducive role in the restoration of the endangered historical sites, including teams from other countries like École française d'Extrême-Orient (EFFO), German Apsara Conservation Project (GACP), Chinese team for Safeguarding Angkor, Italian Geotechnical and Structural Engineering Society (I.Ge.S), Archaeological Survey of India (ASI), Banteay Srei Conservation Project (BSCP) with Swiss Agency for Development and Cooperation, as well as international organizations such as World Monuments Fund (WMF). Given the sprawling archaeological complex of Angkor and adjacent sites, the principal materials used in the construction and decoration of the Angkor temples suffer from various degrees of physical, chemical, biological and human impact. Therefore, individual research on specific type of decay observed in a particular site or structure is called for in the planning and programming of conservation interventions, thus offering a reasonable opportunity for countries and organizations to make good use of their competitive edge. As a result of the collective efforts, Angkor was removed from UNESCO's List of World Heritage in Danger on July 4, 2004.

Aside from the weighted summation pattern in seeking international cooperation, Japan's practice in safeguarding the Angkor relics over the 30 years is found to be characterized by three distinctive features, which may provide great insights into functional cooperation for other countries and in other fields.

Firstly, all Japanese organizations like JSA are working towards the ultimate goal of localizing preservation and restoration of the relics in Cambodia. That is, to focus on knowledge transfer and technique sharing. Or as Professor Yoshiaki Ishizawa, head of Sophia Team, aptly put it, international cultural cooperation goes beyond assistance in terms of funding, technology, and equipment, and shall ultimately be "communication between the people", which shall focus on "reciprocal learning from the differences".[16]

Due to years of war and political unrest, Cambodia has long been suffering from loss of intellectuals and technicians. To prepare the country for independent and self-sufficient cultural heritage management, Japanese specialists and technical staff have been working in close collaboration with local trainees to help cultivate conservation professionals in Cambodia, with local experts mainly in charge of the proposal, administration, operation, as well as report on the restoration projects, and technicians in charge of on-site restoration work. For instance, JSA and Cambodian Royal University of Fine Arts have co-launched a series of training programs, lasting from three or four weeks to one year. A variety of training activities offered plenty of opportunities for students to familiarize themselves with the conservation work, these activities including on-site excavation and research, lectures and courses on measuring, analysis, topographical mapping techniques, as well as on daily record keeping and report writing. These programs aim at preparing the selected Cambodian trainees for future work in conservation and restoration of cultural heritage.

Besides, the "Ta Nei Training Program", which was launched in November 1999, is financially endorsed by Japanese government, and is cooperated by APSARA, International Center for the Study of the Preservation and Restoration of Cultural Property (ICCROM), and

Southeast Asian Ministers of Education Organization (SEAMEO) Regional Center for Archaeology and Fine Arts (SPAFA), with adequate support from UNESCO. The five-month training program involves university graduates from Cambodia and teachers invited from JSA, Kanazawa University as well as universities and research institutes from other countries. The primary goal of the Ta Nei Training Program is to provide advanced on-site training to national technicians in archaeology, architecture and engineering, so as to prepare a professional technical team for site management for the country's cultural heritage preservation.[17]

The student participants from the Departments of Archaeology and Architecture of the Royal University of Fine Arts in Cambodia also enjoy the opportunity to receive on-site training offered by international research team from Sophia University. Some graduates will be admitted in postgraduate programs and conduct research work under the guidance of Japanese supervisors, and advanced trainees will pursue master's or doctoral degrees in Japanese universities, such as Sophia University and graduate school of Tokyo University of the Arts, on scholarships provided by Ministry of Education, Culture, Sports, Science and Technology (MEXT) and consortia in Japan.

Secondly, conservation and restoration of cultural heritage is a systematic and integrated project. It involves a wide range of subjects, including social sciences like history, archaeology, anthropology, architecture, horticulture, art, and museum studies, natural sciences like chemistry, biology, and meteorology, which lend technical support to the work as well as political science and sociology. With considerable experience gained from preserving and restoring its various historical relics, Japan has developed a set of feasible and effective regulations and advanced techniques in cultural heritage management, which has been proven successful in Angkor case.

For one thing, with its clear advantage in such key areas as topography, information processing, and biology, Japan is well prepared to offer professional aid to countries struggling with limited materials and technology for cultural heritage management. For instance, the Cambodian government made an appeal to Japan in 1996 for assistance in a topographic map project of north and east of the Siem Reap Region, which is home to a large concentration of the Angkor relics. In September 1996, Japan International

Cooperation Agencies (JICA) sent their research team to Cambodia for preliminary research work, with APSARA in charge of administration of the project, and Geographical Information Authority of Japan, which is a subbranch of Ministry of Land, Infrastructure, Transport and Tourism, providing technical support. In virtue of the substantial material and technical assistance from Japan, APSARA established its Geographical Information System (GIS) unit in 2000. Operated by Cambodian staff under the guidance of volunteer experts from Japan in operation of the system and topographical map making, the unit had been generating rich and valuable data for preservation of the historical site. From 1998 to 2003, JICA had presented to APSARA comprehensive data generated by GIS, and detailed topographical maps of the Angkor site. Furthermore, APSARA staff had been receiving technical trainings from Japanese technicians and specialists in Cambodia and Japan.[18] Another noteworthy breakthrough was made in digitally archiving cultural heritage by the research team led by Professor Katsushi Ikeuchi form University of Tokyo. Despite the technical challenges presented by sensing huge outdoor structures, they managed to digitally model the Bayon Temple using various kinds of sensors including an aerial laser scanner, which made use of a GPS unit attached to a large helium balloon, to scan the entire surface of the complex, and to collect data for constructing a 3-D model. This helps to establish a solid data base for further restoration of the relics,[19] while leading the way for digitalizing world heritage sites and cultural assets in future.

In addition to its advanced technology, Japan also enjoys its competitive edge in cultural heritage management in virtue of rich experience gained from restoring its own cultural heritage sites. Aside from restoration of the overall appearance, keeping intact the original architectural style is also pertinent to the restoration of cultural relics. The Indian archaeological team, for instance, found their long-practiced techniques and strategies in historical site preservation and restoration literally inapplicable to the Cambodian cultural heritage, merely due to differences in soil structure. Given such practical limitations in human resources and materials, the Japanese team made creative use of the traditional technique by adding hydrated lime to sand in the solidification process, so as to recondition the soil to maintain its favorable permeability and intensity. With the traditional technique successfully transplanted to the conservation work, the historical site was adequately preserved in its original appearance and function.[20] Moreover, the stone structures in the Angkor temples are found similar to traditional techniques in the making of lamp-holders and tomb stones in Japanese culture. In addition to offering professional guidance on the conservation site, experienced Japanese technicians made a unique contribution to the training of Cambodian specialists by opening up training schools to teach specific stone handicrafts and techniques required in the preservation of stone relics.[21] Other restoration projects of stone structures in Japan's cultural heritage sites, such as the Nagoya City and Himeji City also provide rich experience and opportunities for Cambodian technicians.[22]

Apart from the aforementioned government agencies, universities and research institutes, a number of enterprises have also actively engaged in the cooperative projects to safeguard the Cambodian cultural heritage. For instance, the construction machinery manufacturers in Takamatsu, Tadano LTD and Asuka Construction Company, offered firm support to Nara Research Institute for Cultural Properties. In particular, Tadano provided free self-propelled all-terrain cranes, hydraulic lifting platform and cargo ship cranes. It also collaborated with Nara Research Institute for Cultural Properties in the restoration work on the Kitora Tomb, providing specially designed machinery for cautiously handling with the ancient stone structures. Asuka Construction Company has also involved in the restoration of ancient tombs and preservation of frescoes. The effective collaboration among the three institutes has once again offered opportunities for Japanese experts and professionals to contribute to World Cultural Heritage preservation in other countries.[23]

Another helping hand was extended by Aeon, which financially aided Sophia University and APSARA in building the Preah Norodom Sihanouk-Angkor Museum in the Siem Reap Region. Inaugurated on November 2, 2007, the museum showcased excavations like stone statues, kilns, crockery and porcelain unearthed by Sophia Asia Center for Research and Human Development. All these discoveries provide concrete and invaluable evidence to unveil the country's turbulent history. The stone statues, for instance, were found to be buried underground in the 7th century A.D. during which the country's religion was undergoing the transformation from Mahayana to Hinduism. Great significance has been attached to the museum as the reigning King of Cambodia Norodom Sihamoni attended the project's completion ceremony in person.[24]

Conclusion: Cultural Diplomacy and Japan's Cooperation Strategy towards East Asia

Japan's joint efforts in safeguarding the World Cultural Heritage of ancient Angkor relics manifest the development of the country's cultural diplomacy in post-war era. Its successful attempts in the Angkor case adequately demonstrate what forms the core of cultural diplomacy. That is, to stay open to and encourage multiple means of communication with other cultures, while emphasizing on the respect for cultural exchange and cultural diversity. According to the Japanese government, the three primary goals for cultural diplomacy are (1) to foster better understanding of the country and to bolster the country's image; (2) to improve mutual understanding and trust so as to avoid conflict; (3) to contribute to the enrichment of human society and the common values of humanity. In line with this objective, Japan's cultural diplomacy is ambitiously aiming towards a harmonious "symbiosis" of multiple cultural values by mutual communication, "spreading" its own culture and "accommodating" other cultures.[25]

With its dazzling growth of state power and rising international status, Japan's cultural diplomacy entered a new era in the early 1970s, when a more positive cultural diplomacy was deployed in place of more reactive policies aiming at dispelling its pre-war militaristic image. This major shift in Japan's cultural diplomacy was based on the country's renewed identity as an independent and responsible member of the international community. Since cultural diplomacy in its broad sense lays special emphasis on the international cooperation on the World Cultural Heritage, Japan has been actively engaged in various projects to lend support to other countries in restoration and preservation of their cultural heritage. For instance, since 1975 Japanese government has been devoting part of the Official Development Assistance (ODA) to aid the rejuvenation of developing countries' culture and education. In his well-known "London Speech" delivered during his visit to Europe in May 1988, Prime Minister Noboru Takeshita pointed out that Japan ought to engage itself in cooperation with international organizations and contribute to the noble cause of safeguarding World Cultural Heritage and developing local cultures.[26] Therefore, the next stage for Japan's evolving cultural diplomacy started in the early 1990s, with rapid development of its international cooperation in cultural heritage protection.[27]

Since 2000, Japanese government has been focusing its attention on preservation and restoration of cultural relics in addition to offering free assistance to other countries. Striving towards "free cultural cooperation at grass-roots level", it regards safeguarding ancient relics, World Cultural Heritage in particular, as pillar to its cultural communication with other countries. Whether it is motivated by due respect for cultural diversity or the ultimate goal of becoming a "culture valuing great nation", Japan has been playing an active role in promoting activities to "save cultural properties" and in sending humanitarian aid to countries in need.[28] It is in the spirit of such evolving cultural diplomacy that the safeguarding Angkor project smoothly proceeds.

Furthermore, cultural diplomacy could be viewed as a significant part and an effective vehicle in Japan's regional cooperation strategies. In his ceremonial speech at commemorating the 30th anniversary of ASEAN in Singapore in January 1997, Prime Minister Ryutaro Hashimoto made special mention of mutual understanding between the peoples and diverse means of cultural cooperation as one of the three aspects for the future development in Japan's relation with ASEAN. Using the Angkor project as an example, he stressed the necessity to work in close cooperation with other countries in preserving and restoring cultural relics, so as to maintain and develop local cultures.

Three potent factors may have motivated Japan's international cooperation in safeguarding cultural properties in the Asia-Pacific region. First of all, despite the importance that countries in the Asia-Pacific region have attached to protecting their own cultural heritage, many countries are struggling with a serious lack of administrative and technical personnel, inadequate legal system and capital shortage. Therefore, protection against insidious damage and prevention of reckless restoration for tourism purposes are urgently called for to save the invaluable cultural relics in these countries. In comparison, Japan is generally viewed as a model for countries faced with the daunting task of maintaining rapid economic growth while preserving traditional culture, and has received international recognition of its adequately developed system of conservation policies and regulations, fundamental research and advanced restoration techniques. Moreover, several political initiatives have been taken to provide institutional support to its cooperative attempts at safeguarding cultural heritage in Asia-Pacific region. These include the 1992 UNESCO World Heritage Convention, its active involvement in world heritage conservation programs and activities launched by UNESCO and other international organizations, and Prime Minister Ryutaro Hashimoto's "London Speech".[29] Another significant institution for promoting cooperation in cultural heritage conservation in Asia-Pacific region is Asia-Pacific Cultural Center for UNESCO (ACCU), which was founded on August 1, 1999 in Nara, and is co-operated by the Agency for Cultural Affairs, county and municipal government of Nara.[30]

According to a review of all the international cooperative programs Japan initiated from 1990 to 2006, Asia remains its major target, with Vietnam, China, Cambodia, Indonesia and Thailand being the top five countries on the list.[31] Two strategic reasons may have led to this informed decision. One is the fact that as a member of one shared cultural circle, Japan is closely related to other East Asian countries in terms of geography, history and culture. The other reason is the close intimacy Japanese culture and religion enjoy with the cultural heritage in other Asian countries, thus promoting Asia-based international cooperation in cultural heritage has profound significance in deepening understanding of its own history and culture.[32]

Furthermore, seeking international cooperation in research of cultural heritage and preservation and restoration of historical relics is conducive to developing mutual trust between Japan and other countries, which can serve as a solid foundation for peaceful diplomacy, so as to increase its own cultural impact and reinforce its national identity in the international community.[33] Besides, by means of transplanting the mode of domestic governance abroad and encouraging collaboration between officials and ordinary people, Japan has made a successful attempt at enhancing mutual understanding and gaining more power and better image in the international community, regardless of the constraints of geopolitical limitations and historical sentiments.

The symbolic site of Angkor is a unique concentration of features testifying to an exceptional Cambodian culture and its national spirit. Therefore safeguarding it against the impact of Cambodia's turbulent history and political turmoil contains more than high architectural, archaeological and artistic significance. It is also one major step the country takes towards a reestablished cultural identity and national reconciliation, and it may also pave the way for Cambodia to regain its place in the international community and to re-participate in regional cooperation. Since the late 1980s, restoring peace to Cambodia has been high on the Japanese agenda in its foreign policy. As a "unique external player" in the Cambodian peace process, Japan has been playing an increasingly active part, from mild intervention to dispatching self-defense forces, striving towards offering assistance of various kinds to promote reconciliation and reconstruction of Cambodia, which is one of the major achievements in its regional diplomacy since the 1990s.[34]

A fundamental principle of "separating politics from economy" has long been followed by post-war Japan in making its foreign policy towards countries in Southeast Asia. While focusing exclusively on investment and trade, it has remained relatively passive in dealing with political and security issues.[35] However, cultural heritage in general shares an intimate relationship with politics, in which case, seeking international cooperation in safeguarding the Angkor site entails taking into account all the three elements of ancient relics (culture), village (human), and woods (nature), while endeavoring to build "cross-border trust". In light of this statement, cooperative work in world heritage protection has multiple implications, and its significance is also manifold.[36]

The case of Japan's cooperative attempts at safeguarding the Angkor cultural heritage demonstrates the significant role both functional cooperation and regional public goods supply may assume in raising public awareness in cultural heritage protection. The successes in safeguarding the Angkor relics and other historical sites offer countries like Cambodia a sense of regional integration and a sense of "goodwill" in Japan's diplomacy. Noticeably, the favorable changes in its relationship with Southeast Asian countries over recent years ought to be partially attributed to the successful attempts at functional cooperation, which may offer great theoretical and practical insights for China and countries alike.

Notes

1. 日本外務省：「ユネスコ文化遺産保存日本信託基金による実施案件」, http://www.mofa.go.jp/mofaj/gaiko/culture/kyoryoku/unesco/isan/yukei/yukei_1.html.
2. With reference to the official website of APSARA.
3. Japanese Government Team for Safeguarding Angkor, UNESCO and Japanese Trust Fund for the Preservation of the World Cultural Heritage, *Annual Report on the Technical Survey of Angkor Monument*, Tokyo: Japan International Cooperation Center.
4. Unless otherwise specified, resources concerning JSA are attributed to its official website, http://angkor-jsa.org.
5. Yoshiaki Ishizawa and Yasushi Kōno, eds., *Study and Preservation of Historic Cities of Southeast Asia: Study and Preservation of the Cultural Heritage of Southeast Asia: Research Report*, Tokyo: Japan Times, 1986.
6. 石澤良昭:「アンコール遺跡の調査研究と修復保存活動の歴史」, 1998年, http://angkorvat.jp/doc/history/history_outline.pdf.
7. 石澤良昭：「アンコール遺跡環境汚染への対策急げ」,『朝日新聞』、2005 年1月4日、朝刊,上智大学アンコール遺跡国際調査団:「上智大学· 学外共同研究が支援するアンコール· 環境マネジメントシステム(ISO14001) 導入プロジェクトについて」, http://angkorvat.jp/doc/about/ISO14001.pdf.
8. See http://www.autoriteapsara.org/en/apsara/about_apsara/environment.html.
9. 「アンコール遺跡で清掃作業、日本人学生、研究を兼ね」,『日本経済新聞』、2000 年 8 月 2 8日, 夕刊, 18 頁.
10. 東京文化財研究所, http://www.tobunken.go.jp/japanese/gaiyo/gaiyo-topic2013-6.html.
11. 東京文化財研究所, http://www.tobunken.go.jp/~kokusen/JAPANESE/RESEARCH/SEASIA/seasiac01.html.
12. 『東京文化財研究所文化遺産国際協力センター』, 2007 年3 月31 日、10頁.
13. 『東京文化財研究所文化遺産国際協力センター』, 11 頁.
14. 奈良文化財研究所, http://www.nabunken.go.jp/research/cambodia/index.html.
15. 田代亜紀子：「解明がもとめられるポスト·アンコール期の都」,『奈文研ニュース』、第 49 号, 2013 年 6 月, 1 頁.
16. 石澤良昭:「アンコール遺跡の調査研究と修復保存活動の歴史」.
17. APSARA, http://www.autoriteapsara.org/en/apsara/about_apsara/training/ta_nei.html.

18. APSARA, http://www.autoriteapsara.org/en/apsara/about_apsara/gis.html.
19. 「東大など、アンコール遺跡の寺院、デジタル立体画像で保存——修復·研究などに活用」,『日経産業新聞』, 2006 年 2 月 9 日, 9 頁.
20. 日本国政府アンコール遺跡救済チーム:「日本国政府アンコール遺跡救済チーム (JSA)の概要」, 4頁.
21. 「第125話守る、文化財直します(3)カンボジアで信頼関係刻む」,『日本経済新聞』、1999 年 4 月 21 日, 夕刊, 18 頁.
22. 「アンコール遺跡の修復支援、文化庁、技術者研修受け入れ——来秋にも5人」,『日本経済新聞』, 1992 年 9 月 10 日, 朝刊, 38 頁.
23. 奈良文化財研究所, http://www.nabunken.go.jp/research/cambodia/project.html.
24. 「シハヌーク·イオン博物館の案内書」, http://angkorvat.jp/doc/tch/ang-tch1530.pdf, イオン株式会社, http://www.aeon.info/1p/international/others/.
25. 文化外交の推進に関する懇談会報告書:「『文化交流の平和国家』日本の創造を」, 2005 年 7 月.
26. 日本外務省:「竹下総理大臣ロンドンスピーチ」, 1989 年 5 月 4 日, http://www.mofa.go.jp/mofaj/gaiko/culture/koryu/others/kokusai_3a.html
27. For individual projects Japan involved in the world cultural heritage preservation and relevant international conventions, please refer to垣内恵美子:「文化財に関する国際交流·協力と世界遺産条約·無形遺産プロジェクト」, 川村恒明、和田勝彦、根木昭編:『文化財政策概論 — 文化遺産保護の新たな展開に向けて』, 東海大学出版会, 2002 年, 181–216 頁.
28. 国際文化交流懇談会:「今後の国際文化交流の推進について」, 2003 年 3 月 24 日.
29. 日本文化庁:「アジア太平洋地域の文化財保護に関する国際協力の在り方について」, 1998年7月7日, http://www.bunka.go.jp/bunkazai/houkoku/kokusai/index.html.
30. ACCU奈良, http://www.nara.accu.or.jp/index.html. The office is also involved in the conservation and restoration of the Angkor relics by launching training programs, organizing international conferences, and promoting information dissimilation and cross-cultural communication between intellectuals.
31. 豊島久乃、清水真一、青木繁夫、田代亜紀子:「我が国の文化遺産国際協力事業の動向と課題ー財源別に整理した事業実績の集計結果よりー」,『保存科学』, 第 47 号, 2008 年, 238 頁.
32. 日本文化庁:「アジア太平洋地域の文化財保護に関する国際協力の在り方について」, 1998 年 7 月 7 日, http://www.bunka.go.jp/bunkazai/houkoku/kokusai/index.html.

33. 文化財国際協力等推進会議:「文化財の国際協力の推進方策について」, 2004 年 8 月 26 日.
34. Yasuhiro Takeda, "Japan's Role in the Cambodian Peace Process: Diplomacy, Manpower, and Finance," *Asian Survey*, Vol. 38, No. 6, 1998, pp. 553–568.
35. Bhubhindar Singh, "ASEAN's Perceptions of Japan: Change and Continuity," Asian Survey, Vol. 42, No. 2, 2002, p. 287.
36. 石澤良昭:「国際協力は国境のない信頼関係の構築から」,『大学時報』, 第 296 号, 2004 年 5 月.

East Asia and the Global World

Chapter 13

The Korea Policy of Truman Administration (1945–1948)

*Fang Xiuyu, Li Li**

Introduction

Whether on the global level or the regional level, during the Truman administration, earthshaking events happened so often. Bibliographies that specialize in Korean policies are scanty, although monographs about the foreign policies of the United States (U.S.) during this time are numerous. However, if we want to know the history or the current situations on the Korean Peninsula well, it is necessary for us to study the U.S. Korean policy during this time. The first reason is that the analysis of inheritance and adjustment of foreign policies, especially the Korean policy, from Roosevelt to Truman is helpful for us to understand the status of the Korean Peninsula in the U.S. global strategy after the war. In addition, it can also help us grasp the demarcation of Thirty-Eighth Parallel and the origin of the Korean division.[1]

Secondly, the introspection of the sterile U.S.-U.S.S.R Commission, the failure of the U.S. to ally with the moderate groups in the south, the divergent interests among different parties inside the peninsula can edify us about the obstacles that we face today if we try to unify the peninsula. Due to its geopolitics, fluctuations inside the Korean Peninsula consequentially

---

* Fang Xiuyu, Professor, Center for Korean Studies, Fudan University, China. Li Li, Doctorate Student, School of International Relations and Public Affairs, Fudan University, China.

touch the nerves of its coterminous and non-coterminous neighbors. Thus, this essay tries to state how powerful neighbors view the reunification of the Korean Peninsula and explain what internal premises we need to reunify the peninsula.

Last but not least, the Korean foreign policy of Truman's first term was retained during his second term although many high officials in the State Department went through a change during this time. Thus, the study of the U.S. Korean policy from 1945 to 1948 is beneficial for us to comprehend the reason why the U.S. responded so immediately to the outbreak of the Korean War in complete disregard of the "perimeter of defense" speech addressed by the Secretary of State Acheson.

Thus, this essay on the one hand tries to expatiate on Korean policy during Truman's first term; on the other hand, it tries to explain the above three questions according to the tension between the national interests and the national power of the U.S.

Korean Policy of the U.S. from September 1945 to September 1947

Today, experts on international relations generalize Truman's foreign policy to two categories: one opinion claims that Truman's foreign policy steps on Roosevelt administration's foot clumsily;[2] the other opinion claims that he instantly gave up Roosevelt's foreign policy when he was inaugurated.[3] The following part tries to explain the relationship between them and how this relationship affected Truman's Korean policy after the Second World War.

Shortly before and after the end of World War II, issues entangling the U.S. and the Soviet Union (U.S.S.R) centered on four aspects: the Polish issue, the Eastern Europe issue, the Far East issue, and the UN issue. As far as the Far East and the Korean Peninsula issues were concerned, Roosevelt concluded Yalta Agreement with Stalin to win Stalin's commitment to participate in the Pacific War. Roosevelt and Stalin also reconfirmed the implementation of the international trusteeship policy of Korean Peninsula after the war, and allowed it to be independent in due time. The U.S. was concerned about Far East and UN issues since they were most relevant to the anti-Japanese war and the construction of the world order after the war.[4] The Yalta Agreement had encountered much criticism in the domestic America for that it made too many unnecessary concessions to the U.S.S.R. However, some scholars reached the conclusion that the limited options of the U.S. led to that agreement conclusion after they methodically examined the agreement. We will understand these limitations after we retrace the international environment at that time. Firstly, when the Yalta Conference was convened, the U.S. badly needed the U.S.S.R both on the European theater and on the Pacific theater.[5] As a famous American scholar says, the continuation of the war is the key reason why diplomatic and military leaders fail to recognize the complete change of the power balance caused by World War II. The U.S.S.R is still an ally, and cooperation with it is a necessary guarantee to rival Germany and Japan. Common enemies are a paste which solidifies "the great allies". Until the enemies are defeated, Washington, London and Moscow will support cooperation rather than rivalry among their relations. Too much consideration about antagonism after the war will impair the prospect of waging war. Therefore, no country had already prepared for allowing the long-term geopolitical reality to override the need of immediate winning. Secondly, the fact that Russian military force stationed in Eastern Europe was irreversible. Just as Stalin said to the Yougoslavian Communist Party delegate in April 1945, "this war is different from bygones. Whoever occupies a territory can impose his social institutions there. He can impose his own social institutions as far as his army can reach". Then, it had some relations with Roosevelt's personal belief. He agreed with the dominant opinion that the aggression in the East Europe by the U.S.S.R originated with insecurities it suffered. These insecurities were rooted in the fact that East Europe and Poland are natural accesses to invade Russia. Thus, the U.S.S.R made some behaviors aiming at defense rather than aggression. If the U.S. counterbalanced U.S.S.R overtly, the consequence could be a self-prophecy. Lastly, Roosevelt hoped to fuse realistic and idealistic political considerations together after the war to establish a collective security organization which centered on four powers. This organization was titular without the U.S.S.R.

Thus Truman faced a dilemma at the beginning of his term. This dilemma reflected an ambiguous perception held by Truman toward U.S.S.R. Conversely, this perception resided in that although the two states still had common interests, the divergence of interests was enlarging. On the one hand, Truman administration tried to re-elucidate the Yalta Agreement into what incorporated Poland, German, East Europe and Far East issues according to the varied international situations and the U.S. national interests. As far as the Far East regions were concerned, Harriman and high officials in the State Department and War Department adhered to nullify Yalta Agreement and re-negotiate with the U.S.S.R to limit its interests in these regions. On the other hand, Stimson, Marshall and some other officials in the Army supported continuing cooperation with U.S.S.R. The reasons they gave were that not only did the U.S. need the U.S.S.R's cooperation in establishing the UN, but also the abolishment of agreement would expand rather than contain the appetite of U.S.S.R. Furthermore, the time to finish Pacific theater war was unspecified. According to "Olympic", a plan set down by the U.S. government to combat Japan, the U.S. might launch an attack against the Japanese mainland in November 1945 as early as possible.[6] Before defeating Japan, the U.S. needed Russia's cooperation in Far East to reduce the U.S.' casualties and hasten the completion of the war.[7] This dilemma led to volatile attitude of President Truman to Russia. On April 23, 1945, Truman met with Molotov, the foreign minister of the U.S.S.R, and reprehended the U.S.S.R for the violation of Yalta Agreement. When Molotov tried to defend the Russian activities, Truman interrupted him and said that if they wanted to continue the cooperation, they should observe the agreement.[8] However, in May, Truman sent the Hopkins delegation to Russia to confer with Stalin on many issues. Truman also thought highly of their good job. Simultaneously, Truman declined the suggestion made by Churchill and his advisers to disavow Russia's occupations in middle Europe and Northeast Asia in previous agreements.[9] Truman even pointed out that "I diverge with Chancellor Churchill as much as Stalin".[10] But Truman knew very little about the U.S. foreign policies before he assumed office. Thus he decided to continue Roosevelt's foreign policy at the beginning which manifested on three aspects: retaining cabinet members, demanding unconditional surrender of Japan and observing to Yalta Agreement.[11]

The successful detonation of the atom bomb made the dilemma disappear. Since successful detonation took place just one day before Potsdam Conference, several things indicated that the U.S. had inversed its attitude toward the U.S.S.R, and the U.S. tried to haggle with Russia with atom bomb. From the beginning to the end of the conference, five issues intertwined together. During this last meeting of three magnets, however, conflicts increased rather than being resolved. The usual diplomatic flexibility disappeared while the arguments and strife intensified. Obdurate attitude and pomposity dominated the conference.[12] As far as the U.S. Korean policy concerned, the successful detonation of atom bomb resolved the domestic quagmire caused by Russian participation in Pacific War, and even made Joint Chiefs of Staff hope to avoid involvement of the U.S.S.R into Pacific War.[13] Thus at the moment, The U.S. Korean policy aimed at separate occupations to prevent Russia from imposing threats on China and Japan. Just as a scholar says, Washington hoped that the atom bomb could force Japan to surrender before the U.S.S.R intervened. The trust between two countries was disappearing due to their difference on East Europe issue. Thus, Truman began to consider precluding the U.S.S.R from occupying Korean Peninsula.[14]

The strategy of the U.S. would succeed on the premise that it could conquer Japan before Russia intervened. Only this could the U.S. achieve its strategic plan to preclude Russia from Asia. Since the U.S.S.R also viewed the Northeastern Asia as one of its core interests, the U.S. did the following things to achieve its plan. Firstly, Truman sent a telegram to Chiang Kai-shek after he heard the report by Marshall and Stimson about Russian intervention into Pacific War. Truman told him to consider his acceptable limits and the U.S. national interests when he negotiated with Stalin.[15] The reason Truman did this was that Stalin once told him that if he could not conclude an agreement with China in terms of Yalta Agreement, he would not participate in anti-Japanese war.[16] Therefore, Truman hoped to delay China-U.S.S.R negotiation to prolong Russian intervention into war. Secondly, in Potsdam conference, Truman and the U.S. government decided to occupy Japan completely to avoid the repeat of German situation in Japan. In order to get rid of the threats to Japan from Russia, the U.S. government also tried to occupy Korean Peninsula and Chinese littoral areas, including Taiwan. Therefore, during the Potsdam conference the U.S. and Britain refused to discuss international trusteeship and conclude agreements with Russia. This was remarkably reflected when the Russian delegation proposed a proposal about international trusteeship of Italian colonies, the U.S. and Britain did not want to further explore this issue. Lastly, in the Potsdam proclamation, which demanded Japanese unconditional surrender issued by the U.S. after the conference, he skirted Russia, concealed Yalta Agreement, and centered on the U.S., Britain and China to prompt the surrender of Japan.[17] At the moment, Russia still had diplomatic activities with Japan, as Russia waited desperately for an excuse to participate in the war. This excuse was the U.S. invitation. However, Truman disappointed Stalin.[18] We can conclude from this that the successful detonation of atom bomb helped the U.S. resolve the problem of limited power and hold a talisman to pulverize Japan. This directly turned his attitude to Russia. Since the Russia informed the U.S. that it would participate in the pacific war at the middle or late time of August, the U.S. determined to drop an atom bomb earlier in the August to finish the war.[19]

But Japan declined to surrender unconditionally after the drop of the first atom bomb, since on the one hand the U.S. demand of unconditional surrender cannot be tolerated by war parties in Japanese cabinet.[20] On the other hand, Japan hoped to finish the war conditionally via mediation by the U.S.S.R.

Russia declared war to Japan shortly after the drop of the first atom bomb since it wanted to expand its interests in Asia and brush off the mortification it suffered after the defeat in 1904 war. This behavior was unexpected and unwanted by the U.S. Russia put forward on a large scale in the Korean Peninsula, which provided it a good opportunity to build influential areas there, since no concrete agreements existed between Russia and the U.S. on Korean Peninsula and the U.S. soldiers needed time to enter the peninsula.[21] The U.S. government responded with two actions. On the one hand, they modified previous unconditional surrender demand toward Japan. Tough groups represented by Byrnes, Secretary of State, moderated their attitude, and agreed with the modified plan proposed by Stimson. At the same time, they warned Japan of dropping the atom bomb again. However, the U.S. did not clarify the arrangement of Japanese emperor, which made Japanese military departments stick to fight and not respond instantly to the modified plan. Russia took advantage of this time vacuum to forward into Northeastern China and Korean Peninsula. Under this circumstance, options faced by Truman were absolutely limited: the total occupation of Korean Peninsula by Russia or joint occupation. Thus, the other action made by Truman was issuing the "General Order 1", which suggested the Thirty-Eighth Parallel as demarcation line of joint occupation. This line drew two-thirds Korea and its capital into the U.S. occupation territory. "General Order 1" signified a turn of the U.S. Korean policy. Truman supported international trusteeship of Korean Peninsula at first, and then he substituted this policy with separate occupation in to root out Russian expansion in Asia. Lastly, the U.S. had no choices but to temporarily divide the peninsula due to Russia's great military success in this area. Unexpectedly, although Russia had a military advantage in Korean Peninsula, it accepted the arrangement offered by the U.S. Stalin also proffered amendments: Japan transferred the whole Kuril Islands and the northern Hokkaido to the Soviet army.[22]

Concluded from the above, there are two adjustments from Truman to Roosevelt Korean Peninsula policy shortly before and after the victory of World War II. The direct inducements of modifications were successful detonation of atom bomb and Japan's surrender. Successful detonation of atom bomb cracked down a policy dilemma which lingered on Truman's mind when he stepped into White House, that is, whether to urge Russia to participate in the pacific war. Russia's involvement in war with Japan and the latter's rapid surrender made the U.S. government re-pick the international trusteeship policy of Korean Peninsula, since the balance in Northeast Asia leaned over the U.S.S.R now.[23] The underlying reasons of these two turns were structural, that is, Russia and the U.S. had reoriented their national interests and security after the change of international circumstance. As far as the U.S. Korean policy concerned during this time, Truman administration viewed Korean Peninsula as an important place to achieve national interests and preclude Russian presence in Northeast Asia. Thus, the U.S. tried to occupy it separately. However, the fact that Russia was superior in military power than the U.S. on the Korean Peninsula made him withdraw to an inferior choice; that is, supporting joint occupation alongside Thirty-Eighth Parallel. Although this policy was beneficial to the U.S. national interest and indicated high importance he attached to Korean Peninsula, it laid a divisive fuse on Korean Peninsula.

The Korea Policy of the U.S. from September 1945 to September 1947

Truman's Korea policy underwent two changes in the large context of the U.S.-U.S.S.R relationship during 1945. The direct consequence of these changes was that a unified country and nation had been divided by an artificial line. As far as the geographical quality of this line itself was concerned, it did not represent climatic, natural or cultural differences between the south and the north. However, more than thirty years of colonization by Japan had a great effect on Korea. This effect was reflected in the political, economic and social divergence between the two parts of the peninsula.[24] Since the Korean Peninsula already had political, economic and social differences, the Thirty-Eighth Parallel would deepen this division if it was not erased quickly.[25] To eliminate this line and establish a regime beneficial to its own national interests, the U.S. took many measures.

In September 1945, the U.S. officially occupied the south of Korea and established a military government there. General Hodge was the leader of the military government. In contrast to the active up-to-down policies implemented by Russia in northern Korea, the policies took by the U.S. military government in southern Korea were passive. These passive policies were rooted in the fact that, on the one hand, the Capital Seoul lay within the U.S.' occupation territory. Different parties that were active in the capital had diverse interests, thus making it difficult for the U.S. to implement policies in practice. On the other hand, the U.S. Korean policy had no concrete orientations. On August 12, General Hodge received an order to occupy the southern Korea instead of concrete directives about dealing with Korean political and economic problems.[26] He even said that, had he been a civil official, he would not care about this obligation at all.[27] The U.S. passive policies in southern Korea were mainly reflected on the following aspects: keeping the Japanese colonized bureaucracy, dealing with Korean turncoats moderately, changing the farms owned by Japanese partially, without changing old agrarian institutions, without dealing with Japanese properties or solving inflation.[28]

Although the military government did not take any impressive policies during this time, the U.S. government did not vacillate on its decision to put the Korean Peninsula under trusteeship. We can cite two events to substantiate this point. One was a speech made by John Vincent, the director of the Office of Far East Affairs, to the Foreign Policy Association of Washington. His speech revealed that the SWNCC made a decision to put the Korean Peninsula under trusteeship. The other were documents 79/1, 79/2, 101/4 brought out by SWNCC. These documents dictated that the current military occupation should be replaced with the trusteeship policy as early as possible, and the concerned countries should negotiate about the trusteeship policy.[29]

On December 16, 1945, a conference was held in the Moscow which gathered foreign ministers of the U.S., Britain, and the U.S.S.R. The U.S. and the U.S.S.R explicated their own international trusteeship proposal for the Korean Peninsula, which had a common point (i.e., establishing a regime beneficial to itself in the peninsula). The difference was the procedure of trusteeship. The U.S. supported the establishment of a UAK (Unified Administration for Korea) under control of the U.S. and Russian military leaders to prepare for four countries' trusteeship. The duration of trusteeship was five years. If necessary, it could be prolonged to another five years. The U.S. also proposed to establish an executive commission made up of a commissioner and four bureaucrats from the U.S., Russia, China and Britain respectively. On the one hand, the U.S. plan precluded the native Korean force from participating in the UAK at the beginning. Thus, it eliminated the influence of the Korean left-wing force. On the other hand, it insisted that the U.S. should assume the position of commissioner, which would guarantee that the U.S. and its supporters would dominate the executive commission.[30] The U.S.S.R adhered to establishing a Joint U.S.-Soviet Commission. This commission would negotiate with the Korean native democratic and social organizations to assist the latter in founding a temporary Korean government. However, the decision of trusteeship should be made by four countries and the duration of trusteeship could last some time no more than five years. At the conclusion of the conference, they signed a protocol about the Korean international trusteeship policy. The protocol was that the four countries would decide how to establish an autonomous country in the Korean Peninsula in the subsequent five years.[31] This protocol had evoked a hue and cry in Korea. The right-wing parties unified and opposed the international trusteeship despite their different considerations. They demanded the instant Korea independence.[32] The Korean left-wing parties changed their attitude from moderate opposition to support.[33] Korean domestic opposition and other differences, such as the Iranian problem, the East Europe issue and the ideological difference between the U.S. and Russia overshadowed the implementation of the U.S. Korean plan from the beginning. Despite this, the U.S. did make efforts on the U.S.-U.S.S.R relationship and on the southern Korea to implement its international trusteeship policy in Korea.

Firstly, as far as the U.S.-U.S.S.R relationship was concerned, the U.S. and the U.S.S.R had convoked preparatory meetings and two formal meetings of the Joint Commission, endeavoring to put international trusteeship policy into practice. From January 16 to February 16, 1946, the U.S. and the U.S.S.R convened preparatory meetings for fifteen times. However, all were unfruitful. What these preparatory meetings really did was to make the different national interests between these two countries more obvious. The preparatory meetings concluded with a short proclamation. It dictated to set up a ten representatives' commission where the members from the U.S. and the U.S.S.R were evenly distributed. After the preparatory meetings, the Joint Commission would set up a permanent chair in the Seoul in a month.[34] On March 20, 1946 the first formal meeting of Joint Commission was convened. This meeting lasted until May 6. In this meeting, two countries had a common aim, which was establishing a beneficial regime to itself in the Korean Peninsula. Thus, what they did in the meeting was discussing how to achieve this aim. The first step was to build a temporary government in Korean Peninsula. Thereby, international trusteeship policy could be implemented via this government. However, the U.S. and the U.S.S.R differed in the sequence of temporary government and unification. The U.S. claimed to unify the Korean economy and society at first, and then set up temporary government. Russia held a complete opposite stand. Furthermore, General Hodge tried to build a Consultative Union and took in RDC (Representative Democratic Council) to confer with northern Korean parties. Russia opposed to involve Korean native parties in Consultative Union.[35] Because of their intransigence, Joint Commission issued joint communique on April 15, which stipulated that the Joint Commission would consult with Korean democratic parties and social organizations. These organizations, however, should have democratic aims and means, and they should observe to resolutions made by Moscow conference, including the determination to establish temporary Korean government.[36]

The second formal Joint Commission from May 21 to August 21, 1947 still could not alleviate their divergences. They differed and could not reach a compromise on the issue that which party or organization would be chosen as the main partner to confer with. So this conference was also abortive, which engendered a widespread impact. Since U.S. failed to unify Korea peninsula through negotiation with U.S.S.R, it became cogitate to establish a permanent government in Korean Peninsula instead of making a temporary government permanent.[37]

From June 1946 to January 1947, the U.S. also made an effort to ally with moderate parties in the southern Korea to go a "middle way". After the abortion of the first Joint Commission formal meeting, the southern Korean parties diverted their attention from international trusteeship to the debate relevant to establish a temporary government. The debate was headed by Syngman Rhee and Kim Koo respectively. The former had intense anti-communism emotion while the latter supported pan-nationalism. Since parties and organizations in the southern Korea were so divisive and could not be reconciled, the U.S. determined to take dual measures, that is, dividing communist parties while not supporting extreme right parties. The military government decided to support moderate parties to solidify its position in the subsequent Joint Commission.[38] At the same time, the moderate party led by Kim Kyu-sik in the south cooperated with the moderate left party led by Yo Un-hung in the north to launch a United Front Unification Movement. They tried to unify the whole nation through international trusteeship policy backed by the U.S. and Russia. In May and June 1946, Kim Kyu-sik and Yo Un-hung held colloquium respectively. General Hodge attended the colloquium in June to signal his support. He hoped to unify with them and precluded Syngman Rhee and Kim Koo parties. But after the extreme opposition by the right party, Kim Koo was endowed with some duties. However, he declined to participate in the United Front Unification Movement.[39] From October 17 to October 22, 1946, the military government organized the election of the South Korea Interim Legislative Assembly. Due to different parties' manipulation, low public support and absence of democratic procedure, the election did not have true representation. Therefore, the military government's plan to ally with moderate parties via this election failed. The failure of this alliance can be attributed to two aspects: on the one hand, the U.S. disregarded political atmosphere in the southern peninsula, trying to transplant the U.S.' democracy directly into the south while it could not tolerate short-term political chaos at the same time. On the other hand, although South Korea's native parties were willing to unify together to enhance their status, they diverged on issues such as trusteeship, agrarian reform, dealing with Japanese owned possessions, and did not want to abandon their parochial interests to unify the whole nation.[40]

We can conclude from the discussion above that from September 1945 when the U.S. began its formal occupation in the southern Korea to September 1947 when it referred the Korean issue to the UN, its domestic dominant Korea policy was to establish a unified regime beneficial to him via international trusteeship of the peninsula. To achieve this aim, it held Joint Commission conference with the U.S.S.R to discuss concrete trusteeship policy on the one hand. On the other hand, it tried to ally with moderate parties in the south who supported international trusteeship policy. Since both the U.S. and the U.S.S.R wanted to set up a regime beneficial to themselves, and they could not reconcile on the aim, and since Korean internal parties and organizations preferred to their own parochial interests rather than national unification, however, situations inside and outside the Korean Peninsula began to polarize, which predisposed the unsuccessful fate of the U.S. international trusteeship policy. Korean Peninsula lost an opportunity of unification which edifies us about obstacles to unify peninsula today. Due to its geopolitical position, fluctuations inside Korean Peninsula must touch the nerves of its neighbors. Thus, its neighbors would endeavor to influence internal changes according to their national interests. They would cooperate together to promote Korean unification only on the premise that they can compromise with each other on this issue. Besides, both South Korea and North Korea should replace their state interests with national interests. However, it is very difficult to realize these preconditions at this moment since the international politics are determined by interests and power of states.

The Korea Policy of the U.S. from September 1947 to the End of 1948

On August 1947, after the failure of the U.S.-U.S.S.R Joint Commission, the U.S. made a suggestion to the U.S.S.R which was discussing alternative way of the Moscow Agreement, that is, to elect a legislative administrative institution under the surveillance of the UN. The U.S.S.R, however, refused this suggestion. At the same time, some new factors inside and outside the U.S. prompted it to develop a new Korean policy, which was to set up a government in the southern Korea and transfer the administration slowly to native party. As a matter of fact, there was a voice inside the U.S. government, which supported building an independent regime in the southern peninsula since December 1945. This voice rooted in the hopelessness to the U.S.-U.S.S.R cooperation and was represented by Joint Chiefs of Staff. The cooperation involved East Europe, Iran and Poland, Far East issues. In contrast with voice of supporting cooperation, Joint Chiefs of Staff began to consider arming militia in the south and building an independent national army. Although this voice had not been elevated to a national policy, it implied that the U.S. retained an option which was to implement unilateralism in the southern Korea if it could not establish a unified, independent regime beneficial to it via the cooperation with Russia and international trusteeship. The failure to implement international trusteeship through cooperation with Russia plus other reasons provided an opportunity to elevate this voice to national policy. There are also other reasons.

First of all, the U.S. national interests stipulated that it would not abandon the Korean Peninsula, at least the part south of Thirty-Eighth Parallel. These interests were: firstly, from the perspective of the global situation, the deterioration of the U.S.-U.S.S.R relations made Roosevelt's envision, that is, to deal with global problem and guarantee the global peace via cooperation among big powers impractical. Two countries differed in many issues and the "iron curtain" of the Cold War dropped down. As the Truman Doctrine came up on March 1947, the U.S. reoriented its aim of foreign policy as containment of communism. Just as the Truman Doctrine claimed, that is, not only did the U.S. aid Greek and Turkey, it would also support and help all countries in the world who chose free institutions to fight authoritative force. Thus, in consideration of the U.S. credulity, the U.S. would support free institutions worldwide.

Secondly, as far as the geopolitics of Northeastern Asia concerned, on the one hand, since Korean Peninsula could be Japanese gangway to invade China in history, it could also be an access for the U.S.S.R to threaten Japan and Southeastern Asian countries. On the other hand, the southern Korea's economics tied closely with Japan due to Japanese colonized polices. The Japanese domestic produce relied heavily on the export from the South Korea. Thus, the U.S. attempt to revitalize Japanese economy depended on the opportune Korean policy.

Thirdly, the dominant parties and organizations inside peninsula opposed international trusteeship and demanded autonomy and independence. The north peninsula bounded itself with Russia. Consequently, if the U.S. wanted a foothold in the peninsula, it must take the south political atmosphere and the south internal parties' political emotions into consideration.

Fourthly, from the perspective of the domestic the politics, there was a fierce polemic between the State of Department and the War Department. The former worried about the political repercussion caused by the U.S. evacuation and thought Korean Peninsula had a relation to the U.S. important national interests. Thus, the U.S. should guard the peninsula. However, the War Department, which was actually in charge of the Korean affairs, advised to retreat from the peninsula since the military government there was opposed by extremely right parties and faced exasperate Korean economy. An example was in January 1947, General Hodge encouraged Syngman Rhee to go to the U.S. to persuade the latter's support to Korean independence. General Hodge even taught him how to fulfill this aim.[41]

In February 1947, two departments reconciled that they would guard and assist the southern Korea and work actively to get Russia's support on this issue while they would make an alternative plan in case Russia did not cooperate. In April 1947, they minimized their difference further and agreed to negotiate with Russia. At the same time, they launched an election of Interim Legislative Assembly and transferred administration to local temporary government. If negotiation between two countries failed, they would submit this issue to UN or help to build an independent regime in the southern peninsula. Whatever, the U.S. soldiers would evacuate from the peninsula in the following three years, and the tasks of relief and reconstruction of Korea would be delivered to the State of Department at that time.[42]

Since the U.S. global responsibilities grew up, and there were political chaos and inflation in the southern peninsula, and the Congress curtailed fiscal appropriation of government, and the pubic in the U.S. were indifferent to the Korean Peninsula, the U.S. decided to support UN to tackle Korean problems on the premise of not giving it up.

This could draw a huge international attention. If Russia did not cooperate, the U.S. could press it with the help of international society. The U.S. had already appealed to this method successfully in solving Iranian problem.[43] In September 1947, the U.S. delivered Korean issue to the UN. In November 1947, the UN adopted a resolution which determined the process of Korean unification. In January 1948, United Nation's Temporary Commission on Korea (UNTCOK) arrived in Seoul and tried to accomplish and surveillance the election throughout the whole peninsula. However, Russia did not allow them to enter the northern Korea. UNTCOK did not organize the separate election in the southern peninsula instantly. However, the U.S. peddled its idea to United Nation's Temporary Commission on Korea since it wanted to realize its own purpose which was to invigilate election in the southern Korea separately and establish an independent government. Its idea was accepted by the commission. In May 1948, UNTCOK organized an election in the southern Korea despite the legitimacy's problem and constant roar in the southern Korea. On August 15, 1948, the Republic of Korea was founded.

We can conclude from the discussion above that the submission of Korean issue to the UN by the U.S. signified its change of Korea policy, that is, from supporting the establishment of a unified, beneficial regime through cooperation with Russia to implement international trusteeship to set up a separate regime in the southern Korea. Although this change took place after the failure of the second Joint Commission formal meeting, there was always a voice inside the U.S. government supporting this change. This voice was formally elevated to the national policy when the cooperation policy failed. Of course, its elevation to the dominant policy of the U.S. after August 1947 was due to that it could satisfy the needs of the U.S. national interests. In addition, it also considered the difference between the global responsibility and the national power of the U.S. Thus, the U.S. support of separate election in the southern Korea and Syngman Rhee government did not mean its disregard of the peninsula and its desperation of evacuation. The U.S. action was determined by its strategic consideration. On the one hand, it was imprudent to garrison 45 thousand people there when Europe faced heavy shortage of human resources and the U.S.' onus was increasing.[44] In September 1947, the SWCC pointed out, due to the heavy shortage of armies, two divisions which currently garrisoned south of Korean Peninsula could be used in other places.[45] On the other hand, the combination of UN, establishment of ROK and the evacuation of the U.S. soldiers' could cool down the roaring of forwarding northward speech of Syngman Rhee and corresponded with the U.S. war plan. Just as Acheson said in his "perimeter of defense" speech, the U.S. would take actions under the authority of UN when the emergency happened in the Korean Peninsula. Furthermore, the U.S. would increase its relief and aid to the southern Korea to help it defend itself before its evacuation according to the NSC68.[46] Therefore, the delivery of the Korean issue to the UN and the withdrawal of the U.S. to the backdrop did not signify its underestimation of the Korea Peninsula's strategic significance. This policy just illuminated that when national power is not enough to fulfill its complete national interests, the U.S. will restrict its national interests correspondingly. However, when national power increases, the definition of national interests and its desire to fulfill them will expand accordingly. The U.S. evacuation from Korean Peninsula before the Korean War does not mean it forsake ROK. It is the consequence of the struggle between the U.S. national interests and national power. After the outbreak of the Korean War, the highly orientation of Korean Peninsula reoccupied the U.S. Korea policy and propelled it to make an instant response.

Conclusion

Just as Hans J. Morgenthau said, national policies of a state are dependent on its national interests and national power defines national interests.[47] When the national power is insufficient for fulfilling all national interests, the state will always reorder national interests, thus reshaping the agenda of foreign policies. The foreign policies, therefore, are often determined by the tension between the national interests and the national power.

The Korean policy of the U.S. from 1945 to 1948 reflected that tension strikingly. Shortly before and after the end of World War II, Truman confronted a policy dilemma on the Far East issue. On the one hand, he tried to cooperate with the U.S.S.R to finish the Pacific War, which would reduce the causalities for the U.S. On the other hand, he tried to occupy Japan separately without the U.S.S.R. The successful detonation of atom bomb cracked this hard nut, and made Truman have the chip to abandon Roosevelt's Korea policy. As the U.S.S.R declared war with Japan, and Japan surrendered very quickly, however, Truman had to re-pick joint occupation and international trusteeship policy. The division of Thirty-Eighth Parallel corresponded with the national interests of the U.S. while aided the ground of Korean separation.

The U.S. failed to establish a unified regime beneficial to himself in the Korean Peninsula via international trusteeship policy. The reasons for this failure were the divergent national interests between the U.S. and the U.S.S.R, and the opposition from Korean internal parties and people. This failure enabled us to think about the problems of the current Korean Peninsula, although it deprived Korean Peninsula of a unification opportunity. The future unification of the Korean Peninsula is in desperate need of the compromise of neighboring countries. The unification also depends on that the DPRK and the ROK put national interests, instead of state interests, in priority.

After the failure of international trusteeship policy, the U.S. adjusted its Korean policy, supported separate election south of Thirty-Eighth Parallel and the establishment of ROK. However, the U.S.' withdrawal to the backdrop did not mean underestimation of Korea's strategic importance. Thus, when the Korean War broke out, the U.S. made an immediate response.

Notes

1. Professor Shen Zhihua's paper the Origin and the Historical Effect of Thirty-Eighth parallel analyses why America chose Thirty-Eighth Parallel. This

paper focuses on why America makes a decision to demarcate Korean Peninsula according to its adjust of Korea policy which depends on American national interests. As to how Thirty-Eighth Parallel became the demarcation line, please see Shen Zhihua, "The Origin and the Historical Effect of Thirty-Eight Parallel," *Jianghuai Culture History*, 2010, No. 2, pp. 156–165.

2. See Roger Buckley, *The U.S. in the Asia-Pacific since 1945*, Cambridge: Cambridge University Press, 2002, p. 42.
3. James I. Matray, "Captive of the Cold War: The Decision to Divide Korea at the 38th Parallel," *Pacific Historical Review*, Vol. 50, No. 2 (May, 1981), pp. 145–168.
4. Robin Edmonds, "Yalta and Potsdam: Forty Years Afterwards," *International Affairs* (Royal Institute of International Affairs 1944–), Vol. 62, No. 2.
5. Ibid.
6. D.M. Giangreco, "Casualty Projections for the U.S. Invasions of Japan, 1945–1946: Planning and Policy," *The Journal of Military History*, Vol. 61, No. 3 (Jul., 1997), pp. 521–558.
7. Hasegawa, Tsuyoshi, *Racing the Enemy: Stalin, Truman, and the Surrender of Japan*, the Belknap Press of Harvard University Press, Cambridge, Massachusetts, London, England, 2005, pp. 51–53.
8. Harry S. Truman, *Memoirs: Year of Decisions, 1945*, Doubleday, 1956, pp. 96–99.
9. John Lewis Gaddis, *The United States and the Origins of the Cold War, 1941–1947*, Columbia University Press, 1972, pp. 206–211.
10. Robert H. Ferrell, *Off the Record: The Private Papers of Harry S. Truman*, New York: Harper & Row, 1980, pp. 31–32.
11. Tsuyoshi Hasegawa, *Racing the Enemy: Stalin, Truman, and the Surrender of Japan*, pp. 49–51.
12. Charles Rice, *Meeting in Potsdam*, Shanghai: SDX Joint Publishing Company, 1978, p. 2.
13. Tsuyoshi Hasegawa, *Racing the Enemy: Stalin, Truman, and the Surrender of Japan*, pp. 145–154.
14. William Whitney Stueck, Jr., *The Road to Confrontation-American Policy toward China and Korea, 1947–1950*, The University of North Carolina Press Chapel Hill, 1981, p. 21.
15. Ibid.
16. Tsuyoshi Hasegawa, *Racing the Enemy: Stalin, Truman, and the Surrender of Japan*, pp. 174–176.
17. Ibid., p. 137.

18. Harry S. Truman, *Off the Record: The Private Papers of Harry S. Truman*, Columbia: University of Missouri Press, 1997, p. 53.
19. Tsuyoshi Hasegawa, *Racing the Enemy: Stalin, Truman, and the Surrender of Japan*, pp. 183–186.
20. William Whitney Stueck, Jr., *The Road to Confrontation-American Policy toward China and Korea, 1947–1950*, p. 21.
21. Ibid.
22. Shen Zhihua, "The Origin and the Historical Effect of Thirty-Eight Parallell" pp. 156–165.
23. John Lewis Gaddis, *The Long Peace: Inquiries into the History of the Cold War*, translated by Pan Yaling, Shanghai People's Publishing House, 2011, p. 62.
24. Hyung-Kook Kim, *The Division of Korea and the Alliance Making Process-Internationalization of Internal Conflict and Internalization of International Struggle, 1945–1948*, University Press of America, Inc. Lanham, New York, London 1995, pp. 91–119.
25. Shannon McCune, "The Thirty-Eighth Parallel in Korea," *World Politics*, Vol. 1, No. 2 (Jan., 1949), pp. 223–232.
26. U.S. Army, Brief History of the 24th Corps, National Archives, p. 4.
27. Mark Clark, *From the Danube to Yalu*, New York: Harper and Brothers, 1954, p. 52.
28. Hyung-Kook Kim, *The Division of Korea and the Alliance Making Process: Internationalization of Internal Conflict and Internalization of International Struggle, 1945–1948*, University Press of America, Inc. Lanham, New York, London, 1995, pp. 143–153.
29. U.S. State Department, FRUS, 1945, Vol., pp. 1121–1122, transferred from Hyung-Kook Kim, *The Division of Korea and the Alliance Making Process: Internationalization of Internal Conflict and Internalization of International Struggle, 1945–1948*, University Press of America, Inc. Lanham, New York. London, 1995, pp. 143–153.
30. Hyung-Kook Kim, *The Division of Korea and the Alliance Making Process-Internationalization of Internal Conflict and Internalization of International Struggle, 1945–1948*, p. 174.
31. Roger Buckley, *The United States in the Asia-Pacific since 1945*, p. 34.
32. Hyung-Kook Kim, *The Division of Korea and the Alliance Making Process-Internationalization of Internal Conflict and Internalization of International Struggle, 1945–1948*, p. 176.
33. Ibid., p. 175.

34. FRUS, 1946, Vol. 8. A telegram sent by Lieutenant General John R. Hodge to the War Department, pp. 611–612.
35. RDC: Representative Democratic Council.
36. Hyung-Kook Kim, *The Division of Korea and the Alliance Making Process-Internationalization of Internal Conflict and Internalization of International Struggle, 1945–1948*, p. 182.
37. Ibid., p. 209.
38. Military government supported mild parities because they support international trusteeship policy.
39. Hyung-Kook Kim, *The Division of Korea and the Alliance Making Process-Internationalization of Internal Conflict and Internalization of International Struggle, 1945–1948*, pp. 195–196.
40. Ibid., pp. 195–200.
41. William Whitney Stueck, Jr., *The Road to Confrontation-American Policy toward China and Korea, 1947–1950*, p. 75.
42. Ibid., pp. 79–81.
43. Ibid., p. 88.
44. John Lewis Gaddis, *The Long Peace: Inquiries into the History of the Cold War*, p. 114.
45. Forrestal to Marshall, September 29, 1947, *FR: 1947*, VI, p. 818.
46. William Whitney Stueck, Jr., *The Road to Confrontation-American Policy toward China and Korea, 1947–1950*, p. 99.
47. Morgenthau, Hans J, *Politics among Nations: The Struggle for Power and Peace*, Peking University Press, 2007, pp. 47–49.

Chapter 14

China's Proposing Behavior in Global Governance: The Cases of the WTO Doha Round Negotiation and G-20 Process

*Liu Hongsong**

Introduction

As "the collective management of common problems at the international level",[1] global governance aims to address global issues as well as buttress and shape global order. Due to the absence of central authority in the international system, states play a central role in global governance, though non-state actors are indispensible participants. By creating and acting through various international institutions, states manage global issues beyond borders collectively, thus constructing and maintaining global order. As such, the relationship between states and international institutions and states' behavior in international institutions are crucial aspects of their engagement in global governance. Accordingly, the key aspect of China's participation in global governance intertwined with the evolution of its involvement in international institutions lies in its interaction with international institutions.

---

*Liu Hongsong, School of International Relations and Public Affairs, Shanghai International Studies University, China.

Since China recovered its legitimate seat in the United Nations in 1971, it has been gradually integrated into the international institutional order and become a systematically important actor on nearly all issues of global governance. Within this context, China's participation in global governance has entered into the research agenda of International Relations and Chinese Foreign Policy. With regard to the theme of China's participation in global governance, the existing studies primarily focus on (1) China's participation in international institutions, (2) China's compliance with the rules of international institutions, and (3) the impact of international institutions on China's domestic politics and foreign policy. Admittedly, taking the relationship between China and international institutions as the research focus fits with the fact that international institutions play key role in global governance. However, the aforementioned three questions do not cover all the aspects of China's engagement in global governance.

Apart from being integrated into the international institutional order and shaped by international institutions, China's shaping efforts in international institutions are also essential part of China's participation in global governance. This chapter will explore the aspect of China's participation in global governance which has not been paid sufficient attention to, and examine China's proposing behavior in global governance and its main features by clarifying China's reform proposals in the WTO Doha Round negotiation and the G-20 process.

The rest of this chapter proceeds as follows. The second section reviews the state of research on the theme of China's participation in global governance and illustrates the justification for choosing the cases of the WTO Doha Round negotiation and G-20 process. The third and fourth sections clarify China's reform proposals in the WTO Doha Round negotiation and the G-20 process respectively. The fifth section discusses the main features of China's proposing behavior in global governance based on the two cases. The conclusion summarizes the research findings.

State of Research: China and Global Governance

Along with the emergence of various global issues and the transformation of China's political economy and foreign policy, China's participation in global governance is increasing both in extensive and intensive way.

Owing to the need to participate in global governance, China's coping with its foreign relations is increasingly conducted through the channel of international institutions. In light of this, the relationship between China and international institutions has been given close attention to by Chinese and international academia.

In international academia, Samuel Kim and Gerald Chen were forerunners in this research field. Their works entitled *China, the United Nations and World Order and China and International Institutions* were published respectively in 1979 and 1989. The former examined China's voting and diplomatic behavior in the United Nations in the context of West-East confrontation and North-South relationship after China recovered its legitimate seat in the UN.[2] The latter considered the relationship between China and non-governmental organizations since 1971.[3] From the 1990s on, more scholars delved into the research on the relationship between China and international institutions. Harold Jacobson and Michael Oksenberg published a book entitled *China's Participation in the IMF, the World Bank, and GATT*. This book discussed China's participation in these international economic institutions and the domestic impetus behind its participation.[4] Afterwards, *China Joins the World*[5] edited by Elizabeth Economy and Michael Oksenberg and *Engaging China*[6] edited by Alastair Iain Johnston and Robert Ross were published one after another in the 1990s. The works in the two volumes were focused on China's participation in international institutions in a range of issue areas such as international trade and finance, human rights, energy and arms control as well as the change of China's domestic politics and foreign policy behavior in the process of its interaction with international institutions. Besides the research focusing on China's participation in international institutions, some scholars followed with interest in China's commitment in and compliance with international institutions. Regarding this issue, *China's Compliance in Global Affairs*[7] and *Beyond Compliance*[8] are typical works. Moreover, Johnston systematically examined China's socialization in the Conference on Disarmament, the Comprehensive Nuclear Test Ban, the Convention on Conventional Weapons, and the ASEAN Regional Forum in his more recent book *Social States*. In Johnston's view, it is the effect of socialization that caused the major change of China's attitude toward international institutions.[9]

Chinese scholars have also been doing a lot of work in this research field. Yizhou Wang *et al.* expounded China's interaction with a variety of international institutions in the issue areas of international economy, arms control, human rights and environmental protection in a relatively comprehensive manner.[10] In his more recent book, Wang stressed China's creative involvement by various means including diplomacy in international institutions.[11] In the book entitled *Institutionalized Survival*, Jie Liu pointed out that participating in international institutions actively is a strategic choice for China intending to rise peacefully.[12] Honghua Men provided a historical overview of the relationship between China and international institutions, and proposed that China not only need to participate in international institutions but also ought to play a leading role in agenda-setting and institution-building.[13] Changhe Su's series of articles on the relationship between China and international institutions explored the profound change of China's diplomatic thinking and behavior and the impact of China's participation in international institutions on its domestic political economy, given that China is undergoing the transformation of domestic political economy in a rising trend of international institutionalization.[14] Ye Tian and Jing Lin did a more specific work which explained China's choice of joining International Labor Organization in order to strengthen state autonomy from a political economy perspective.[15] Yaqin Qin and Ling Wei analyzed how China was attracted by Asian regional cooperation process and thereby participated in regional institutions by employing a theoretical model of process constructivism.[16]

The existing studies primarily dealt with three questions: China's participation in international institutions, China's compliance with the rules of international institutions, and the impact of international institutions on China's domestic politics and foreign policy. All of them presumed that the relationship between China and international institutions is a process of being integrated, shaped, and impacted. Nevertheless, with the rise of China's overall power and influence, China has not accepted all the arrangements in terms of form and substance in international institutions in an entirely passive manner, but rather manifested in an increasingly proactive posture by putting forward proposals for institutional design or reform or proposing to create international institutions with particular form and substance. To a large extent, this phenomenon is ignored by the existing studies.[17]

The purpose of this chapter is to examine China's proposing behavior in global governance based on illuminating the reform proposals China put forward in the WTO Doha Round negotiation and G-20 process. Choosing the cases of the WTO Doha Round negotiation and G-20 process is justifiable on the following grounds.

First, global economic governance is more salient compared to global governance in other issue areas in contemporary world politics. Economic issues such as trade and finance have not been incorporated into the range of high politics as security issues have been. Nevertheless, given that most states, especially big powers, are not facing pressing security threats, economic issues closely related to the people's living and welfare are definitely in the spotlight in global governance, and therefore in a relatively salient position.

Second, the WTO Doha Round negotiation and G-20 process are critical junctures in the reform of global economic governance.[18] In such critical junctures, reform proposals have access to the agenda for negotiation or discussion, which encourages states to put forward reform proposals. In the WTO Doha Round negotiation, members attempted to revise some WTO rules. Specifically speaking, developing countries attempted to address the issue of development deficit, while developed countries aimed to further trade liberalization. Nonetheless, the purpose of all the negotiating parties is revising WTO rules and reforming global trade governance. The G-20 mechanism formed shortly after Asian financial crisis in 1997 was initially a forum where the finance ministers and central bank governors of the members discussed how to coordinate macro-economic policies among them. After the eruption of global financial crisis in 2008, the G-20 mechanism was elevated to a regularly held summit in which the leaders of developed economies and developing countries, particularly emerging countries, discussed how to deal with the crisis and coordinate their economic and financial policies. In the G-20 process, the leaders actively engaged in discussion on how to stabilize global financial order, strengthen international financial regulation, resist trade protectionism and rebalance global economy among other issues, set forth their views on the direction and means of the reform of global economic governance, and achieved consensus in some aspects. Therefore, the G-20 process became a critical juncture for the reform of global economic governance.

China's Reform Proposals in the WTO Doha Round Negotiation

In the WTO Doha Round negotiation, developed countries and developing countries put forward different reform proposals by virtue of the opportunity for revising the WTO rules. The core difference of their proposals is that developing countries desired to get special and differentiated treatment, while developed countries aimed to further trade liberalization. This difference in principle hindered developing countries and developed countries from reaching consensus on many issues, including special safeguard mechanism and agricultural subsidy. In general, China supported the development-oriented proposals put forward by developing countries, albeit it was not reluctant to make appropriate compromise for the development of trade liberalization.

In addition, it is evident that China put forward some reform proposals proactively. China's proposals concentrated on the issues of the ruling bodies for the Doha Round, dispute settlement mechanism and anti-dumping rules.

1. The Ruling Bodies for the Doha Round

The Trade Negotiation Committee for the Doha Round which could exert major influence on agenda-setting was largely controlled by developed countries. To restrain developed countries from influencing agenda-setting by controlling the Trade Negotiation Committee, China together with many other developing countries put forward a proposal for reforming the selection procedure of the chair of the committee. China demanded that the chairmanship of the Trade Negotiation Committee be rotated among member ambassadors rather than be appointed by the Director-General of the WTO.[19] In the same vein, China together with many other developing countries proposed jointly that: (1) the discretionary authority of the chairs of the six Trade Negotiation Committee subcommittees negotiation subcommittees' chairs in determining which alternative positions are included for consideration in draft proposals should be restrained; (2) alternative draft proposals for negotiation should be determined through deliberation process, not by the chair of the Trade Negotiation Committee.[20]

Despite the fact that China collaborated in proposing together with other developing countries in the two instances, there was much evidence that China actually exercised positive influence on the formation and pursuit of the two proposals for reforming the ruling bodies for the Doha Round.[21]

2. Dispute Settlement Mechanism

The dispute settlement mechanism (DSM) provides the WTO members with a legalized procedure for solving trade disputes, and thereby plays an extremely important role in managing the trading relationship among the members. However, due to the lack of necessary expertise and administrative capacity, many developing countries, especially least developed countries, have much difficulty in utilizing this mechanism effectively as developed countries do. For this reason, China put forward four proposals which were designed to protect and promote the interest of developing countries in the working group for DSM.

First, China proposed that: (1) developed countries should maintain a proper restraint from starting the cases against developing countries; (2) developed countries cannot submit more than two cases against the same developing country to the Dispute Settlement Body (DSB) in a calendar year; (3) this restriction should not apply to the cases that developing countries start against developed countries or other developing countries.

Second, regarding the provision about the duration of the consultation procedure, the reform proposal China put forward was that if one or more parties involved in consultation are developing countries, the duration should be prolonged to a maximum of thirty days when the complaining party requests.

Third, with regard to the provision about the establishing time of a panel in *Understanding on Rules and Procedures Governing the Settlement of Disputes*, China proposed to revise it as follows: (1) if the complaining party requests, the panel shall be established at the DSB meeting at which such a request first appears as an item on the DSB's agenda, unless the DSB decides by consensus not to establish a panel; (2) if the defending party is a developing country, the current procedure on the establishment of a panel remains to apply, that is, a panel shall be established at the latest at the DSB meeting following that at which the request as an item on the

DSB's agenda. Fourth, China proposed that: (1) a general provision applicable to all the developing countries should be added in Understanding on Rules and Procedures Governing the Settlement of Disputes; (2) the provision about special and differentiated treatment for developing countries should be further consolidated so as to be more effective; (3) due to the principle of special and differentiated principle, any stricter provision engendered in the negotiation for the DSM should not apply to developing countries improperly; (4) developed countries should also help developing countries to participate in the DSM of the WTO by providing technical assistance and capacity training programs; (5) in order to avoid undermining the WTO system more severely, the revision of *the Understanding on Rules and Procedures Governing the Settlement of Disputes* should encourage the disputing parties to seek mutually acceptable solutions, rather than resort to retaliation.[22]

These reform proposals China put forward are in conformity with the principle that the DSM should particularly consider the special situation of developing countries. China's proposing behavior for reforming the DSM is a manifestation of pushing the development-oriented reform of the WTO rules and promoting the development agenda of the Doha Round.

3. Anti-Dumping Rules

The fact that some WTO members abuse the anti-dumping rules in practice is widely denounced by developing countries and some developed countries. As a consequence, the reform of the anti-dumping rules was placed on the agenda of the WTO Doha Round negotiation. In the Doha Round negotiation, Friends of Anti-Dumping (FANS), the US, Canada, Australia, Egypt, India among some other WTO members put forward lots of reform proposals. Soon after joining the WTO, China in collaboration with fifteen WTO members submitted a written report about the anti-dumping of the textiles. Thereafter, China put forward four reform proposals regarding the reform of the anti-dumping rules.

The proposal put forward in 2003 is the most important one. The main content of this proposal was about enforcing anti-dumping discipline more rigorously. On this issue, China proposed: (1) to renew a back-to-back investigation provision, specify the meaning of the terms "special market situation" and "structural normal value" in more detail, and specify the factors which need to be considered when assessing the condition of competition among the imported products from different members or between imported products and domestic products; (2) to restrain the initiating member's investigating authority from assessing the damage arbitrarily, ensure that the causal relationship between dumping imported products and domestic damage is affirmed only if the former is the substantive cause of the latter, prohibit the application of the return-to-zero method explicitly, establish clear guidance for dealing with the normal value of related party transactions, and improve the method of confirming all other tariff rates of the non-sampled targeted countries' exporters or manufacturers; (3) to make a further explanation on the commitment provisions, restrain the initiating member's investigating authority from rejecting the pricing commitment, and improve the review rules.[23] Taken together, these reform proposals aimed to restrain the WTO members' discretion over initiating anti-dumping investigation arbitrarily and abusing anti-dumping measures as well as prevent anti-dumping rules from impeding free trade among the WTO members.

Likewise, the main purpose of the two proposals China put forward in 2007 was restraining the WTO members' discretion. More specifically, for instance, on the issue of the applicants' qualification, China proposed that the circumstance in which the application for anti-dumping is considered as being delivered by domestic industries should be defined clearly; on the issue of sun-set review, China proposed that its use should be restricted to no more than once, that means, the duration of any anti-dumping measure is no more than ten years.

In addition, China put forward some proposals for special and differentiated treatment for developing countries. On this issue, China proposed that: (1) when a developed country adopt anti-dumping measures against a developing country's products, the lesser tariff rate rule should be enforced; (2) the percentage of negligible imports and de minimus dumping margin should be improved; (3) when a developed country adopts anti-dumping measures against a developing country's products, as long as the proposed pricing commitment of the exporters can offset the confirmed dumping margin, the developing country's investigating authority should accept the proposal; (4) if an anti-dumping measure is adopted by a developed country against a developing country's products, the measure should terminate automatically after five years.[24]

From the content of China's proposals on the reform of anti-dumping rules, it can be found that China's proposing behavior was dedicated to offering developing countries more substantive special and differentiated treatment.

China's Reform Proposals in the G-20 Process

Since the eruption of global financial crisis in 2008, G-20 has become the primary platform for global economic governance gradually. At all the past G-20 summits, issues concerning the reform of global economic governance, such as strengthening international financial regulation, reforming international financial institutions, rebalancing global economy, were focal points of the leaders' discussion. As such, the G-20 process became a critical juncture for the reform of global economic governance. In the G-20 process, China expressed its ideas for the reform of global economic governance proactively.

At the first G-20 summit in 2008, China pointed out clearly that the reform of international financial system should aim at the direction toward establishing a fair, just, inclusive and orderly new international financial order, should strive to create an institutional environment conducive to sound global economic development, and should adhere to comprehensive, balanced, progressive, and effective principles.[25] At the G-20 London summit in 2009, China emphasized the direction toward establishing a fair, just, inclusive and orderly new international financial order again.[26] Revolving around this direction, China put forward a series of reform proposals in G-20 summits. China's reform proposals concentrated on the reform of international financial regulations, international financial institutions reform and international monetary system reform.

1. Reform of International Financial Regulation

At the first G-20 summit, to strengthen international financial regulatory cooperation and improve international regulatory system, China put forth four reform proposals: establishing code of conduct for credit rating agencies, increasing the level of monitoring global capital flows, strengthening the supervision of various financial institutions and intermediary organizations, and enhancing the transparency of financial markets and their products.[27] At the following G-20 summits, China put forth more specific reform proposals on the issues of establishing an early warning mechanism, monitoring the shadow banking system, strengthening the regulation of credit rating agencies, and put forth a principle of simplicity, practicability, accountability, and balancing financial regulation and financial innovation.

With regard to how to implement the principle of simplicity, practicability, and accountability in the reform of international financial regulation, China proposed: (1) to establish an international financial system conducive to the development of the real economy; (2) to establish and enforce strict capital and leverage ratio requirements, incorporate the shadow banking system into the regulatory system, and reformulate unified global accounting standards; (3) to strive to strengthen the supervision of systemically important financial institutions, and take the necessary precautionary measures to prevent the risk of excessive speculation; (4) to emphasize the standards of international regulation in consistency with its core principle while taking the differences among financial markets in different states into full consideration, and improve the relevance and effectiveness of financial supervision; (5) to strengthen the supervision of credit rating agencies, reduce reliance on credit rating agencies, improve code of conduct and system of accountability for credit rating agencies, and in particular develop objective, fair, reasonable and unified sovereign credit rating methods and standards so that the rating results accurately reflect a country's economic situation and credit level.[28]

With regard to how to balance financial regulation and financial innovation, China proposed: (1) to endeavor to solve the systemic and fundamental problems in international financial system, and make the financial system rest on, serve, and promote the development of the real economy; (2) to adhere to high standards and strict requirements, and assess the implementation of the new regulatory standards of each member consistently.[29]

2. International Financial Institutions Reform

China's reform proposals concerning international financial institutions reform were designed to increase the representation and voice of developing countries in international financial institutions. At G-20 summits, China proposed: (1) to reform the generating mechanism of the executive board in international financial institutions so as to increase the representation and voice of developing countries in international financial institutions;[30] (2) to reform the governance structure of the IMF and World Bank so as to increase the representation and voice of developing countries;[31] (3) to strive to increase the representation and voice of developing countries, continue to promote the reform to achieve substantive progress, reform the existing decision = making procedures and mechanisms of international financial institutions, and promote more extensive and effective participation of all parties;[32] (4) to continue to promote the reform of international financial institutions, accelerate the completion of the IMF quota adjustment, and push more persons from emerging countries and developing countries to be appointed as executives in international financial institutions so as to increase the representation and voice of developing countries;[33] (5) to continue to be committed to choose the high-level executives in international financial institutions based on a fair principle, increase the proportion of middle-level and high-level executives from developing countries, and resolve the problem of executive deficit for developing countries in the institutional framework of international financial institutions.[34]

Largely as a result of China and other developing countries' efforts, the G-20 members committed to increase emerging countries and developing countries' quota share in the IMF to at least 5% and increase developing countries and transition economies' voting rights in the World Bank to at least 3% at the G-20 Pittsburgh summit in 2009. At the G-20 Toronto summit in 2010, the G-20 members committed to increase the proportion of officials and scholars from emerging countries appointed as high-level executives in the IMF, World Bank and other international financial institutions, and complete the IMF quota reform at the Seoul Summit.[35]

In addition to increasing the representation and voice of developing countries in international financial institutions, China has put forward some proposals on the issues of establishing a timely and efficient crisis response and rescue mechanism, reinforcing the IMF's aid to developing countries, increasing the total capital of the IMF, strengthening the IMF's supervision on the macroeconomic policies of all the parties especially the major reserve currency issuing economies, strengthening the IMF's role in monitoring and warning capital flows early, and so on. These reform proposals covering a wide range of content suggest that China not only attached importance to the interests and voice of developing countries, but also underscored the capacity building and effective monitoring of international financial institutions.

3. International Monetary System Reform

Prior to the G-20 London summit in 2009, Chinese Central Bank Governor Xiaochuan Zhou called for reform of the existing international monetary system and the creation of a super-sovereign international reserve currency which can replace the U.S. dollar hegemony, and suggested that the issuing and the available range for the use of Special Drawing Rights (SDRs) should be expanded in the short term in order to reduce the global economy's dependence on the U.S. dollar in his published article.[36] This proposal was paid close attention to internationally, and gained support of some emerging countries including Brazil and Russia. Xiaochuan Zhou's radical proposal on international monetary system reform did not represent the official position of Chinese government. In the G-20 process, China advocated reform of the existing international monetary system, but did not acknowledge the feasibility and operability of a super-sovereign international reserve currency.

Regarding international monetary system reform, China proposed to improve the regulatory mechanism of reserve currencies, maintain relative stability of major reserve currencies, and promote the diversification and rationalization of international monetary system.[37] Given that the U.S. launched quantitative easing monetary policies, China proposed that major reserve currency issuing economies should adopt responsible policies to maintain a relatively stable exchange rate.[38] On the issue of expanding the available range for the use of SDRs, at the Cannes summit in 2011, China proposed: (1) to push forward reform of the existing international monetary system steadily, expand the available range for the use of SDRs IMF special drawing rights, and restructure the composition of the basket of SDRs; (2) to establish an international reserve currency system with stable currency value, orderly supply and adjustable total amount.[39]

The Main Features of China's Proposing Behavior

The WTO Doha Round negotiation and G-20 process provided window of opportunity for China to put forward proposals on the reform of global economic governance. China took advantage of the critical junctures to put forward a series of reform proposals. In terms of China's proposing behavior, three main features are worth noting.

First, China advocated the proper adjustment of global governance institutions, instead of seeking to change the basic principles of the existing system of rules. The multilateral trading system in the framework of the WTO set the following basic principles: (1) non-discrimination principle meaning that the WTO members cannot discriminate trading partners, must give the same treatment to other members (ie MFN principle), and must give equal treatment to domestic and international products and services (national treatment principle); (2) freer trade principle meaning that tariff and non-tariff barriers should be reduced continuously through multilateral trade negotiations; (3) more transparency principle; (4) fair trade principle (anti-dumping and anti-subsidy); (5) pro-development principle which means developing countries should be given special and differentiated treatment.[40] On the above basic principles of the WTO, China did not requested reforms. More importantly, China desired to formulate more explicit and specific rules so as to implement the principles more effectively.

China's reform proposals aiming at the managing board procedure were designed to make agenda-setting in the WTO Doha Round negotiation more transparent. The reform proposals aiming at the dispute settlement mechanism were designed to allow developing countries for reasonable differentiated treatment and prevent developing countries from failing to use this mechanism resulting from lack of technical and administrative capacity. Last but not least, the reform proposals aiming at the anti-dumping rules were designed to reduce the likelihood of being abused in practice and thereby promote fair trade. In a nutshell, China's proposed rule adjustment was to revise the WTO rules in such a way that the revised rules would conform to the basic principles to a larger extent.

In the G-20 process, China's reform proposals included strengthening international financial regulation, increasing the representation and voice of developing countries in international financial institutions, and promoting the diversification and rationalization of international monetary system among others. Such a proposing behavior was an endeavor in establishing a fair, just, inclusive and orderly international financial system without intention of changing the basic principles of the existing international financial system. If the proposals were implemented, the existing international financial system would be more effective in promoting the healthy development of global economy under the circumstance that the embedded liberalism would remain the basic principle. Put it differently, China manifested itself as a reform-minded constructor for global economic governance institutions without revisionist intention.

Second, China did not take the lead in the process of proposing jointly with other countries. While proposing jointly with other countries, it was evident that China participated actively and tried to make a difference. In the process of proposing jointly, however, China did not play a leadership role. China's performance in the G-20[41] in the WTO Doha Round negotiation was typical in demonstrating the fact that China did not take the lead while proposing jointly with other countries. At the Cancun Ministerial, China joined the G-20 and proposed jointly with Brazil, India and other G-20 members. They proposed that developed countries should reduce huge subsidies for their farmers and other domestic support for agriculture, and developed countries should take effective and measurable means to substantially improve market access for agricultural products of developing countries.[42] China participated actively in information exchange and mutual discussion inside the G-20, coordinated negotiating positions with other members, and gave strong support to collective bargaining. Nevertheless, China neither took part in the drafting of the first proposal led by Brazil and India, nor took the lead in choosing specific issues for negotiation and designing negotiating strategy.

In the case of proposing jointly in the G-20 in the WTO Doha Round negotiation, China's reluctance to play a leadership role, on the one hand, partly resulted from its diplomatic style, on the other hand, was partly due to the fact that its interest in agricultural issues differed from other G-20 members'. Unlike most other G-20 members, China was both seller and buyer in agricultural trade. For the seller's standpoint, China wanted developed countries to reduce agricultural subsidies. As a seller, it was in

China's interest to pressure developed countries to improve market access for agricultural products of developing countries. As a buyer, however, it was not in China's interest to exert too much pressure on agricultural issues. As such, participating actively in proposing jointly with other G-20 members while refraining from taking the lead was a more reasonable choice which could strike a balance between a seller's interest and a buyer's. In a similar vein, in the process of proposing for improving developing countries' representation and voice in international financial institutions jointly with other BRIC/BRICS countries, China did not play a leadership role, which was linked to the intention to avoid conflicting directly with European countries on the issue of the IMF quota adjustment. Seen from this perspective, if taking the lead would serve China's interest better in proposing jointly with other countries in the future, China would be likely to play a leadership role.[43]

Third, China upheld the principled idea of pro-development in proposing behavior. China's reform proposals in the WTO Doha Round negotiation concentrated on the pro-development principle. This is not only because giving developing countries special and differentiated treatment is in China's interest, but also results from China's identification with the principled pro-development idea. China's reform proposals concerning the DSM in the WTO were based on the consideration that developing countries lack expertise and administrative capacity. As China could mobilize sufficient resources to provide intellectual, technical and administrative support for its use of the DSM, and had familiarized and understood the rules of the DSM well since its accession to the WTO, unlike some small developing countries, China did not lack the necessary expertise and administrative capacity for the effective use of the DSM. Therefore, China's proposing behavior on the issue of the DSM reform was not entirely for the sake of its own interest. To some extent, it was guided by the pro-development idea China upheld.

At the G-20 London summit in 2009, China proposed that International financial institutions should provide more assistance to developing countries and IMF should ensure that the new funding is preferred for the less developed countries.[44] Also, this proposal showed China's identification with the principled pro-development idea, because as the largest developing country with a large amount of foreign currency reserves, China is extremely unlikely to become a bailout object of international financial institutions.

Conclusion

The WTO Doha Round negotiation and G-20 process were critical junctures for the reform of global economic governance. China put forward a series of proposals on the reform of global economic governance by actively engaging in the critical junctures. This suggests that shaping the rules of international institutions proactively has become essential part of China's engagement in global governance. In global governance, China is not only impacted by the rules of international institutions, but also evident in proposing to reform the rules.

In proposing behavior, China advocated the proper adjustment of global governance institutions, rather than seeking to change the basic principles of the existing system of rules. Partly for national interest, China did not take the lead in proposing jointly with other countries. As the largest developing country, China had no strong interest in revising the existing rules of global economic governance in a development-oriented manner, but still upheld the principled idea of pro-development.

Notes

1. National Intelligence Council and European Union Institute for Security Studies, *Global Governance 2025: At a Critical Juncture*, Washington, DC: National Intelligence Council, 2011, p. iii.
2. Samuel Kim, *China, the United Nations, and World Order*, Princeton: Princeton University Press, 1979.
3. Gerald Chen, *China and International Organizations: Participation in Non-Governmental Organizations since 1971*, Oxford: Oxford University Press, 1989.
4. Harold Jacobson and Michael Oksenberg, *China's Participation in the IMF, the World Bank, and GATT: Toward a Global Economic Order*, Ann Arbor: University of Michigan Press, 1990.
5. Elezabeth Economy and Michael Oksenberg, eds., *China Joins the World: Process and Prospects*, Washington DC: Brookings Institution Press, 1999.

6. Alastair Iain Johnston and Robert Ross, eds., *Engaging China: The Management of an Emerging Power*, London: Routledge, 1999.
7. Gerald Chen, *China's Compliance in Global Affairs: Trade, Arms Control, Environmental Protection, Human Rights*, Singapore: World Scientific, 2006.
8. Ann Kent, *Beyond Compliance: China, International Organizations, and Global Security*, Stanford: Stanford University Press, 2007.
9. Alastair Iain Johnston, *Social States: China in International Institutions (1980–2000)*, Princeton: Princeton University Press, 2008.
10. Yizhou Wang, eds., *Mohe Zhong de JianGou: Zhongguo yu Guoji Zuzhi Guanxi de Duoshijiao Toushi (Construction in Contradiction: A Multiple-dimensional Examination on the Relationship between China and International Organizations)*, Beijing: Zhongguo Fazhan Chubanshe (China Development Press), 2003.
11. Yizhou Wang, *Chuangzao Xing Jieru: Zhongguo Waijiao Xin Quxiang (Creative Involvement: A New Direction in China's Diplomacy)*, Beijing: Beijing Daxue Chubanshe (Peking University Press), 2011.
12. Jie Liu, Jizhi Hua Shengcun: *Zhongguo Heping Jueqi De Zhanlue Xuanze (Institutionalized Survival: A Strategic Choice for China Intending to Rise Peacefully)*, Beijing: Shishi Chubanshe (Current Affairs Press), 2004.
13. Honghua Men, "Guoji Jizhi Yu Zhongguo De Zhanlue Xuanze" (International Regimes and China's Strategic Choice), *Zhongguo Shehui Kexue (Social Sciences in China)*, No. 2001, pp. 178–187.
14. Changhe Su, "Zhongguo yu Guoji Zhidu: Yixiang Yanjiu Yicheng" (China and International Institutions: A Research Agenda), *Shijie Jingji yu Zhengzhi (World Economy and Politics)*, No. 10, 2002, pp. 5–10; Changhe Su, "Faxian Zhongguo Xin Waijiao: Duobian Guoji Zhidu yu Zhongguo Waijiao Xin Siwei" (Discovering China's New Diplomacy: Multilateral International Institutions and China's new Thinking on Diplomacy), *Shijie Jingji yu Zhengzhi (World Economy and Politics)*, No. 4, 2005, pp. 11–16; Changhe Su, "Zhoubian Zhidu yu Zhoubian Zhuyi: Dongya Quyu Zhili Zhong de Zhongguo Tujin" (Neighborhood Institutions and Neighborhoodism: China's Approach to Governance in East Asia), *Shijie Jingji yu Zhengzhi (World Economy and Politics)*, No. 1, 2006, pp. 7–14; Changhe Su, "Zhongguo yu Quanqiu Zhili: Jincheng, Xingwei, Jiegou yu Zhishi" (China and Global Governance: Process, Behavior, Structure and Knowledge), *Guoji Zhengzhi Yanjiu (Studies of International Politics)*, No. 1, 2011, pp. 35–45.
15. Ye Tian and Jing Lin, "Guoji Laogong Biaozhun yu Zhongguo Laodong Zhili: Yizhong Zhengzhi Jingji Xue Fenxi" (International Labor Standards

and Labor Governance in China: A Political Economy Perspective), *Shijie Jingji yu Zhengzhi (World Economy and Politics)*, No. 5, 2009, pp. 6–16.

16. Yaqin Qin and Ling Wei, "Jiegou, Jincheng yu Quanli De Shehui Hua: Zhongguo yu Dongya Diqu Hezuo" (Structure, Process and the Socialization of Power: China and Asian Regional Institutions), *Shijie Jingji yu Zhengzhi (World Economy and Politics)*, No. 3, 2007, pp. 7–15.
17. Although Gregory and Ramesh Thakur raised the question whether China will change the rules of global order, their discussion focused on whether, rather than how. See Gregory Chin and Ramesh Thakur, "Will China Change the Rules of Global Order?," *Washington Quarterly*, Vol. 33, No. 4, October 2010, pp. 119–138.
18. Critical juncture is an important concept of historical institutionalism. In critical junctures, institutional change is apt to occur. See Giovanni Capoccia and Daniel Kelelmen, "The Study of Critical Junctures: Theory, Narrative and Counterfactuals in Historical Institutionalism," *World Politics*, Vol. 59, No. 3, April 2007, pp. 341–369.
19. Margaret Pearson, "China in Geneva: Lessons from China's Early Years in the World Trade Organization," in Alastair Iain Johnston and Robert Ross, eds., *New Directions in the Study of China's Foreign Policy*, Stanford: Stanford University Press, 2006, p. 253.
20. Ibid.
21. Gregory Chin, "Reforming the WTO: China, the Doha Round and Beyond," in Amrita Narlikar and Brendan Vickers, eds., *Leadership and Change in Multilateral Trading System*, Leiden: Brill/Martinus Nijhoff Academic Publishers, 2009, p. 139.
22. Yanqiong Mao, "Lun Zhongguo Yingdui WTO Zhengduan Jiejue Jizhi Gaige de Celue" (China's Strategy in Response to the Reform of Dispute Settlement Mechanism of the WTO), *Jianghuai Luntan (Jianghuai Forum)*, No. 6, 2008, pp. 55–57.
23. Fei Yu, "WTO Fan Qingxiao Guize Gaige Shuping: Yi Doha Fazhan Yicheng Fan Qingxiao Tanpan wei Zhongxin" (Discussion on the Reform of the WTO Anti-dumping Rules: With a Focus on the Negotiation of the Anti-dumping Rules in Doha Development Agenda), *Fashang Yanjiu (Studies in Law and Business)*, No. 4, 2009, p. 73.
24. Ibid., p. 74.
25. "Hu Jingtao Zai Ershi Guo Jituan Lingdao Ren Di Yici Fenghui Shang de Jianghua" (Jingtao Hu's Speech at the First G-20 Leaders' Summit), available at http://news.xinhuanet.com/newscenter/2008-11/16/content_10364070.htm (accessed 12 March 2013).

26. "Hu Jingtao Zai Ershi Guo Jituan Lingdao Ren Di Erci Fenghui Shang de Jianghua" (Jingtao Hu's Speech at the Second G-20 Leaders' Summit), available at http://news.xinhuanet.com/newscenter/2009-04/03/content_11122834.htm (accessed 12 March 2013).
27. "Hu Jingtao Zai Ershi Guo Jituan Lingdao Ren Di Yici Fenghui Shang de Jianghua" (Jingtao Hu's Speech at the First G-20 Leaders' Summit), available at http://news.xinhuanet.com/newscenter/2008-11/16/content_10364070.htm (accessed 12 March 2013).
28. "Hu Jingtao Zai Ershi Guo Jituan Lingdao Ren Di Sici Fenghui Shang de Jianghua" (Jingtao Hu's Speech at the Fourth G-20 Leaders' Summit), available at http://news.xinhuanet.com/world/2010-06/27/c_12269632.htm (accessed 18 March 2013).
29. "Hu Jingtao Zai Ershi Guo Jituan Lingdao Ren Di Wuci Fenghui Shang de Jianghua" (Jingtao Hu's Speech at the Fifth G-20 Leaders' Summit), available at http://news.xinhuanet.com/world/2010-11/12/c_12766973.htm (accessed 18 March 2013).
30. "Hu Jingtao Zai Ershi Guo Jituan Lingdao Ren Di Yici Fenghui Shang de Jianghua" (Jingtao Hu's Speech at the First G-20 Leaders' Summit), available at http://news.xinhuanet.com/newscenter/2008-11/16/content_10364070.htm (accessed 20 March 2013).
31. "Hu Jingtao Zai Ershi Guo Jituan Lingdao Ren Di Erci Fenghui Shang de Jianghua" (Jingtao Hu's Speech at the Second G-20 Leaders' Summit), available at http://news.xinhuanet.com/newscenter/2009-04/03/content_11122834.htm (accessed 20 March 2013).
32. "Hu Jingtao Zai Ershi Guo Jituan Lingdao Ren Di Sanci Fenghui Shang de Jianghua" (Jingtao Hu's Speech at the Third G-20 Leaders' Summit), available at http://news.xinhuanet.com/politics/2009-09/26/content_12112502.htm (accessed 20 March 2013).
33. "Hu Jingtao Zai Ershi Guo Jituan Lingdao Ren Di Sici Fenghui Shang de Jianghua" (Jingtao Hu's Speech at the Fourth G-20 Leaders' Summit), available at http://news.xinhuanet.com/world/2010-06/27/c_12269632.htm (accessed 20 March 2013).
34. "Hu Jingtao Zai Ershi Guo Jituan Lingdao Ren Di Wuci Fenghui Shang de Jianghua" (Jingtao Hu's Speech at the Fifth G-20 Leaders' Summit), available at http://news.xinhuanet.com/world/2010-11/12/c_12766973.htm (accessed on March 2013).
35. Xiao Li and Yongqi Feng, "Guoji Huobi Tixi Gaige de Jiti Xingdong yu Ershi Guo Jituan de Zuoyong" (The Collective Action of International Monetary System Reform and the Role of G-20), *Shijie Jingji yu Zhengzhi (World Economy and Politics)*, No. 2, 2012, p. 137.

36. Xiaochuan Zhou, "Guanyu Gaige Guoji Huobi Tixi De Sikao" (Thoughts on International Monetary System Reform), *Dangdai Jingji (Contemporary Economy)*, No. 4, 2009, p. 1.
37. "Hu Jingtao Zai Ershi Guo Jituan Lingdao Ren Di Erci Fenghui Shang De Jianghua" (Jingtao Hu's Speech at the Second G-20 Leaders' Summit), http://news.xinhuanet.com/newscenter/2009-04/03/content_11122834.htm (accessed on 20 March 2013).
38. "Hu Jingtao Zai Ershi Guo Jituan Lingdao Ren Di Wuci Fenghui Shang De Jianghua" (Jingtao Hu's Speech at the Fifth G-20 Leaders' Summit), http://news.xinhuanet.com/world/2010-11/12/c_12766973.htm (accessed on 20 March 2013).
39. "Hu Jingtao Zai Ershi Guo Jituan Lingdao Ren Di Liuci Fenghui Shang De Jianghua" (Jingtao Hu's Speech at the Sixth G-20 Leaders' Summit), http://news.xinhuanet.com/world/2011-11/04/c_122235131.htm (accessed on 20 March 2013).
40. See WTO, *Understanding the WTO*, fifth edition, Geneva, 2010.
41. The G-20 in the WTO Doha Round negotiation is an informal group composed of 21 developing countries.
42. Amrita Narlikar and Diana Tussie, "The G-20 at the Cancun Ministerial: Developing Countries and Their Evolving Coalitions in the WTO," *World Economy*, Vol. 27, No. 7, July 2004, p. 952.
43. Collective bargaining can enhance the group members' bargaining power, provided that their interests converge. See Amrita Narlikar, *International Trade and Developing Countries: Bargaining Coalitions in the GATT & WTO*, London: Routledge, 2003.
44. "Hu Jingtao Zai Ershi Guo Jituan Lingdao Ren Di Erci Fenghui Shang de Jianghua" (Jingtao Hu's Speech at the Second G-20 Leaders' Summit), available at http://news.xinhuanet.com/newscenter/2009-04/03/content_11122834.htm (accessed 25 March 2013).

Chapter 15

Analysis of Trade Commodity Structure and Complementarity of the Regional Cooperation between China and Russia

*Kang Chengwen**

Introduction

The political relations of China and Russia, two geopolitical and strategic cooperation partners who are connected with 4,300 km continental borderline, have entered their best period in history. In August 2012, Russia's official "Accession to the WTO" means that Russia welcomed the new starting point for its economic development and foreign trade and economic cooperation. This study, based on the analysis of the development and current situation of the Sino-Russian trade as well as the UN Comtrade data, analyzes Sino-Russian bilateral trade commodity structure and its change, relative comparative advantage in trade and bilateral comprehensive trade complementarity from the angle of both exports and imports. The analysis revealed the potential and trend of Sino-Russian trade.

---

* Kang Chengwen, IBER, Harbin University of Commerce. This paper is supported by the national social science fund project (Issue no. 13BGJ015) and Heilongjiang Province social science fund project (Issue no. 14B019).

The Present Status and Development of the Bilateral Trade

Since the 1990s, along with the improvement of relations between China and Russia, the Sino-Russian trade has expanded and developed. In recent years, the bilateral trade has been growing rapidly, with Heilongjiang province's trade to Russia accounting for more than 25% of the amount of China's total trade with Russia for many years. The consolidation of political relationship between Russia and China and the Russia's accession to the WTO provide new opportunities and challenges to further expand bilateral trade and regional economic cooperation. Figure 1 represents the variations of Sino-Russian total amount of export and bilateral trading export during 1992–2012.

As shown in Figure 1, the Sino-Russian trade has experienced the development process of "W" type curve. During 1992–1993, trade between China and Russia developed rapidly. Bilateral exports soon reached 7.7 billion USD in 1993. In 1993, China became the second largest trade partner of Russia, while Russia became China's seventh largest trading partner. But thereafter, the bilateral trade from 1994 to 1999 was in the low volatility around the states, due to several reasons: the large increase of the Russian tariffs, the change of barter trade into cash trade, etc. After 2000, along with the commencement and continuation of a series of favorable situations, such as the signature of "Sino-Russian

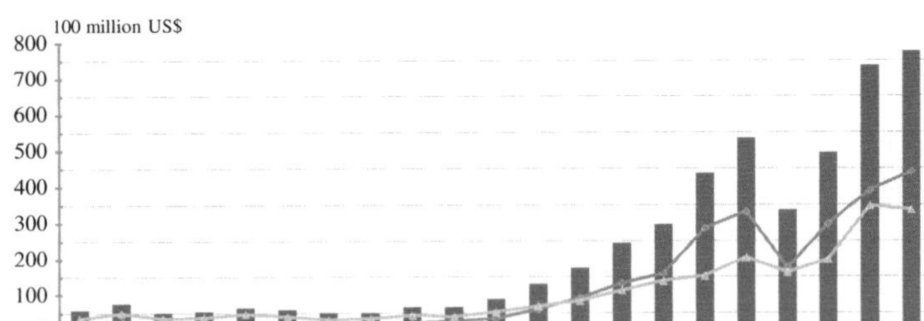

year	92	93	94	95	96	97	98	99	00	01	02	03	04	05	06	07	08	09	10	11	12
Sino -Russia trade	59	77	51	55	64	60	50	50	66	67	88	130	175	244	296	437	534	336	494	736	776
China export	23	27	16	17	17	20	18	15	22	27	35	60	91	132	158	285	331	175	296	389	441
Russia export	35	50	35	38	48	40	32	35	44	39	53	69	84	112	138	152	203	161	198	347	336

Figure 1. Development of Sino-Russia Bilateral Trade (1992–2012).

Source: Plotted based on UN Comtrade Data.

governmental trade agreement for 2001–2005" and "good neighborly friendship and cooperation treaty", the high-level visits between the two countries and the accession to WTO successively, the Sino-Russian trade has experienced rapid growth. In 2005, mutual exports between the two countries broke the 10 billion mark for the first time. From 2000 to 2012, the Sino-Russian bilateral trade continuously hit the record highs (except 2009). At present, China is Russia's largest source of imports, while Russia is China's fifth largest trading partner.

Analysis of the Sino-Russia Bilateral Trade Commodity Structure

By definition, the foreign trade commodity structure refers to the proportion or status of all categories of goods or a specific type of goods in a country's foreign trade during a certain period, i.e. the ratio of import and export trade value in each category of goods to the national total amount of the import and export trade value. In the study of commodity structure in the bilateral trade, it is used to calculate the portion of export trading value between a country and its partner country comparing with the total export value to all other countries. This ratio is employed to analyze the imported or exported commodity structure. The analysis of the trade between the two countries can be taken in two steps: the first is to calculate the ratio of the total mutual import and export trading amount in all commodity departments between China and Russia to the total amount of each country with all other trading countries as a whole; the second step is to determine and calculate the proportion of the major commodities in the major departments by comparing the magnitude of the calculated proportions. In order to reduce errors and to unify the dimensions, this chapter used UN Comtrade SITC1 departments data and other related data. Based on UN Comtrade data and calculation with Excel software, the information of Sino-Russian mutual import and export commodities in all departments, i.e. the total value of SITC1 departmental commodities as well as its proportion to the total value of the foreign import/export trade in all departments of each country, is shown in Table 1.[1]

It can be seen from Table 1 that on the export side, especially since 2005, China's exports to Russia have mainly focused on "labor intensive

Table 1. The Mutual SITC*1* Departmental Import and Export Trade Value of China and Russia and the Comparison of the Magnitude of their Proportions.

Year	Total	SITC*0*	SITC*1*	SITC2	SITC*3*	SITC*4*	SITC*5*	SITC*6*	SITC*7*	SITC*8*	SITC*9*
1. China's exports to Russia								Unit: 100 million US$, % (in percentage)			
1996	16.9	4.4 (26)	0.08 (0)	0.4 (2)	0.2 (1)	0.008 (0)	0.4 (2)	1.2 (7)	0.9 (5)	9.3 (55)	0 (0)
2000	22.3	1.4 (6)	0.2 (0)	0.4 (2)	0.5 (2)	0 (0)	0.8 (4)	1.5 (7)	1.5 (7)	15.9 (71)	0 (0)
2005	132.1	6.3 (5)	0.1 (0)	1.0 (1)	1.3 (1)	0.005 (0)	4.6 (3)	17.7 (13)	23.6 (18)	77.5 (59)	0.002 (0)
2010	296.1	13.8 (5)	0.2 (0)	1.3 (0)	2.2 (1)	0.03 (0)	15.0 (5)	60.6 (20)	101.4 (34)	101.5 (34)	0.08 (0)
2011	389.0	17.5 (4)	0.3 (0)	2.2 (1)	3.5 (1)	0.06 (0)	20.3 (5)	80.2 (21)	144.7 (37)	120.0 (31)	0.2 (0)
2012	440.6	17.5 (4)	0.3 (0)	1.9 (0)	3.0 (1)	0.06 (0)	21.9 (5)	90.1 (20)	172.0 (39)	133.8 (30)	0.02 (0)
2. China's imports from Russia								Unit: 100 million US$, % (in percentage)			
1996	51.5	2.2 (4)	0 (0)	3.6 (7)	2.3 (4)	0.05 (0)	15.3 (30)	16.6 (32)	9.2 (18)	1.6 (3)	0.7 (1)
2000	57.7	4.2 (7)	0.002 (0)	10.4 (18)	7.7 (13)	0 (0)	11.5 (20)	17.4 (30)	2.4 (4)	1.0 (2)	3.1 (5)
2005	158.9	11.4 (7)	0.005 (0)	32.6 (21)	65.4 (41)	0 (0)	22.0 (14)	23.8 (15)	3.2 (2)	0.3 (0)	0.1 (0)
2010	259.1	13.7 (5)	0.02 (0)	53.1 (20)	128.3 (50)	0 (0)	28.4 (11)	31.5 (12)	3.3 (1)	0.7 (0)	0.07 (0)
2011	403.6	16.7 (4)	0.02 (0)	85.6 (21)	228.9 (57)	0.004 (0)	31.6 (8)	37.7 (9)	2.2 (1)	0.8 (0)	0.1 (0)
2012	441.4	14.9 (3)	0.02 (0)	68.6 (16)	295.1 (67)	0.03 (0)	31.0 (7)	28.2 (6)	2.3 (1)	1.2 (0)	0.1 (0)

3. Russia's export to China

Unit: 100 million US$, % (in percentage)

1996	47.5	0.2 (0)	0.03 (0)	2.8 (6)	0.4 (1)	0 (0)	11.2 (24)	18.9 (40)	5.0 (10)	1.3 (3)	0.01 (0)
2000	44.0	0.6 (1)	0 (0)	7.2 (16)	3.4 (8)	0 (0)	7.5 (17)	14.9 (34)	5.9 (13)	1.9 (4)	2.5 (6)
2005	112.2	1.5 (1)	0 (0)	23.3 (21)	43.8 (39)	0 (0)	15.7 (14)	17.6 (16)	9.0 (8)	1.3 (1)	0 (0)
2010	197.8	9.4 (5)	0.02 (0)	41.4 (21)	102.7 (52)	0 (0)	21.3 (11)	7.9 (4)	10.0 (5)	1.1 (1)	4.0 (2)
2011	346.9	9.6 (3)	0.02 (0)	63.3 (18)	227.1 (65)	0 (0)	26.6 (8)	6.7 (2)	7.8 (2)	0.9 (0)	5.0 (1)
2012	335.6	9.9 (3)	0.03 (0)	52.3 (16)	248.9 (74)	0.03 (0)	27.0 (8)	5.1 (2)	11.2 (3)	0.8 (0)	2.4 (1)

4. Russia's imports from China

Unit: 100 million US$, % (in percentage)

1996	10.0	3.9 (39)	0.1 (1)	0.5 (5)	0.2 (2)	0.01 (0)	0.5 (5)	1.1 (11)	1.0 (10)	2.6 (26)	0 (0)
2000	9.5	1.0 (11)	0.3 (3)	0.4 (4)	0.6 (6)	0 (0)	1.2 (13)	2.2 (23)	1.0 (10)	2.8 (29)	0 (0)
2005	72.5	5.2 (7)	0.3 (0)	1.1 (2)	0.9 (1)	0.01 (0)	4.0 (5)	10.3 (14)	32.3 (44)	18.6 (26)	0 (0)
2010	389.6	12.2 (3)	0.6 (0)	1.6 (0)	1.6 (0)	0.02 (0)	18.2 (5)	59.9 (15)	180.8 (46)	113.7 (29)	1.1 (0)
2011	480.4	15.5 (3)	0.7 (0)	2.3 (0)	2.1 (0)	0.04 (0)	23.8 (5)	76.5 (16)	232.4 (48)	127.1 (26)	0.01 (0)
2012	487.8	14.7 (3)	0.6 (0)	2.3 (0)	1.6 (0)	0.04 (0)	25.9 (5)	81.2 (17)	256.9 (53)	134.4 (28)	0.04 (0)

Source: Plotted based on the UN Comtrade data.

products" and "technology and capital intensive products", such as "Manufactured goods classified chiefly by material", "Machinery and transport equipment" of SITC6 department and "Miscellaneous manufactured articles" of SITC8 department. Among them, the proportion of the SITC7 sector has raised slightly, the proportion of SITC8 sector has declined obviously and has been in trend of decline. The Russian exports to China were mainly focused on "primary products" of "Crude materials, inedible, except fuels" of SITC2 department and "Mineral fuels, lubricants and related materials" of SITC3 department. Among them, the proportion of SITC3 sector grew obviously, even reached 74% in 2012. Amount the goods Russia exported to China, the proportion of "Chemicals" of SITC5 department and "Manufactured goods classified chiefly by material" of SITC6 department dropped greatly, among which SITC6 department has changed the export sector into import goods sector. On the import side, the two countries mutual imports and exports and the respective proportion are basically agreed with each other, which shows the complementary advantage and mutual benefit of bilateral trade.

Under the condition that the species and quantity of import and export commodities conform to each country in the bilateral trade, the calculation of the proportion of the major trading commodity between the two countries and its variation can be made by using the statistics data of any one of the two countries'. Table 2 shows the first five trade commodities calculated by using statistics in UN Comtrade database of import and export from China to Russia every five years.

As it can be seen from Table 2, among the exports from China to Russia in 1996 to 2007, SITC84 "Clothing" ranked first with the average proportion being 39%, which was replaced by SITC71 "Machinery, other than electric". Especially since twenty-first Century, "Electrical machinery, apparatus and appliances" of the SITC71 and SITC72 and "Transport equipment" of SITC73 have become new "growth points" of China's exports to Russia. In addition, export of "Miscellaneous manufactured articles, nes" of SITC89 shows a steady increase trend.

On the import side of China from Russia, especially in the new century, "Petroleum and petroleum products" of SITC33 replaced "Iron and steel" of SITC67 and took the first place. Although the proportion of SITC24 "Wood, lumber and cork" dropped, its volume significantly increased. In recent years, SITC68 "Non ferrous metals", SITC28

Table 2. Top 5 Commodities and their Variations in Sino-Russia Trade Every 5 Years from 1996.

Year 1996–2002[a]			Year 2003–2007			Year 2008–2012		
SITC Code	Description	Trade Value	SITC Code	Description	Trade Value	SITC Code	Description	Trade Value
1. China's exports to Russia						Unit: 100 million US$, % (in percentage)		
84	Clothing	67.2 (43.3)	*84*	Clothing	252.4 (34.7)	*71*	Machinery, other than electric	259.9 (15.9)
85	Footwear	19.2 (12.3)	*72*	Electrical machinery, apparatus and appliances	85.2 (11.7)	*84*	Clothing	259.6 (15.9)
89	Miscellaneous manufactured articles, nes	8.4 (5.4)	*71*	Machinery, other than electric	53.8 (7.4)	*72*	Electrical machinery, apparatus and appliances	234.3 (14.4)
01	Meat and meat preparations	8.2 (5.3)	*85*	Footwear	52.0 (7.1)	*89*	Miscellaneous manufactured articles, nes	93.8 (5.8)
72	Electrical machinery, apparatus and appliances	7.4 (4.8)	*89*	Miscellaneous manufactured articles, nes	40.5 (5.6)	*73*	Transport equipment	90.6 (5.6)

(*Continued*)

Table 2. (*Continued*)

Year 1996–2002[a]			Year 2003–2007			Year 2008–2012		
SITC Code	Description	Trade Value	SITC Code	Description	Trade Value	SITC Code	Description	Trade Value
2. China's imports from Russia						Unit: 100 million US$, % (in percentage)		
67	Iron and steel	61.6 (15.7)	*33*	Petroleum and petroleum products	313.5 (41.8)	*33*	Petroleum and petroleum products	788.5 (50.7)
56	Fertilizers, manufactured	55.5 (14.2)	*24*	Wood, lumber and cork	93.7 (12.5)	*24*	Wood, lumber and cork	143.3 (9.2)
73	Transport equipment	46.4 (11.8)	*67*	Iron and steel	53.8 (7.2)	*68*	Non ferrous metals	120.3 (7.7)
33	Petroleum and petroleum products	38.3 (9.8)	*56*	Fertilizers, manufactured	51.0 (6.8)	*28*	Metalliferous ores and metal scrap	92.8 (6.0)
68	Non ferrous metals	27.1 (6.9)	*03*	Fish and fish preparations	50.9 (6.8)	*32*	Coal, coke and briquettes	66.7 (4.3)

Source: Plotted based on the UN Comtrade data.
Note: [a]Data for 7 years (1996–2002).

"Metalliferous ores and metal scrap" and SITC32 "Coal, and briquettes import coke" have increased significantly, and has the tendency of expansion. To sum up, the commodity structure of Sino-Russian trade can be summarized as follows: (1) bilateral trade commodity mainly focused on "industrial manufactured goods", such as SITC6, 7, 8 and "primary products" such as SITC2 & 3; (2) China mainly exports "industrial manufactured goods", such as SITC6, 7, 8 and import "primary products" such as SITC2 & 3, while Russia is the opposite; (3) trade division of labor between China and Russia becomes increasingly obvious and stable.

Differences of Comparative Advantage and Complementarity between China and Russia

Comparative advantage is the foundation of international division and international trade, as well as the leading cause of differences and complementarity in bilateral trade. Main indicator of measuring a country's comparative advantage is the index of revealed comparative advantage (Revealed Comparative Advantage, RCA), which is the ratio of share of a certain product of a country in the total export to the share of this product of the whole world in the total world exports.

However, this index reflects the advantage of export of a certain product of a country in the world export trade. In order to measure a country's comparative advantage comprehensively, according to the definition by Iso gai *et al.* (2002), Revealed Comparative Disadvantage (RCDA) and Relative Revealed Comparative Trade Advantage (RTA) is introduced to measure comparative advantage of Sino-Russian Trade comprehensively. Formulas of three different indices are as follows:

Revealed Comparative advantage: $RCA_{aj} = X_{aj}/X_a X_{wj}/X_w - 1 \times 100$ (1)

Revealed Comparative Disadvantage: $RCDA_{aj} = M_{aj}/M_a M_{wj}/M_w - 1 \times 100$ (2)

Relative Revealed Comparative Trade Advantage: $RTA_{aj} = RCA_{aj} - RCDA_{aj}$ (3)

where, X_{aj} represents the total *j* product exports of country *a*, X_a represents total exports of country *a*. X_{wj} represents the total *j* product exports of the whole world. X_w represents total exports in the world. M_{aj} represents the total j product imports of country a, M_a represents total imports of country a. M_{wj} represents the total j product imports of the whole world. M_w represents total exports in the world. Relative Revealed Comparative Trade Advantage equals to RCA_{aj} minutes $RCDA_{aj}$. $RCA_{aj} > 0$ illustrates that the share of j product export is larger than the average share of j product export in the world export which means country a has comparative advantage on j product. The larger ratio indicates the greater advantage. $RCDA_{aj} > 0$ illustrates that the share of j product import is larger than the average share of j product import in the world import which means country a has comparative disadvantage on j product. The larger ratio indicates the greater disadvantage. $RCA_{aj} < 0$ and $RCDA_{aj} < 0$ illustrates import and exports structure of product j are similar and there is Intra industry trade of product j in country a. The larger ratio of RTA_{aj} shows the stronger comparative advantage of j product in country a. On the contrary, that comparative disadvantage is stronger. If RCA_{aj}, $RCDA_{aj}$, RTA_{aj} is zero, then there is no comparative advantage or disadvantage. If there is difference in comparative advantage (disadvantage) on the same commodity of both parties, then complementarity is existed in bilateral trading according to the definition of comparative advantage.

According to the above formula (1), (2), (3), trade complementary index (TCI) of both sides can be calculated by the difference of TCI of the same commodity.[2] The calculation formula is as follows:

$$TCI_{abj} = RTA_{aj} - RTA_{bj} \quad (4)$$

In the formula, TCI_{abj} represents the TCI on product j in countries a and b; RTA_{aj} and RTA_{bj} represents RTA on product j in countries a and b respectively. $TCI_{abj} > 0$ is called Trade Complementary Index of RCA. The larger ratio, the greater trading complementarity on product j in both country a and b. $TCI_{abj} < 0$ is called Trade Complementary Index of RCDA. The smaller the ratio, the greater trading complementarity on product j in both country a and b. If TCI_{abj} equals to 0, then there is no trading complementarity on product j in both country a and b.

According to the above formulas (1), (2), (3), (4), RTA_{aj} and trading complementarity of Sino-Russian trading commodities calculated by Excel shown in Table 3.

Table 3. Comparison of RTA and TCI Data of SITC1 Departmental Commodities of China and Russia.

Item	SITC Code & Description		2000 Year		2005 Year		2010 Year		2011 Year		2012 Year	
	Code	Description	China	Russia	China	Russia	China	Russia	China	Russia	China	Russia
	0	Food and live animals*	55	−270	30	−222	18	−179	16	−146	7	−148
	1	Beverages and tobacco*	15	−385	5	−276	−7	−174	−12	−156	−16	−154
	2	Crude materials, inedible, except fuels*	−195	26	−263	71	−319	40	−315	42	−304	27
	3	Mineral fuels, lubricants and related materials*	−58	464	−65	424	−73	469	−76	418	−77	547
R	*4*	Animal and vegetable oils and fats*	−122	−338	−128	−190	−122	−107	−108	−74	−130	−35
T	*5*	Chemicals***	−90	−86	−66	−85	−44	−75	−37	−64	−42	−68
A	*6*	Manufactured goods classified chiefly by material**	−10	30	31	11	45	−9	58	−19	54	−27
	7	Machinery and transport equipment***	−26	−47	−6	−97	23	−104	29	−120	21	−131
	8	Miscellaneous manufactured articles**	236	−43	158	−55	145	−98	155	−94	155	−106
	9	Commod. & transacts. Not class. Accord. To kind***	−15	13	−5	23	−46	−25	−115	−53	−113	57

(Continued)

Table 3. *(Continued)*

	SITC Code & Description		2000 Year		2005 Year		2010 Year		2011 Year		2012 Year	
Item	Code	Description	China	Russia	China	Russia	China	Russia	China	Russia	China	Russia
	0	Food and live animals*	325	−325	252	−252	197	−197	162	−162	155	−155
	1	Beverages and tobacco*	400	−400	281	−281	167	−167	144	−144	138	−138
	2	Crude materials, inedible, except fuels*	−221	221	−334	334	−359	359	−357	357	−331	331
	3	Mineral fuels, lubricants and related materials*	−522	522	−489	489	−542	542	−494	494	−624	624
T	*4*	Animal and vegetable oils and fats*	216	−216	62	−62	−15	15	−34	34	−95	95
C	*5*	Chemicals***	−4	4	19	−19	31	−31	27	−27	26	−26
I	*6*	Manufact goods classified chiefly by material**	−39	39	20	−20	54	−54	77	−77	81	−81
	7	Machinery and transport equipment***	21	−21	91	−91	127	−127	149	−149	152	−152
	8	Miscellaneous manufactured articles**	279	−279	213	−213	243	−243	249	−249	261	−261
	9	Commod. & transacts. Not class. Accord. To kind***	−29	29	−27	27	−21	21	−62	62	−170	170

Source: Plotted based on the UN Comtrade data.

Note: *Preliminary product; **: Labor intensive product; ***: Capital and technology intensive product.

Through comprehensive comparison and analysis of the data in Table 3, the current characteristics of RTA and TCI in two countries can be summed up as follows:

First, in terms of RTA: China has strong comprehensive comparative advantage on products of SITC0, 6, 7, 8 department, among which commodity of SITC6, 7 department is transferred from comparative disadvantage and SITC8 has the strongest comparative advantage. Commodities of SITC1, 2, 3, 4, 5, 9 department have comparative disadvantages, among which commodities of SITC2 has the strongest disadvantages. Russia has comparative advantage in commodities of SITC2, 3, 9 departments, among which commodities of SITC9 has the strongest advantages. Commodities of SITC0, 1, 4, 5, 6, 7, 8 department have comparative disadvantages.

Second, in terms of TCI: China has great Trade Còmplementarity of RCA in commodities of SITCO SITC0, 1, 5, 6, 7, 8 departments (Russia has great Trade Complementarity of RCDA); China has great Trade Complementarity of RCA in commodities of SITC0, 2, 3, 4, 9 departments (Russia has great Trade Complementarity of RCDA).

Conclusion and Prospect

Through the empirical analysis of the current state and prospect, and bilateral trade commodity structure of the Sino-Russian trade, as well as the RTA and the complementarity of the trade (TCI), the following conclusions are obtained.

Firstly, after undergoing the "low volatility period of wandering", the Sino-Russian trade goes into the fast-developing period. In the situation that the bilateral relation is getting closer, bilateral trade is getting better, which is conducive to the bilateral political economy development for both of the countries.

Secondly, the mutual structures of import and export commodities are different. China's major export commodities, i.e. comparative advantage products are concentrated in the departments of SITC6, SITC7 and SITC6. However, this in Russia is on the contrary, which means that the bilateral trade between China and Russia belongs to trading among industries of low reverence of trading commodities structure. It is difficult to form an intimate relationship between the two countries.

Thirdly, the trade complementarity is great between the two countries. Russia's representatives of the export commodities are energy, mineral products (such as SITC2 & 3) and resource intensive products like this. While China's main export advantage goods are industrial manufactured goods. Therefore, complementarity of the two countries is shown as advantage among industries.

In conclusion, the trade complementarity is great between the two countries, and there is great potential in the development of bilateral trade. However, there also exists a realistic problem that the correlation in the trade structure is relatively low. Facing the problem of opportunity and reality, China and Russia should learn and rearrange the bilateral structure of the commodity trade, as well as change and enlarge the content, structure and style of the trade cooperation. Improving the relevance of bilateral trade structure can realize the mutual benefits for both of the countries.

Notes

1. SITC (Standard International Trade Classification) Rev.1 Code 0–9 are named as follows: 0: Food and live animals; 1: Beverages and tobacco; 2: Crude materials, inedible, except fuels; 3: Mineral fuels, lubricants and related materials; 4: Animal and vegetable oils and fats; 5: Chemicals; 6: Manufactured goods classified chiefly by material; 7: Machinery and transport equipment; 8: Miscellaneous manufactured articles; 9: Commod. & transacts. Not class. Accord. To kind.
2. Complementary index of trade is calculated in accordance to the comparison advantage index used. Refer to Peter Drysdale (1967), based on the premise that the import and export values meet each other for the same category of commodities in the bilateral trade, the complementary index is defined as the product of import and export RCA index.

References

Dong Rui (2010), "An Empirical Analysis of China-Russia Trade Complementarity," Northeast Asia Forum, 2010 (3), pp. 51–57.

Lu Nanquan (2009), "The Analysis on the Trend of Sino-Russia Regional Economic and Trading Cooperation Development", *Russian Central Asian & East European Market*, 2009 (9), pp. 1–16.

Peter Drysdale (1967), "Japan, Australia and New Zealand: The Prospects for Western Integration," *Economic Record*, September.

UN Comtrade database, http://comtrade.un.org/db/default.aspx.

Sino-Russian economic & trade cooperation network, http://www.crc.mofcom.gov.cn/index.shtml.

Yang Xiyan and Wang Di (2005), "Complementary Analysis of Sino-Russian Trade," *World Economy Study*, 2005 (7), pp. 71–77.